The Hard Problems of Management

Gaining the Ethics Edge

Mark Pastin

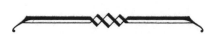

The Hard Problems of Management

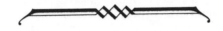

Gaining the Ethics Edge

 Jossey-Bass Publishers

San Francisco • Oxford • 1991

THE HARD PROBLEMS OF MANAGEMENT
Gaining the Ethics Edge
   by Mark Pastin

Copyright © 1986 by: Jossey-Bass Inc., Publishers
                     350 Sansome Street
                     San Francisco, California 94104
                              &
                     Jossey-Bass Limited
                     Headington Hill Hall
                     London OX3 0BW

Epigraph for Chapter Three taken from J. Patrick Wright,
"How Moral Men Make Immoral Decisions," Chapter Four
from *On a Clear Day You Can See General Motors.*
Copyright © by J. Patrick Wright, 1979. Reprinted with
permission from Multimedia Product Development, Inc.

Library of Congress Cataloging-in-Publication Data

Pastin, Mark (date)
   The hard problems of management.

   (The Jossey-Bass management series)
   Bibliography: p. 229
   Includes index.
   1. Business ethics. 2. Industrial management—Moral
and ethical aspects. I. Title. II. Series.
HF5387.P37 1986   174'.4   85-45911
ISBN 0-87589-688-X

Manufactured in the United States of America

The paper in this book meets the guidelines for
permanence and durability of the Committee on
Production Guidelines for Book Longevity of the
Council on Library Resources.

JACKET DESIGN BY WILLI BAUM
FIRST EDITION

HB Printing   10 9 8 7 6 5

Code 8617

The Jossey-Bass
Management Series

Consulting Editors
Organizations and Management

Warren Bennis
University of Southern California

Richard O. Mason
Southern Methodist University

Ian I. Mitroff
University of Southern California

Preface

The problem with the hard problems of management is that we know that the tools we bring to bear on these problems do not work. We continue using them because we believe it is better to do something than to just let the problems grow worse. But the problems continue to grow worse. What are the hard problems of management? Today countless external constituencies demand a say in how firms are managed. But there is no way to understand what makes these constituencies tick and how to get them to listen to reason. Environmentalists demand pollution controls from a nearly bankrupt copper industry, government regulators compete among themselves to control a biotechnology industry struggling to be born, public prosecutors hold executives criminally responsible for the acts of their employees, consumer groups demand an endless supply of electricity without rate increases to build new power plants, and the media label every industrial accident as intentional corporate malfeasance.

The hard problems of management also reach inside of firms. Managers have experimented with everything from theories X, Y, and Z to various grids, culture changes, back-to-basics programs, and transcendental meditation to somehow make their

organizations work. Critics charge that managers fail because
they are obsessed with short-term results at the expense of long-
term objectives. But the strategies that state long-term objectives are in disrepute as inapplicable, irrelevant academic exer-
cises. Performance appraisal systems are in a constant state of
revision, with no one believing that they will really get any better. It is as if some missing ingredient keeps our organizations
from working. One of the hardest problems of management is
simply finding this missing ingredient. The very persistence of
the hard problems suggests something is radically wrong—in the
dictionary sense of "radical," meaning to the very root. My objective is to say what is wrong and, more important, to start
making it right.

The reason managers face so many hard problems is that
the basic socioethical rules governing businesses and other organizations have shifted and continue to shift, altering the manager's job, often for the worse. By socioethical rules, I mean the
fundamental principles that guide our decisions and actions, not
the abstract maxims of philosophers. If it seems odd to speak of
the basic principles by which organizations operate as *ethical*
principles, that is because managers have bought the "big lie"
that business and ethics are incommensurable. But business and
ethics can work together for managers who have the will to
tackle the hard, ethically colored problems that make up the
current business environment.

Are the hard problems of management really ethically
colored? Kenneth Andrews, editor of the *Harvard Business Review,* found the following ethical problems discussed in just one
issue in 1985: Do the economic benefits of hostile takeovers for
shareholders justify their costs for others? Do the traditional
financial goals of corporations undermine their long-term competitiveness, and, thereby, their value to society? Are accounting procedures deliberately narrow and arcane to shelter management from scrutiny by shareholders and other constituencies?
Does the collective bargaining process give the interests of management and labor an undue priority over the interests of other
affected groups? The list could be extended to reveal that many
more of the hard problems confronting managers are ethical

problems. This signals a fundamental shift in the *kind* of problems managers face.

This book is not about being a "nice guy" manager. It is about thinking outside the no-ethics box of standard management tools. Managers willing to think outside the box reap a two-fold advantage. First, they can address hard, ethically colored problems in positive, nondefensive terms. For example, the "unethical" defense contractor who is actually struggling to break even on a primary contract with the Defense Department can start to make his legitimate case. Second, managers who think outside the no-ethics box can see the hard problems of management through a different "filter" than that of their ethics-blind competitors. There is no advantage in looking at the same problems in the same way as your competitors. The ethics edge is the competitive advantage available to managers who are willing to see problems in their hardest real terms, with their ethical blinders off.

The heroes of this book have taken problems invisible to their competitors and solved them. We think of the Dow Chemical Company managers who solved their pollution problem by seeing plant emissions as an unexploited by-product rather than a regulatory mess. We think of the Cadbury Schweppes managers who operate in a hostile labor environment without labor discord by concentrating mainly on ethics. We think of Milos Krofta, the immigrant entrepreneur who has cleaned up America's water by seeing that regulations blinded his competitors to the problem's cause. And we think of Kathy Kolbe who beat the odds and defied the experts to reform elementary education through her for profit firm, Resources for the Gifted.

Many of the lessons in this book are based on a three-year study of high-ethics, high-profit firms in the United States and Great Britain. Academics and managers jointly conducted the study, with managers leading research teams and shaping the observations into usable tools. The managers, academics, and consultants who worked on the study carried the lessons back to their own organizations and consulting clients in order to test them. In short, the new approach to the hard problems of management offered here has been conceived with action in mind.

I begin the process of tackling hard problems by debunking the myth that ethics is an ethereal subject at best irrelevant to business and at worst debilitating to sound management practice. I demystify ethics by offering a new way of looking at hard business problems through ethics. In my conception, the ethics of a person or firm is simply *the most fundamental ground rules by which the person or firm acts.* Understanding these ground rules is the key to understanding how organizations function and to changing the way they function.

To see problems in a new light, it is often necessary to break up old ways of looking at them. Drawing on Joseph Schumpeter's view of capitalism as a process of creative destruction, I describe giving up no-ethics management as Constructive Destruction. Thus I attack several management myths. I attack the myth that managers fail ethically and economically because they emphasize the short run at the expense of the long run. I attack the myth that strong cultures are good for organizations. And I attack the myth that individuals should assume collective responsibility for the actions of the firm. I seek the element of truth in these myths and address the problems masked by the myths. Thus I show how seeking present alignment, rather than future goals, makes strategy work; how fair agreements achieve the supposed benefits of strong cultures; and how restoring individual responsibility infuses organizations with creativity and genuine responsibility.

I also ponder the next generation of organizations and technologies and the threats they will pose for managers who think inside the box. I use the ethics-as-ground-rules concept to expose the changing rules of business and society and to ask how managers can steer these changes in a direction that tolerates the existence of new organizations fostering new technologies.

Thinking inside the no-ethics box is comfortable, even as we notice the hard problems of management eroding our companies' competitiveness. It is comfortable because we can pretend to be doing "all that can be reasonably expected," with fellow managers readily agreeing that "everything is fine." After all, they too are comfortable inside the no-ethics box. When the

hard problems begin to overwhelm us, we seek an outside villain, be it the Germans, the Japanese, the regulators, the unions,
the pace of technological change, or the mysterious forces that
unpredictably drive economies. In short, many of us will accept
the costs of thinking inside the box to avoid giving up comfortable habits of mind and management.

    This is not a comfortable book and it is not for everyone.
It is for a select group of managers, consultants, academics, and
students. It is for managers who see that life in most firms exists
in the gap between how it should be and how it is. It is for managers who see this and are deeply offended by it. It is genuinely
puzzling why organizations quickly and predictably settle into
this gap and then explain why this is the best that can be expected. This puzzle motivated the writing of this book and
forms the heart of it. This book is also for managers who realize
that managing "external relations" is a sterile description of the
one factor that most determines the success or failure of firms.
My aim is to undermine the false security of an internal-external
dichotomy and get managers back to the job of managing the
factors that truly determine success.

    There are two types of consultants. Some consultants de-
vise a model, chart, or assemblage of buzzwords that can be
resold to client after client. All is well with these consultants so
long as their story does not grow stale and their billable hours
do not decline. When this inevitably happens, they try one gim-
mick after another on unsuspecting clients until they find "the
next great thing." I offer little to this group.

    Others pursue consulting, often accepting lower pay and
insecurity, because they sense how profoundly debilitating life
inside most organizations is. These consultants may also hawk
charts, grids, and buzzwords if only because clients expect them
to. But they live outside the organization because they cannot
accept life inside. They are consultants out of a commitment to
the quality of life of those who live inside. To these consultants
I offer a fresh, comprehensive view of the hard problems they
are dedicated to solving.

    Academics divide into two analogous groups. Familiar
ideas, and their minor variations, lend themselves to contained

studies, articles in journals safe from the eyes of practicing managers, and a secure career. But the job of academics is to seek the truth without prejudice and with courage. To academics who accept the tough job of seeking the truth about organizations, I have assembled ideas from several disciplines to connect my action-oriented discussion with the concerns of researchers.

Students are in a tough spot. They recognize the sterility of the tools they must learn to get the chance to work as managers or management researchers. They must please the guardians of the past while accepting responsibility for the hard problems they will inherit. To the student who wants to be part of the solution, not one of the problems, I have tried to portray hard problems as accurately as possible and invite thinking that will still be relevant when he or she is face to face with a hard problem.

Managers, academics, and students willing to tackle the hard problems of management look beyond solutions to today's problems. They seek a model or picture of the firm that takes hard problems in stride, lives up to its potential, and allows individuals to live up to their potential. There are pitfalls in idealized pictures. There is a tendency to use the picture of the organization that might be as an excuse for not addressing the problems of the organization that is. And it is easy to be misled by the simplicity of an ideal picture into underestimating the intertwined problems of conflicting interests, nonadaptive ground rules, and sloppy thinking hiding behind precise methodology. These warnings given, I offer a picture of an ideal organization. My standard is straightforward: An ideal organization adds to the autonomy and value of the individuals who are the organization. It does not require that individuals sacrifice some of their integrity to belong to the organization. The ideal is straightforward, but the path from today's hard problems to this ideal organization is tortuous.

Overview of the Contents

The Hard Problems of Management has three parts. Part One provides a rationale for the approach to hard problems taken in this book. Part Two deals with the actual process of tackling hard problems. Part Three previews the hard problems organizations will face in coming years and consolidates the lessons of this book. The reader who is anxious to attack some problems may want to start with Part Two and pick up the rationale and projections later. If you are anxious to know exactly what you will get out of the book, you may want to skim Chapter Ten before reading the rest.

Part One introduces the ideas I will be using and emphasizes understanding prior to action. It focuses on ethics as a tool for understanding why organizations face so many hard problems. The Introduction asks why, in the face of utter confusion on many fronts, we repackage so many of the problems we face as ethical problems. Chapter One argues that ethics has become a powerful antibusiness tool. Managers need to understand what lies behind this phenomenon to get off the defensive and begin thinking outside the box of standard management tools. Chapter Two introduces the concept of ethics as the ground rules that determine which actions are possible for organizations and which are not. This concept is used to get to the root of how decisions are actually made and how to change the way they are made.

Part Two surveys some of the hardest problems of management and brings the concept of ethics as ground rules to bear on them. The emphasis is on concepts and tools for tackling hard problems. Chapter Three looks at the gridlock of conflicting interests that undercuts management in all organizations and asks how to break it. Chapter Four examines the ethics that developed in response to the industrial revolution. This ethics provides a powerful tool for discovering who really counts in difficult decisions. Chapter Five focuses on why corporate strategies so often fail. This chapter shows why managing for the long run is the wrong approach, both economically and ethically, and argues that present-oriented management leads to goal achievement and to integrity of action.

Chapter Six returns to the rules by which firms operate and shows how these rules are at the root of recalcitrant organizational conflicts. I show how these rules are sometimes intentionally misunderstood to the detriment of business. This chapter also addresses the hard problems of managing across borders, cultures, and diverse ethics. Chapter Seven looks at organizational cultures and argues that most "culture changes" decrease the firm's vitality and adaptability. This chapter shows that the supposed benefits of culture change are best achieved by establishing fair, basic agreements in organizations. Chapter Eight explores three critical factors in management success—purpose, responsibility, and creativity. This chapter provides a practical approach to fostering responsibility at all levels of organizations.

Part Three asks what hard problems lie hidden in the current business environment and how managers can use the lessons of earlier chapters to manage "ahead of the curve" of organizational and technological change. Chapter Nine examines the changes in the ground rules of doing business that will accompany emerging forms of organization, the advance of information systems, the proliferation of corporate tragedies, and the commercial application of biotechnologies. This chapter argues that the problems managers will face in the near future are not the familiar problems of regimenting conflicting interests and allocating resources, but are instead problems of design. Chapter Ten consolidates the lessons of the book. We ask how managers can approach the hard problems of coming years and how they can create an organizational atmosphere that is more receptive to outside-the-box thinking about hard problems. Chapter Eleven provides an agenda for managers who wish to create organizations that take hard, ethically colored problems in stride.

A Note on the Cases

I discuss many organizations, some by actual name and some by fictitious name. Many organizations are sensitive about even being mentioned in the same breath as ethics. My principle in naming or masking names is to give due credit to organizations that are exemplars of good management practices. In a few cases, I name organizations whose troubles are a matter of well-known public record. If I am not speaking positively, or when I rely on confidential information, I use fictitious names. All cases are based on fact.

Acknowledgments

Roderick Firth directed my off-beat dissertation at Harvard University on the role of experience in decision making. Graduate students referred to Rod Firth as the faculty's token human being. This was our way of saying that he is a man of extraordinary personal and intellectual integrity. I owe Rod not only a large part of my perspective on ethics but also my confidence that the rewards of living with integrity dwarf the costs.

Philip Theibert is a writer and a colleague in the Critical Thinking Group. He taught me to write ten times better than I used to, critiquing almost every page of the earliest of three drafts of this book. Phil taught me that writing is an art that requires very hard work.

Three people forced me to take my thinking out of the classroom and academic journals and into the world. Michael Hooker, president of Bennington College, literally dragged me before groups of public and private sector managers ten years ago. He is one of the finest managers I know and an inspiration. Dwight Frindt, a top manager for several firms and a colleague in the Critical Thinking Group gave me the benefit of his broad experience. He forced me to realize that I was writing in part from anger at how the world failed to live up to my expectations. Steve Larsen, one of the manager-heroes of this book, is not only a close personal friend but also an important teacher. He created and tested some of the new approaches to management at the core of the argument.

Three consulting editors have been critically important to my work, independent of this project. Ian I. Mitroff is my nominee for a Nobel Prize for innovative thinking in the interests of the betterment of life on the planet. Ian's intellectual brilliance is exceeded only by his dedication to genuinely improving the quality of life in all organizations. His influence runs through all of my work. Richard O. Mason is a puzzling hybrid. He is an absolutely first-rate philosopher, a master of contemporary management, and a stunningly fine person. More than anyone else, he has concretely helped me in writing this book. Warren Bennis is the leader in bringing the worlds of management research, great thought, and the practice of management together in fine thinking and writing. He has influenced me more than he knows. On the way to the Phoenix airport, he helped me develop the key idea of ethics as ground rules.

I have taught at several universities and found colleagues at each who became important teachers. At Indiana University I worked with John D. Donnell and Harvey Bunke. John taught me how business, the law, and ethics are interrelated parts of a whole. By example and exhortation, Harvey taught me that business provides a good environment for novel thinking. At the University of Maryland, Rudi Lamone, dean of the College of Business, befriended me, offered tough criticism, and had faith in my abilities.

Other academic friends have played a central role. H. J. Zoffer, dean of the Graduate School of Business at the University of Pittsburgh, took me on as collaborator on the project that led to this book. West Churchman is an inspiration in several ways. He once asked me a question that changed my life. West is known for arguing that questions are important, but his power as a questioner cannot be appreciated until experienced. Charles Dellheim, a business and cultural historian, has been my closest academic collaborator and has helped with every topic, often forcing me to adopt a more moderate view through the strength of his arguments. He taught me what I know of British business.

Many fine executives have helped. Jack Whiteman, Sr., chief executive of Empire Machines took the time to read parts of this book and gave me detailed, occasionally crushing criticisms. W. R. Schulz, former head of W. R. Schulz Apartments, taught me about the spirit of the entrepreneur. Bill Schulz would have been the next governor of Arizona except for the priority he gives to love of his family. Bill Jamieson, who worked under President Carter and Bruce Babbitt (present Governor of Arizona) and is now an entrepreneur, forced me to believe that integrity in government is possible, if not easy. Roy Serpa of Borg Warner Chemicals taught me a lot and helped me through a number of hard times. Richard Class of the Garrett Corporation read a great deal of the preliminary material, commented in detail, and taught me about the complicated process of managing business-government relations. Once, when I almost gave up, he saved me.

Much of the research for this book was done at the Center for Ethics at Arizona State University. I owe a great deal to L. W. Seidman and William E. Reif for creating a place for this research in the College of Business. Dean Reif has demonstrated confidence in me for a long time and has also served as a teacher. Dean Seidman encouraged me, in no uncertain terms, to get on with it before I was no longer "ahead of the curve," to use his phrase. J. Russell Nelson, president of the university, has consistently supported the practice of ethics. Robert Payton of the Exxon Education Foundation believed in the work of the center before he had much company.

Bruce and Paula Hilby, both of whom are executives, entrepreneurs, and visionaries, have stood by me through thick and a lot of thin. Their personal friendship and intellectual challenges have been invaluable.

My immediate co-workers, Viswanath Narayan and Mary Kohut, have helped me in many ways. Vish Narayan taught me more than I ever thought I could learn about information systems and their impact on management. He made especially important contributions to the discussions of management across cultures. Mary Kohut helped me manage the whole writing process, preserving my sanity a few times.

My debts to my family are specific. My father, Joseph Pastin, read the entire manuscript and gave me helpful comments. A retired steel industry manager, he added realism to my understanding of the steel industry's problems. My mother, Patricia Pastin, is a manager in a firm engaged in international trade. She taught me a lot about the complexities of international trade and about managing small firms. Both of my parents taught me to think from the heart as well as the mind.

My wife Carrie endured a first year of marriage in which I was an absentee husband. She was especially helpful in renewing my belief in practical individualism and in shaping my thought on that topic. I owe her the peace of mind to complete this work. The last words she wants to hear are "In my next book . . ."

These acknowledgments describe an organization of sorts. The most important question to ask about any organization is: Who is responsible? The only possible answer is: We all are.

Tempe, Arizona   Mark Pastin
February 1986

Contents

Part Two: Tackling Hard Problems

The Author

Mark Pastin is professor of management and director of the Center for Ethics at Arizona State University. He received his B.A. degree (1970) from the University of Pittsburgh in philosophy and psychology and his A.M. degree (1972) and Ph.D. degree (1973) from Harvard University in philosophy (decision theory). He has taught at the University of Michigan, the University of Maryland, Indiana University, and in many executive programs. Pastin is also founder of the Critical Thinking Group, a research and consulting firm specializing in strategic planning and issues management.

Pastin's research interests are in tools for critical management thinking, issues management, and the influence of new technologies on organizations. He has held fellowships from the National Science Foundation and the National Endowment for the Humanities. With the support of the Exxon Education Foundation, Pastin developed a training program on ethics for practicing managers offered through the Center for Ethics. He is a member of the Academy of Management, the Philosophy of Science Association, the American Philosophical Association, and several boards of directors.

Pastin is the author of over fifty articles on decision theory, management of technology, strategy, business and medical ethics, and methods for asking questions. Pastin has served as a consultant to many Fortune 500 companies, to state and national political candidates and agencies, to hospitals and medical groups, entrepreneurial firms, and industry organizations. He currently heads a research team applying expert systems technology to job design and performance appraisal and a regional executive network on new ideas in management.

The Hard Problems
of Management

Gaining the Ethics Edge

Introduction

How Ethics Has Been Turned Against Business— and How to Regain the Ethics Edge

I keep six honest serving men
(They taught me all I knew);
Their names are What and Why and When
And How and Where and Who.
—*Rudyard Kipling,* The Elephant's Child

My aim is to help managers tackle some of the hard problems they now confront. Of course, many people say they are going to do this to sell another new approach to management. I spend a lot of time living with managers as they struggle with hard problems, and I see how little good—and often how much harm—such "bright" ideas produce. I will help you to look behind the problems to find out why there are so many hard problems and why the problems have proven so resistant to managers' best efforts to solve them.

There are two stages to tackling hard problems. The first is to see why these problems are now painted in ethical colors. We find that the problem of effectively redeploying corporate assets—through mergers, acquisitions, plant closings, plant openings, buyouts, and so forth—is an ethical problem. The ethical issues here include: Do managers have the *right* to close out-dated plants? Does the acquisition of an oil company by a steel company, or by another oil company, violate the rights of employees and managers of one or both companies? Even the point spread between the cost and price of funds became an ethical issue during the recent recession when builders charged banks with *unfairly* profiting during bad times and not doing their part to foster recovery. This last case is noteworthy since one ordinarily free-market group, builders, asked the government to stop the unethical practices of another group. Managers need to see what is behind the repackaging of hard problems as ethical problems in order to get off the defensive in meeting these problems.

The second stage is to break open the box of standard management tools that have proven ineffective against hard problems. The box of standard management tools does not include the powerful tools of ethics. By adding ethics to the box of management tools, managers can view these problems in a new light and use ethics to gain competitive edges over ethics-blind competitors.

To see how these two stages go together to provide a double ethical edge to managers, we need to see how managers have been pushed onto the ethical defensive.

Big Lies

Today, few people believe that business is ethical. The lead editorial in the morning paper is entitled "Business Ethics' Time Has Come in Era of Defense Contract Overcharging" (Murphy, 1985). A recent *New York Times*-CBS News poll (June 9, 1985) finds that 55 percent of the public think executives are dishonest and that only 33 percent think they are honest. Perhaps few people have ever believed business to be ethical, but there has been a significant change: Instead of seeing an occasional black sheep in business, we see herds of them grazing the business pasture.

The ethics of business per se is in question. People are

challenging the ethical legitimacy of business in conversation, in the press, in classrooms and training sessions, in Congress, and in the courts. Peter Drucker calls this "ethical chic" (1981). Is this talk of business ethics idle academic and journalistic chatter, or does it signal an unraveling of the fabric of American business? The verdict depends on American business. It cannot continue to meet ethical challenges in a self-defeating, defensive posture.

A symptom of the eroding ethical legitimacy of business is the prevalence of corporate tragedies—from Three Mile Island to Rely Tampons to Bhopal. The difference between an industrial accident and a corporate tragedy is ethical. Tragedies involve an element of "evil." When an accident involves intentional violation of basic social ethics, such as the mandate not to imperil innocent bystanders, we see it as evil. The public and the media today seem almost ready to believe that accidents are intentionally planned by malevolent corporate executives. This willingness to see accidents as involving evil, instead of inadvertence or bad luck, signals an important shift in society's attitude toward business.

Business can halt the erosion of its ethical legitimacy and regain the advantage in discussions of ethical issues. Ethical challenges to particular businesses or industries can be met without conceding everything to the critics.

For example, it is now generally accepted that defense contractors, including General Dynamics, Hughes Helicopters, General Electric, and McDonnell Douglas, unscrupulously abuse the contracting process. The media hastily concluded that defense contractors were ripping off the Defense Department and the public. The public was only too happy to believe this. Rather than make their ethical case, these firms conceded and ran for the hills. The costs to these firms to date are great. Given the wave of regulations to follow, costs over time will be staggering.

Defense contractors have a credible ethical response. These contractors seldom make money on a principal contract. The Defense Department retains patent rights on all new technologies, devises detailed specifications with scant knowledge of their engineering implications, and then changes specifications willy-nilly. Contractors dare not complain for fear of being locked out of future contracts, so they try to make money on peripherals and spare parts. The game is no secret. Everyone involved in defense contracting knows why there are and, by the present rules, must be $400 toilets. Is it unethical to charge $400 for a $30 toilet when you must deliver a $2.5 million airplane for $2 million? Defense contractors must forthrightly raise this question or be regulated into bankruptcy.

The overall consequences of a steady retreat on ethical issues can be oppressive. Intensifying ethical attacks on business may collectively create a big lie that business and ethics are incompatible. A *big lie* is a lie that must constantly expand to avoid being uncovered as a lie. Once the lie expands to its limit, it becomes "the truth" in the minds of those who buy it. One master of big lies stated: "The size of the lie is a definite factor in causing it to be believed. . . . The vast masses of the nations are . . . a more easy prey to a big lie than a small one, for they themselves often tell little lies but would be ashamed to tell a big one" (Hitler, [1926] 1939, p. 313).

Remember the other small lies that became "the truth." Prior to Hitler's rise, it was easy to ignore talk of Aryan supermen as ineffectual bigotry wrapped in pseudo-intellectual jargon. Prior to the war in Vietnam, the domino theory seemed a toy of journalists, eggheads, and Pentagon analysts. Prior to the regulatory strangling of American business in the 1970s, talk of environmental destruction seemed the province of zealous college students and professional gadflies thriving on media attention. Proliferating attacks on the ethics of business may come together in a big lie that seriously undermines American business. In the environment of that big lie, regulations may be passed that make today's most noxious regulations seem like minor irritants.

Think Outside the Box

Thinking in ethical terms will help managers meet ethical attacks and expose the big lie that ethics and business are enemies. But my aim in bringing ethics into the picture goes beyond checking ethical attacks. To think in ethical terms is to think "outside the box." The box in question is the box of standard tools of management thinking. The very factors that give prominence to ethics in business also make standard business tools irrelevant to the nonstandard problems that managers regularly confront. These factors mark a fundamental change in the business environment.

Today's talk of ethics in business, medicine, law, journalism, and most professions is not accidental. Ethics becomes a major topic of discussion when a society is undergoing fundamental change and the basic agreements that govern it are disintegrating. A high level of ethical controversy strongly indicates a society undergoing radical change. The last peak of ethical controversy was at the front edge of the industrial revolution, when society renegotiated its understandings of work, family, church, and government. The function of ethics in society is to provide a context for considering basic changes, renegotiating agreements, and restoring order.

Ethics again permeates the air. We are renegotiating basic social agreements at the front edge of the revolution in information systems and biotechnology. Organizations modeled on armies—the model of industrial-era organizations—are outmoded. Property is no longer defined by physical boundaries. Where exactly is a piece of information, or an idea, and who owns it? Corporate tragedies are displacing industrial accidents. Instead of facing problems of dramatic scarcity, we ask what sort of people and environment to design genetically. Our standing ethical rules no more address these problems than reading pig innards explains the weather. It is not a good idea to ignore this discussion of ethics. Doing so allows the critics of business to draw up the rules that you will live by.

Because of these basic changes and renegotiations, managers relentlessly search for new ideas about how to manage. They prowl the business section of local bookstores like teenagers looking for the dirty magazine that will unlock the secret. Tried-and-true ways of business thinking are not working on today's hard problems. So we grasp at straws. These straws include the portfolio approach, matrix management, theory Z, corporate cultures, the seven-S model of *In Search of Excellence* (Peters and Waterman, 1982), and industrial policy in liberal and conservative dress. One panacea follows another at an accelerating pace. The moral? When we face truly fundamental changes, minor tune-ups and quick fixes do not work.

What does work? My answer is that there is no answer—except to ask the right questions. The "ethics edge" is the edge available to managers who use ethics to ask the right questions. Managers cannot solve resistant problems because they think "inside the box" of standard business tools. This box just does not contain the tools we need. It is time to break out of the box and ask some hard questions.

Thinking about ethics is profitable. It breaks open the box of customary ways of thinking and allows new ideas in. Ethics forces managers to think outside the box, which is just to say that it forces them to think. Thus I call our hero the thinking manager. Ethics is not the only box opener. But it is a potent one. It is potent because it digs to the most basic premises by which we think and work and asks why? Managers have fired Kipling's honest serving man Why. They desperately need him back on the payroll.

The lie that ethics and business do not mix has made so much headway that it seems odd to suggest that ethics "pays off." The lie has gone far enough that this suggestion even strikes some as immoral. Yet I guarantee that managers who think ethics will gain two critical advantages over their ethics-blind peers. First, they will be able to address ethical issues from a positive, nondefensive stance. Second, they will be able to find competitive opportunities that are invisible to those locked inside the no-ethics box.

This is not to say that managers who think ethics are sure to profit. This makes no more sense than saying that managers who think accounting are sure to profit. Ethics, like accounting, opens the possibility of addressing certain issues and seeing certain opportunities. Neither ethics nor accounting guarantees that addressing issues and seeing opportunities will result in sound choices being made. They only guarantee that you will see what is at issue in making a choice.

Let us now consider an example of an ethics edge to see how it works. It is a down-to-earth example to show that ethics is as relevant to the practical problems of small, low-tech businesses as it is to Fortune 500 companies.

Case: Shopping Mall Ethics

Shopping mall developers are not held in high ethical esteem. Mel Howard is no exception. He is about to lose a dream. He is waiting for the phone call he does not want to get.

Mel has worked tirelessly for three years, and spent $3.5 million, planning an innovative shopping mall for Bloomington, Indiana. This project means everything to Mel. He has a reputation as a "strip-mall" developer. This project is his chance to break into the big time and do something he is proud of.

Mel knows that pleasing city hall is the key to development projects. He tried to do everything right: He agreed to widen streets, build a playground, and fund the city's study of the mall's impact. By now, most of the profit is squeezed out of the project, but this matters little to Mel.

The project is up for final consideration by the city council, and at this point everything is unraveling. So Mel has a problem. The problem is solvable if he will look at it in terms of ethics; otherwise, he has wasted three years and lost $3.5 million.

What happened?

City planners and council members, despite their anti-developer bias, came to favor the project. The impact study impressed them. It showed that the benefits to the city would far exceed the costs.

Then a citizens' group—mainly doctors, lawyers, and other professionals who live near the mall site—commissioned their own study. Their study agreed with the city's study, with one critical exception: The benefits of the mall would go mainly to people who *moved* to Bloomington to build the mall and manage its stores. Present residents would pick up only construction and clerking jobs. Increased tax revenues would underwrite services for new residents. Considering only *present resi-*

dents, the costs and benefits are even, but the citizens do not want traffic snarling their neighborhood or mall lighting invading their privacy. Who needs a mall? The council now agrees with the citizens' group. They refuse to underwrite jobs for immigrants from Gary.

The phone rings. The council postponed action.

Mel, granted a one-week reprieve, still expects execution. But he still believes in his mall. Why? The mall is important to him. He regards city planners and council members as closet Bolsheviks out to get developers. But that is not the whole story. For Mel sees an ethical issue. He thinks the likely outcome is *unfair,* and not just to him.

Bloomington's populace forms two equal factions. (This division in Bloomington's populace was the focus of the film *Breaking Away.*) One faction is academics and professionals. The other is townies. The townies are the offspring of limestone workers. Most are unemployed, with little prospect of employment. While the construction companies who will build the mall and the managers who will run its stores will be nonresidents, the construction workers and store clerks will be townies. This may not seem like much to doctors, lawyers, and dentists, but it is a lot to the townies. Mel knows how it feels to be an unemployed townie, since he was a street kid himself.

Mel's point is ethical. Ethically, all present residents are not equal. Mel makes his case. While conceding that the mall imposes costs on present residents, especially residents of the upscale neighborhood near the mall site, he argues that the benefits indeed balance these out. More important, the benefits go to unemployed townies. And the trade-offs are better than the numbers show, for how can one measure the difference between life as a state dependent and having a good job? Mel does not question the city's or the citizens' studies, but he does have the numbers to show *who* will receive the benefits and *who* will pay the costs.

It is not smooth sailing. Mel is accused of hypocrisy: "When did you become a friend of the poor?" But Mel sticks to the facts and his argument.

Some liberal council members felt vindicated in their initial stand favoring the project, but the citizens' group pressed on as if Mel had said nothing.

Mel offered more concessions, including light barriers, to the citizens' group. But the group was not to be placated. The citizens' group began to look selfish.

The project won approval in a close vote. Mel had fought on ethical grounds and won. Instead of arguing straight benefits versus costs, he argued just distribution. He was right.

"Too easy," you say.

Not easy at all. But effective. And not just in Mel's case.

"Not ethics," you say. "It was self-interest masquerading as ethics."

Perhaps. As an ex-townie, I like their cause. The citizens' group hardly acted from humanitarian motives. This group—people quite driven by profits in their own professional fields—exploited the reputation of developers as rapacious capitalists. The citizens' group gave not a thought to the townies.

Mel used ethics to even the playing field for himself and the townies. He found a new approach to an issue he was otherwise sure to lose. Mel was self-interested, but his self-interest respected others more than did the selective "community interest" of the citizens' group. My point is not that Mel is the paragon of moral virtue but that he had a legitimate perspective that deserved a hearing. Because Mel thought ethics, he got his hearing.

I do not expect you, on the strength of Mel's case, to accept the idea that managers who think ethics can gain business advantages—and that it is a good idea to use ethics for business advantage. I expect you to accept it on the basis of a clear argument with cases to back it up.

Is the ethics we are talking about the Real Thing? Or is it some strange New Ethics? What is ethics?

People love to talk about ethics, especially when they think you are at a disadvantage. "Is it ethical to continue operating in South Africa?" (This, of course, is not a question. It is a taunt, reeking of moral superiority.) But they do not say what they mean by *ethical*. I will probe this curious silence in the following chapters. A few words are in order now.

Over five thousand executives have participated in my

Ethics Edge seminars. Each seminar begins with an exercise to determine what each person thinks ethics is. Each participant writes his or her own definition of ethics. I ask participants to avoid posturing and to be accurate about what they really mean when they talk about ethics. (For details on this exercise, see "The Ethics Test" at the end of this Introduction.) Many participants discuss their definitions in the course of the seminar. Their definitions cover the range of what we all mean by ethics.

The most common conception of ethics is that ethics is what our society or group says is right and wrong. Managers often say, "Ethics is what society accepts as right and wrong" or "It's what comes down to us as right and wrong, our customs" or "Right and wrong are the limits our culture sets." Managers who take this line emphasize the variability of ethics from society to society, group to group, and time to time.

Another common conception is that ethics is what a person's conscience says is right or wrong. "It's what I know is right and wrong, what I hear myself say is right or wrong." "It's what I feel good or bad about doing—what sits well with me." "It's what my conscience tells me." Managers who think this way associate ethics with morality. Although there is no difference in meaning between ethics and morality, we tend to speak of morality in assessing the ethics of a *person* rather than of a specific *action*. These managers emphasize that ethics is personal and "up to the individual."

A final group says that ethics is what God commands. "God says what is right and wrong; our job is to do God's will." There are many variations on this theme, emphasizing prayer, scripture, inspiration, and so on, matching the precepts of different religions and attitudes toward religion. These managers see one ethical truth for all times and all people; the job of the individual is to conform to this truth.

None of these common conceptions of ethics is of much use to managers. The idea that ethics is what society considers acceptable does not help unless you know what society considers acceptable and want to go along. Since managers belong to multiple societies (the societies of the organization, the community, professional groups, political parties, and foreign countries), each with different and conflicting standards, the manager who views ethics as a social norm has a confusing, inconsistent guide. That is as good as no guide.

Neither conscience nor religion is a more consistent guide. Assuming that a manager's conscience speaks clearly to him (my conscience often speaks with a forked tongue), this leaves the problem of those whose consciences disagree. Even if the manager is the chief executive, forcing the dictates of his or her conscience on others is not a winning approach to management. If the manager is not the chief executive, he or she can comply, rebel, or take ulcer medicine.

God may tell some managers what is right and wrong, but God tells other managers other stories. There are so many religions and versions of God's Word that managers are not likely to get far resolving ethical issues by claiming they speak God's Word.

It is no news to managers that these conceptions of ethics do not help them resolve ethical issues. These conceptions are a tribute more to our ethical confusion than to our moral insight.

If we are so unclear about ethics, why do we "talk ethics" so much? Why do we talk ethics more at times of broad social and industrial change? Indeed, why do we talk ethics at all? And why is talk of ethics taking the form of a big lie? To understand this, let us look briefly at ethics' underside.

Agreement-Racket Ethics

Managers need to grasp clearly that a lot of ethics is an *agreement racket*. That is, we often talk ethics to ensure that some person, group, or organization agrees with us on a basic issue or principle; if they do not agree, we seek to exclude them, oppose them, or nullify their influence. Sociologists call this the in-group–out-group ploy. The best way to consign someone to the out group is to point out a basic ethical difference between that person and the in group. Carried to its logical conclusion, this ethical agreement racket produces a big lie.

Here is how it works. When you talk ethics, you seize the high ground. "I'm interested in ethics. What are you interested in? Profits? Your career? Preserving the status quo?" By declaring an interest in ethics, you relegate opponents to arguing economics, politics, or self-interest. No one can challenge your premises, since these are ethical rather than factual. But you can challenge the premises of others, since they must argue economic, political, or organizational facts.

A good example of an ethics agreement racket is the discussion of U.S. corporations in South Africa. Critics state that they are ethically opposed to U.S. corporations operating in South Africa. The government of South Africa is immoral because it is racist, brutal in its treatment of minorities, and unwilling to change. The conclusion: It is unethical for U.S. corporations to operate in South Africa since this supports South Africa's immoral government. Since the premise that South Africa's government is immoral is clearly true, critics gain the agreement of much of the public and position U.S. corporations as unethical outsiders. This leaves corporations the unsavory option of arguing that it is ethical to support a racist government. What corporations actually do is to ignore the issue, point lamely to compliance with the Sullivan principles (standards for operating in South Africa), or ask the public relations department to bury the issue.

Ethics is conceded to the critics. It should not be. U.S. corporations operating in South Africa may be responsible for more social change than all the protest groups and governmental initiatives together. The strongest force for social change and justice in any society is envy. When U.S. corporations provide jobs, education, and management opportunities that minorities could not otherwise dream of, including the opportunity to manage whites, minorities get direct evidence of how good life without apartheid could be. They envy those who have these opportunities and demand them for themselves. Ironically, U.S. corporations may have caused the unrest in South Africa that has fueled recent demands for disinvestment. I do not suggest that the issue is simple. It is complex. I suggest that U.S. corporations have an ethical case and should not comply with the agreement-racket ethics of their critics.

The agreement-racket picture of ethics is not pretty, but

it accurately depicts much that passes under the title "ethics." Because ethical concepts—fair and unfair, right and wrong, good and bad—are used to run agreement rackets, there is often a vested interest in keeping ethics unclear. That is why managers face critics who talk ethics but who will not say what they mean. By allowing this to go on, managers buy into agreement rackets in which they are the designated victims, and thus they buy into the business-is-unethical lie.

Managers are unclear about ethics. This sets them up to lose at agreement-racket ethics. But ethics is more than an agreement racket. If managers can see the rest of ethics, what ethics really is, they cannot only immunize themselves against agreement-racket ethics but also use ethics to ask critical questions about the agreements that govern the firm and its environment. By using ethics to ask hard questions, managers can reinvigorate their firms internally and reposition them externally. This book offers a new way of looking at ethics that clears up the confusion and looks beyond agreement-racket ethics.

The first step in getting off the ethical defensive and breaking up agreement-racket ethics is to start to observe ethics at work in your business. The following ethics test describes one way of getting into your ethics and seeing where you stand.

The Ethics Test

People greatly enjoy talking about ethics; however, they seldom bother to say what they are talking about. I therefore start my ethics for executives seminars with a simple exercise designed to determine the ethical awareness level of the participants.

The exercise opens with the observation that we use ethical language in every paragraph we speak: "What he did to get them to go along with the deal wasn't right, don't you agree?" "It's not fair to say that participation counts, and then give the biggest raise to Henri the autocrat." "It's the wrong way to run the department, but we have to play by the same rules as the other departments." The words *right, fair,* and *wrong* signal that these common comments have ethical content. Indeed, I challenge you to carry on a few moments of normal conversation without using several ethical terms.

Furthermore, we often frame our concerns in ethical terms when we perceive an issue to be critical—when we consider going to war, firing someone, quitting, or putting someone out of business. Given that we speak in ethical terms when we face critical issues, we should know what we are saying when we talk ethics.

The exercise proceeds with the instruction to pick a few common ethical words from your vocabulary and write a brief definition stating exactly what *you* mean and when *you* use them. I commend this exercise to the reader. Pick a few words such as *right, wrong, unjust, fair,* or whatever ethical words you commonly use, and say on paper exactly what you mean when *you* use them. It is important not to fudge the exercise. Write down what you have to say. Do not write down some high-minded nonsense you use to impress your friends.

When trying to write something that does not sound silly, the participants discover that they lack a firm understanding of what they mean when they use ethical words.

Some standard responses are: "It doesn't agree with my principles," "It violates basic norms," and "I wouldn't deal with anyone who did that."

"But why," I ask them, "are *your* principles or *our* basic norms, as opposed to those of others, so important or right? And why does it matter who you would or would not do business with? Perhaps you don't like doing business with certain people or kinds of people. It does not follow that there is anything wrong with them or what they do."

After a discussion of this sort, anger and embarrassment permeate the seminar's atmosphere. The participants feel that they are being made to look foolish. They are embarrassed to admit that they do not know what they are talking about in ethics.

The point of the exercise, of course, is not to anger or embarrass anyone. Rather, it is to demonstrate that we need to pay attention to this part of our ordinary thinking and speaking, a part we turn to when our bets are down. More importantly, we must note that our ethical talk often rebukes someone or something that we do not like or agree with. By saying someone is unethical, we serve notice that we regard it as OK to do something to that person or business.

Also, we are seeking the agreement of others (ethical judgments characteristically are followed by "Don't you agree?") that it is okay to discipline the supposedly unethical individual, and we may even be seeking cohorts in forming the lynch mob.

Finally, we use ethical talk to signal whether someone is in our group or outside our group. To label you as unethical states that you are not part of our group and thus are fair game for members of our group, because in-group protections do not apply to you. I realize that this is not a pretty depiction of ethics. But it is a component of ethics, long recognized by psychologists and philosophers, that managers must acknowledge and deal with. As we will see in later chapters, it is neither the totality nor the core of ethical thinking.

As the Ethics Test makes clear, it is not always fun or easy to probe one's ethics. Recognition of this fact, together with the expectation that business will come out the loser in any ethical confrontation, is the heart of managers' fear of ethics. The technology for overcoming fear is familiar: Expose yourself to what you fear, and allow the fear to dissipate.

Of course, all of us would be happy not to overcome some of our fears. I am perfectly content with my fear of sky diving. But fear of the basic ethical grounds from which you act and evaluate can only be debilitating. This is especially true when the opponents of business have detected this fear and are drawing the lines of conflict on the field of ethics.

1

The Competitive Advantage
of Ethics-Based Thinking

The master knows the rules without suffering them;
the servant suffers the rules without knowing them.
—*Chinese proverb*

Agreement-racket ethics can put us on the defensive as
managers and trap us in the big lie that business is unethical. In
order to counteract agreement-racket ethics, we must become
acquainted with true ethics and its powerful tools. This will enable us not only to take a positive, informed stand against agreement-racket ethics but also to get to the very core of hard problems and begin solving them.

Ethics enables us to get at the core of these problems
because it deals with the most fundamental principles by which
individuals and organizations act. We will see in Chapter Seven
that since the ethics of an organization is more fundamental
than its culture, organizations would do best to have weak cultures and strong ethics. In order to understand the way in which
ethics is a powerful practical tool for managers, we look first at
how ethics, through its historical evolution, came to be viewed
as opposed to business. We then introduce the idea of ethics as
ground rules and show how this idea enables managers to beat
the agreement racket and create competitive advantages.

16

Ethics in the Market

Ethics began in the marketplace in ancient Athens. Socrates was the first ethicist. Before Socrates, thinkers pondered the nature of physical reality (What are its constituents and what is its origin?). Socrates turned critical thought on man under the motto "Know thyself."

Socrates was a member of Athen's elite, and he was an elitist. The marketplace was his workshop. He visited the market to pose questions to the citizens he met there. Socrates' message was that it is far more important to know what you do *not* know than it is to know what you do know. His point? If you think you know something when you do not, you are led around by false belief. Indeed, you are forced to surround the false belief with other false beliefs to protect yourself from admitting your misdirection. Stanley Davis (1982) learned the same thing in an important study of chief executives. Their consensus was that the most important quality that managers can have is knowing what they do not know. Only then can they ask the critical questions that need asking for their organizations to survive and prosper.

Although Socrates was reluctant to give pat answers to complex questions, we can infer that virtue, in the sense of good living, was at the heart of his ethics. To live with virtue was to have reason rule the other components of the psyche. Socrates was also concerned with ethics in the state, in business, and in other organizations. His approach was consistent throughout: The ethical, or virtuous, organization is ruled by its rational part in the interest of all of its parts. (For a sample of Socrates' thought, see Plato, 387-367 B.C.)

Socrates may have been the high point as well as the first point in the history of ethics. Plato, Socrates' great pupil, turned ethics from a practice into an academic discipline. (See Grube, 1974.) Given the intriguing questions posed by Socrates, it is understandable that people with the leisure to do so would devote attention to these questions. But academics have proven reluctant to return ethics to those in whom it lives, those who act.

The transformation of ethics into an esoteric discipline was completed by Aristotle, a student in the academy founded by Plato. Although Aristotle's views are extremely complex, his general line of thinking is sensible. For Aristotle, ethics is about living well. To live well is to seek that which it is one's nature to seek; hence, reason and satisfaction figure centrally in human relations. Aristotle put a high value on public life and was a functionalist; he maintained that living well for the individual is partly determined by what the individual does and why. Organizations live well if they have a function and are directed toward achieving it. (See Aristotle, 335-323 B.C.) While Aristotle made a great intellectual contribution, his academization of ethics created a gap between ethics and practice that has proven hard to close.

Ethics Against Good Living

The history of ethics after Aristotle is not a happy one. For many centuries, ethics was the province of scholars arguing the correct interpretation of the views of Plato or Aristotle. Then religion took over. Every religion has an ethical code as part of its world view and recommended way of life. As ethics came to be dominated by priests and theologians, it became a matter of faith rather than reason and was made to serve the institutional needs of religion. Struggles among religions focused partly on ethics. The only common ground among religions was that ethical thinking should be limited to textual interpretation. To seek more revealed a lack of faith. (See Russell, 1965.)

This is not to condemn religion. It is just that when religions become institutionalized, they struggle for place with other institutions. They struggle with other religions, states, businesses, and any other group that aspires to institutional preeminence. This is not so much the nature of religion as it is the nature of institutions. Religion simply excels at using ethics in its struggle for institutional survival and preeminence. Religions use ethics in the way that public interest groups do today—to assume the high ground and condemn dissenters as infidels.

During this period, ethics earned its reputation for guiltmongering and for rigid observance of rules. Religions and cultures fend off questioning of their ethical codes by educating members to experience guilt for transgressions against "the code." Guilt becomes a badge of honor, signifying one's acceptance of the standards of morality. The code must be simple and rigid if it is to be inculcated effectively. Is it any wonder that ethical codes founder and lose their relevance in complex times?

Ethics Shrugged

Ethics began to emerge with new vigor during the Renaissance. One notable work was Machiavelli's famous and infamous *The Prince* (1513). Contemporary thinkers often read *The Prince* in the way Marxists read *The Wall Street Journal*—in search of the devil. *The Prince* has its merits. It is based on reason and on Machiavelli's observations of how governments work. He was largely concerned with shaking institutions (particularly the state) loose from their ecclesiastical moorings and giving them a firm secular foundation. Machiavelli's work illustrates a crucial lesson about ethics: Ethics is a prominent subject when the fundamental institutions of society are radically challenged and forced to change. Today we hear a lot about business ethics, medical ethics, legal ethics, work ethics, police ethics, media ethics, and every other kind of ethics. It is no accident.

Ethics as we now know and breath it took shape in the seventeenth to nineteenth centuries. The dominant ethical models, rule ethics and end-point ethics, were explicitly stated during this period.

Rule Ethics. Rule ethics is the view that there are basic rules which determine the rightness or wrongness of actions. John Locke, to whom the framers of the U.S. Constitution owe so much, stated the most powerful version of rule ethics, or what he termed *social contract ethics.* Locke stated that the rules by which people ought to live are those that they would agree to live by if given the opportunity to make a choice based on reason and knowledge. Social contract ethics was a powerful challenge to kings and aristocrats because it maintained that they could not rely on divine right to back their claims to power; although Locke himself was not a revolutionary, his ideas broke ground for democratic society. (See Locke, 1690.) In some respects, understanding of governance in organizations lags behind understanding of the processes of formal political governance (electoral, legislative, and judicial processes). Today, as managers and researchers are giving more attention to the issue of governance within organizations, Locke's idea of the social contract is providing a basis for a new model of organizations that sees them as networks of contracts (Keeley, 1980). (This model is discussed in Chapter Seven.)

There are as many varieties of rule ethics as there are cultures, religions, and sects. Whether one or the other ethical code is the correct one is less important than how the codes attempt to establish their correctness. Locke distinguished his social contract ethics by arguing that it grows out of voluntary, reasoned choices; thus, the authority of the code derives from its claim to express the reasoned choices of free people. Locke's ethics is open to many criticisms, not the least of which is that it shortchanges the need to correct injustices. For the reasoned choices of free people may still be influenced by prejudices and false beliefs, and thereby yield a social system that treats some groups inequitably.

The final great rule ethicist, Immanuel Kant, tried to correct this wrong and counteract the overbearing influence of science. Kant felt that the scientific view of man as a complex mechanism was pulling the rug out from under ethics. He also insisted that ethics address issues of fair distribution of goods. Kant's supreme maxim says essentially that only rules that apply equally to everyone are ethical. While Kant's ethics is a masterpiece of philosophical reasoning, it is a step backward in its reliance on intuition unsupported by empirical observation to justify itself. Kant's ethics is an esoteric one, most at home in the armchair and classroom. (See Kant, 1785.)

Rule ethics established the lasting sense that ethics is more concerned with the rules governing people than with the pursuit of wise and satisfying living. This undoubtedly reflects the positive role of rule ethics in overturning tyrannical rules of state, church, and society. But there is something missing from an ethics more concerned with procedure than with outcome.

End-Point Ethics. A complete turnabout from the ethics of the Dark Ages was achieved with John Stuart Mill's *Utilitarianism* (1861). Mill, a philosopher, economist, public administrator, and strident defender of the East India Company, was as much a man of action as of thought. Mill articulated utilitarianism, the dominant form of end-point ethics. The idea of utilitarianism is simple: To determine whether an action is right or wrong, one must concentrate on its likely consequences. End-point ethics grew up to be the familiar cost-benefit and risk-benefit analyses (discussed in Chapter Four).

Just as rule ethics was a response to the rise of science, end-point ethics was a response to the industrial revolution. The industrial revolution was forcing shifts in the family (away from the extended family), in government (toward greater involvement in commerce), and in business (with industrialists replacing merchants as the model business managers). It forced people to question their basic social institutions.

Mill asked of any rule or institution: Does this rule (institution) promote a greater balance of benefit over harm than do other rules (institutions) we might live by? If the answer is no, then the rule or institution should not be adopted—or, if it already exists, should be overthrown. Mill thus opposed state paternalism, slavery, and the oppression of women (he coauthored with Harriet Taylor a defense of women's rights). Mill's utilitarianism removed barriers to the progress of the industrial revolution by challenging the ethics of the past and providing a positive way of looking at ongoing ethical changes. (See Mill, [1861] 1948; Ryan, 1970.)

Ethics Today

We are now in a time of transition. The changes in our means and forms of production are as radical as those of the industrial revolution. Some call the current revolution the information revolution; others think of it as a transition to a service-based economy. We are too close to this revolution to pin down its exact character. Predictably, there is wide interest in ethics for business, government, the professions, and society at large. But there has been no new model of ethics to sweep away the resisting past and help make sense of the future.

Rule ethics and end-point ethics persist, just as the forms of organization and the management models appropriate to the passing industrial era persist. Rule ethics, with its focus on the rules by which we act, indicts current business for transgressing the rules of business past; thus business is criticized for playing by different rules in different countries, as if current businesses could enforce ethics across borders as in colonial times. While the greatest virtue of capitalist business is its productivity, rule ethics continues to worry about how the spoils are divided, no matter how meager the spoils would be if the precepts of rule ethics prevailed. End-point ethics can give the productive capacity of business its due, but with its tunnel-visioned concern with the common good, it ignores contractually based property right in a redistributional frenzy almost equal to that of rule ethics. The common good is now the most frequently invoked concept in restricting property rights.

With more and more business managers receiving functional training in business schools, managers are incapacitated in the face of all-out ethical attacks on business. Hence, ethics appears to indict business, with business saying little in its own defense. This unanswered ethical indictment of business is the heart of the antibusiness agreement racket which leads to the lie that business is unethical.

The first thing that managers need to do in order to break up the agreement racket is to reclaim mastery of the ethical tools now turned against them. Both rule ethics and end-point ethics can treat business fairly if business seeks its day in court. Further, if managers think *creatively* in ethical terms, they can play their role in seeing that the emerging ethics tolerates and even supports the constructive power of business.

To reclaim mastery of ethical tools, managers need a practical concept of ethics to apply to the problems they face in the workplace. This book develops such a concept—the concept of ethics as ground rules—so that managers can use the tools of ethics to beat the agreement racket and open up new perspectives for dealing with hard management problems.

Ethics as Ground Rules

Ethics is simpler than people with a vested interest in complicating it would have you believe. Ethics racketeers, as well as the academics, theologians, and writers allied with them, want to keep ethics mysterious. If the racket is exposed, it is hard to run it. If ethics is demystified, those who interpret ethics for the uninitiated are out of work.

All individuals and organizations have ethics. It is fair to say that President Reagan has an ethics of independence, whereas Lee Iacocca has an ethics of interdependence; 3M has an ethics of innovation and Motorola an ethics of participation. Even highly unethical persons or firms have ethics. If you find this difficult to accept, then consider the fact that motorcycle gangs have cultures. Just as it is one thing to have a culture and quite another to have a commendable culture, so it is one thing to *have* ethics and quite another to have *good* ethics. Since what counts as good ethics is debatable, unambiguous examples are hard to come by. But it is clear that Jonas Salk has good ethics and that Muammar Kaddafi does not. The Nixon White House was an organization having bad ethics; Caterpillar Tractor has good ethics. Let us start with the idea that a person has ethics, be that ethics good or bad.

Ethics of Individuals. The ethics of a person is the set of basic ground rules by which that person acts.

Despite the complex explanations we give of our actions, we act for fairly simple reasons. One reason for offering complex explanations of what we do is to mask the underlying simplicity from others and from ourselves. When we talk about the ethics of a person, we are talking about the principles which the person's actions reveal to be fundamental for that person. I call these fundamental principles the person's ground rules. *Ground rules* are a framework delimiting those actions that are possible for the person and those that are not. Just as the rules of a game determine what moves are possible and what each move means, so a person's ground rules determine what actions the person may take and what these actions mean.

Personal ground rules that I have observed in training and consulting include: "What I do and how I do it makes no difference," "What happens to me is what really counts," "If I cooperate with others, I'll eventually get my way," and "If I do things the right way, I'll eventually be rewarded."

For example, I once worked with David Farnswarth (fictional name), an entrepreneur who achieved great success by the age of thirty-five. Farnswarth had a knack for hiring people who shared his entrepreneurial drive and ability. But when they presented their best ideas to him, he accused them of using his name and resources to build their own reputations. Farnswarth acted on the simple ground rule: Only trust people you can control. (This case is examined in detail in Chapter Two.)

It is clear that not all ground rules are commendable. It is also clear that some ground rules are quite commendable. Observing that a person has ethics—a set of ground rules—is not to say whether that ethics is good or bad.

Ethics of Organizations. Organizations also have ethics: 3M has an ethics of innovation, Motorola an ethics of participation, and Amtrak an ethics of survival. The ethics of an organization is the set of basic ground rules by which that organization acts.

There are fundamental principles, or ground rules, by which organizations act. Like the ground rules of individuals, organizational ground rules determine which actions are possible for the organization and what the actions mean. Buried beneath the charts of organizational responsibility, the arcane strategies, the crunched numbers, and the political intrigue of every firm are ground rules by which the game unfolds.

Nothing is more important to the aspiring middle manager or savvy top manager than knowing the ground rules or ethics of the firm. Lacking this knowledge, the manager plays the game without knowing the rules. When consulting to a division of Techtron (fictitious name of a leading office technology company), I was told about their commitment to providing opportunities for women and minorities. A code of conduct underscored this commitment, and managers signed off on this code annually. A training program urged managers to take this commitment seriously. Later in the day, the division head showed me the all-white, all-male executive offices. This division operated on the ground rule: When it comes to high-level positions, ignore the rules and follow your judgment. The judgment of the division management was biased. Aspiring minority and women employees needed to know this ground rule to assess their careers, and Techtron's corporate management needed to know it to produce change in the division.

If you query the ground rules, it is easier to produce change. Motorola, a leading semiconductor and electronics firm, decided to infuse the entire company with the participatory management style that proved very successful in certain divisions. It met a problem best characterized as the "Despite the upbeat talk and best efforts at every level, nothing is happening" syndrome. Motorola had to discover that one of its ground rules was: All that really matters are the numbers. This ground rule translated into a management commitment to what could be measured in quarterly reviews, and nothing else. Once Motorola took note of this ground rule, it moved quickly to make the participation program and ground rule compatible (adjusting both). If Motorola had ignored this ground rule, it would still be paying consultants to give participation training programs.

It may seem that what one person calls the ethics of a firm is what another calls its culture. Although ethics and culture are connected, they are not the same. Ethics is the core of a culture, but it is possible for a firm to have strong ethics and a weak culture. Organizational cultures are slow-footed, hard to change, and frequently offensive. If ethics is the heart of a firm, then culture is the fat that strangles its heart and clogs its arteries. But every organization has, and must have, ethics. This ethics, if acknowledged, helps the organization learn quickly and adapt to a complex, changing world. (Chapter Seven delves further into the connections between ethics and culture.)

The most valuable lesson of this book is to learn to read the ethics of individuals and firms. It follows from the definition of *ethics* as ground rules that the way to discover the ethics of a person or firm is through their actions. How do we observe actions to discover ground rules? In subsequent chapters, we outline a reverse-engineering process: Start with actions, trace them back to decisions, prod decisions to uncover their premises, and sift the premises for ground rules. The method is to be interrogative, asking "Why?" at each step: Why is the office white and male when the written rules say that opportunity is the game? Why is it costing so much to implement a participation program when everyone says they want it? As in all reverse engineering, the trick is to develop an eye for looking at the product and seeing the underlying process.

If you read the ethics (ground rules), you know the rules by which the game is played. You can use the standing ground rules to get where you want to go. This is what Mel did to win approval of his shopping mall (described in the Introduction). He knew the ground rules of the council and the citizens' group. Instead of fighting these ground rules, he framed his argument in terms of them and won.

But not all standing ground rules should be accepted as is. I will be saying quite a bit about changing ground rules. Changing them is a lot like blowing up the nonphysical reality of the organization. But before you set out to change the ground rules for the better, you need to ask what good ground rules are. As we explore ground rules in relation to some of the hard problems of management, we develop a working model of good ground rules for an adaptive high-ethics organization. This model is based on extensive study of high-ethics, high-profit firms.

Taking It to the Street

The successful manager is a good street fighter. Perhaps it would be better if this were not so, but this book is not about wishful thinking. It is popular to portray the "new manager" as a privatized flying nun, but it just does not look or feel that way on the line. The manager who can make a difference ethically is the manager who seeks results.

I offer no *One-Minute Ethicist.* A one-minute guide to

ethics is as useful as *The One-Minute Lover*. But I do say a lot about how to get it done—about what to do if you want to think outside the no-ethics box, get off the defensive, and manage "ahead of the curve."

Viewing ethics as ground rules does not result in cookie-cutter solutions. It results in new ways of approaching problems, making decisions, and anticipating future problems. It is not that the manager who thinks ethics has the answers. Rather, this manager has the questions that enable the organization to find answers. That is why I shall call the ethical manager the thinking manager.

My aim is to provide you with the tools for taking ethics to the street, where it can do some good. A tool is used for a purpose. The purpose of these ethical tools is to allow you to take ownership of the ethical issues that affect you and to build businesses that are better in the broadest sense, economically and ethically. The way to take ownership of ethical issues is to use ethical tools to ask the critical questions—to ask yourself where you stand on an issue and what you want to do about that issue.

Let us look at one way that the thinking manager uses ethics to ask questions and create opportunities. He begins by querying the ground rules; he queries his ethics, the ethics of the firm, and the ethics of the constituencies the firm interacts with. The thinking manager does not settle for the pat answers we are all too ready to give. Instead, he observes, reverse engineering from actions to decisions, from decisions to premises, and from premises to ground rules. By so doing, he learns why he and others do what they do, what to anticipate from himself and others, what moves are possible, and how they will be viewed.

Consider a case in which a thinking manager, using the tool of querying ground rules, achieved a result that was unexpected, ethical, and economic.

Case: Grow Your Own Rules

The senior management of Diesel Engines Inc. (fictitious name for a leading diesel engine manufacturer) is worried. Already staggering under countless federal regulations, they have

learned that Congress may pass strict emission regulations for
diesel engines to match the existing regulations for gasoline
engines.

Senior management gathers for a meeting. After exchang-
ing wisecracks about stupid regulations and idiots at the Environmental Protection Agency, they search for a solution. The
public relations vice-president recommends a publicity campaign against the regulations. The engineers gripe that it is impossible to test for compliance with the new regulations, let
alone comply with them. The vice-president for legal affairs pro-
poses lobbying to block the regulations. Similar scenes occur
across the industry, with predictable outcomes.

But things take a surprising turn in the present meeting.
The chief executive officer (CEO) stuns everyone by asking,
"How do you like driving behind a diesel truck? How would
you like it if you weren't in the business? Let's get the junk out
of the air. I would have done something sooner, but nobody
would have followed us. Now you want to screw it up. You
can't believe gasoline engines are going to be tightly regulated
while we get off scott-free. Have the guts to handle this."

The CEO is learning from the ground rules of the public
and Congress. The public will see it as unfair that they pay for
emission controls while trucks and trains demonstrably continue polluting. The public operates on the ground rule "Don't
ask us to do it if you aren't going to make business do it." Congress acts on the ground rule "Don't appear to favor big business at the expense of the public," a corollary of the ground
rule "Job number one is to stay in office." The CEO also correctly observes that the ground rules for the industry will shift.
The new ground rules will allow Diesel Engines Inc. to design
emission controls into their engines without assuming an economic disadvantage vis-à-vis competitors.

Once their ears cool, the managers agree that, in part,
they always felt the same way. It just seemed disloyal to say so.
They order the lawyers to work with the engineers to draft
stringent but technically sound regulatory proposals. A vigorous
lobbying effort will support these proposals. The lobbyists will
argue that regulation is desirable and technically feasible, that

they have their own model proposals in hand, and that Congress's proposals are technically unsound. Meanwhile, the company begins redesigning its products to meet the more stringent environmental standards.

This is a variant of Mel's strategy. Diesel Engines Inc. will argue from the ground rules of Congress and the public to obtain a result acceptable in terms of its own ground rules. Instead of operating on ground rules destined for extinction, the company has anticipated the emerging ground rules of competition in the industry.

The outcome? Regulations almost identical to the company's model regulations passed after a tough legislative battle. The company was a year ahead of its competitors in getting products to market that complied with the regulations, and its share of the market for large diesel engines increased dramatically. In fact, the next issue it faced was how much of the market it could take without generating the false perception that it had rigged the regulations.

Diesel Engines Inc. gained an ethics edge—a competitive advantage available to an individual or firm willing to face ethical issues and think them through. It probed ground rules, recognized its dependence on external constituencies, and sought fairness. It asked questions that nobody else in the industry could fit into their no-ethics craniums, and it found answers.

You can, if you are so inclined, argue that a concern for ethics was not a critical factor in producing a favorable outcome in this case. The CEO was partly motivated by his accurate assessment of legislative reality. This factor and the awareness of an industrywide need to redesign products explains the company's choice of and success in pursuing an ethical strategy. Perhaps. But it is unclear why we should want to view the case this way, aside from the agreement-racket prejudice that ethics does not contribute to corporate performance.

Try viewing the case as follows: The CEO realized that the ethics of his industry and of his own company's managers was not the ethics of society at large on the issue of pollution. He realized that it was not within the company's power to change the ethics of society to suit the company. The fact that the CEO's personal ethics fit society's ethics better than it fit the ethics of his own company helped. (A conflict between individual and organizational ethics can be constructive.) By forcing a higher ethics at the company level, the CEO produced a more ethical and more profitable outcome.

It is important to note that the role of ethics in this case was not limited to meeting an ethical attack, the potential imposition of restrictive regulations. It also provided the basis for a new competitive strategy: Fight for fair regulations and be the first to the market with a product that complies. In fact, I shall argue that ethics is one of the strongest strategy-making tools available to managers.

When I advise you to think ethics, I am asking you to look at more than employees and products. When you think ethics in observing an automobile, think oil imports, pollution, accidents, hospitals, police officers, residents of foreign countries, and transportation for future generations. Think of the consequences for all; for those encompassed in your ground rules, for those who agree or disagree, in short, for whole systems of connected people and organizations. Think of the questions they will ask and try to ask them first.

By thinking ethics, by thinking of systems under the many guises they present to diverse constituencies, we fight entropy. An organization must create new ideas and intentions to connect it to new realities or it will stagnate within an ever-contracting circle. It is the new questions posed by ethics that break the circle and allow the organization a breath of the fresh air of its environment.

Ethical concepts and tools provide a framework for asking the questions that enable us to probe the ethical reality of a firm and its environment, to find ethics edges, and to convert them into business advantages. The positive role of ethics is to help us explode unworkable assumptions and replace them with more adaptive assumptions and a more adaptive attitude toward assumptions.

In order to put ethics to work, we must look at how managers can systematically discover their own ground rules, the ground rules of those with whom they work, and the ground rules of the organizations they work in and interact with. In short, managers must master the art of reverse engineering actions to uncover underlying ground rules. They can then do some forward engineering to meet hard management problems and design organizations that take these problems in stride.

2

Uncovering
and Taking Control
of Organizational
Ground Rules

Morality is the custom of one's country and the current feeling of one's peers. Cannibalism is moral in a cannibal country.

—*Samuel Butler*, Notebooks

Golfer 1 (food conglomerate executive): What do you do for a living?

Golfer 2 (consultant): I consult to companies on ethical and value issues.

Golfer 1: We never bother with that ethics stuff. We're too busy trying to keep the business running.

Golfer 2: Why has your company been successful for so long?

Golfer 1: We work hard to maintain good long-term relationships with our suppliers. This shelters us from the ups and downs of the grain markets. And we work with our distributors to improve our ability to plan grain purchases.

Golfer 2: Sounds like you have an ethics strategy, one that emphasizes long-term relationships of an informal, trust-based character.

32

Golfer 1:   If that's ethics, that's what we're about. Our prob-
             lem is getting our new people to understand this.
Golfer 2:   A standard ethical problem—one you can solve if
             you recognize it as such.
Golfer 1:   Understand that most companies are not like us.
             We're successful enough to take this ethics stuff
             seriously.
Golfer 2 (to himself): I've heard this somewhere before.

All too often, managers avoid thinking in ethical terms because they are unsure what ethics is and why it matters. Many are frustrated by the vague, nebulous term *ethics* and find that trying to define it is like nailing down Jell-O. I address their confusion by asking them to explain how they think of their company and why it has been successful; that is, I probe their ground rules. When the food conglomerate executive stressed long-term relationships with suppliers and distributors, he was citing ground rules that contributed to his firm's success. Without realizing it, he stated a short definition of the conglomerate's ethics.

Ethics can also be frustrating because it offers few black-and-white solutions; instead, it offers complex problems, hard choices, and uncertain outcomes. In accounting, 2 + 2 = 4, or is supposed to, but in ethics there is no cookbook formula. We can only learn to read ground rules, apply ethical tools, blend them with responsibility and creativity, and take our best shot—which is better than taking no shot or being shot at.

In part, it is just this vagueness of ethics that gives it its potential value to business. Every business can come up with cookbook answers for cookbook questions, but what separates the good companies from the mediocre ones is the ability to think creatively—to develop innovative solutions to problems that are not even problems for one's competitors (for example, how to make a radio to take on a walk). This ability creates unique market, production, and management niches that can "stun" competitors.

Like the food conglomerate executive, managers become comfortable with ethics when they discover that their ground rules have already played a part in their success and can provide further sustainable competitive edges.

When we have difficulty coming up with reasonably plausible definitions of *right* and *wrong* or *fair* and *unfair,* it is upsetting—for if we cannot clearly define what right and wrong or fair and unfair mean, our business decisions (which are saturated with ethical jargon) rest on shaky foundations. If a manager cannot clearly define what is fair and unfair, the basis of his or her decisions may shift overnight. Today's fair deal becomes tomorrow's "It's unfair; you can't do it." This is not a pedantic point. Business critics and regulators flip-flop too. For example, it was "right" for businesses to pay "consideration fees" to foreign governments, but suddenly these fees became "bribes" and were "wrong." Businesses were "caught" with their hands in the wrong pockets.

Thus, while we realize that everybody has "ethics," it makes sense to take the trouble to get as clear as we can about "ethics." In Chapter One, we observed that both individuals and organizations have ethical ground rules. It makes sense to ask what a person's ground rules are and to observe ethical differences among types of individuals. The ground rules of high-level managers in large bureaucratic organizations (such as banks, insurance companies, utilities, and large hospitals) likely emphasize loyalty to the group or the boss, interest in the community, and responsibility (understood in terms of tenure and reliability). The ground rules of managers in entrepreneurial firms emphasize autonomy, individuality, and reward for achievement. The ground rules of individuals also vary by religious background, community, national or ethnic origin, and many other factors.

The ground rules of an individual may also vary from role to role. One of the most eminent tax accountants in the United States got trapped by just such a role variation. As a tax expert, his opinion was that the tax advantages offered to churches were excessive and unproductive and violated the intentions of the lawmakers who had created the tax advantages. He was elected to a very high position in his church at a time when the church was deciding what public position to take on tax advantages to churches. If he pushed the church to accept his professionally considered position or if he even stated his position publicly, he would do grievous harm to the church. He was thus caught between the ground rules of two important roles and had to fall back on more basic ground rules. (His basic ground rules did not help, so he sentenced the issue to death by committee.)

We emphasized that organizations also have ground rules and that these ground rules vary in accordance with organizational character. Motorola's ground rules emphasize participation, quality, and patriotism. The ground rules of an executive government office (president, governor, or mayor) emphasize keeping information inside the office, remembering friends, deferring to authority, and putting the boss above all others. To say that organizations have ethics (ground rules) is not to say that they are some sort of mysterious superpersons inhabited by some sort of superconscience. It is to say that when individuals act as part of an organization, their actions take on characteristics that do not match what they do outside of that organization.

But how do we determine exactly what the ethics of a person or corporation is? The answer I gave in Chapter One is ground rules. I coupled this with the advice that if you want to discover an individual's ground rules, observe him. Do not listen to him. The same holds true for organizations. If a company brags about its concern for employee safety, it is trying to make a point about its ethics. Yet the fact that five employees a week go to the hospital because of unsafe conditions at the plant tells the true story about the company's ethics.

Unfortunately, most companies and most managers do not take the time to analyze their true ground rules, and this can be costly. If you do not know what truly motivates you to make a decision, you are condemned to making mistakes that you could easily have avoided. And you make the same mistakes over and over.

We now look a little more closely at ground rules—what they are and how to find them. And we focus on one important application of an understanding of ground rules—application to the internal workings of the firm and your career. In particular, we explore the implications of gaps between a manager's ground rules and those of his or her firm.

The Technique of Reverse Engineering

Let us start sharpening our ability to observe ground rules with a process for reverse engineering the actions of persons and organizations to discover the underlying ground rules of action.

Actions have their roots in decisions. Of course, not every action results from a conscious decision, but we do consciously decide before taking important actions, and less significant actions reflect conscious and implicit choices that we have made in the past. I do not decide to exercise rigorous candor with each of my consulting clients each time I interact with them. That is how I have decided to practice as a consultant. So the best place to find our ground rules is in our decisions.

A decision has several components. A decision occurs whenever we face alternatives or think we face alternatives. One component of a decision is to try to get clear about what the alternatives are. We sometimes misassess the alternatives. We often think that an alternative is open to us when it is not. (I once thought that one of my alternatives was to be a professional golfer. Alas, my genes did not carry the size chromosomes to make this alternative realistic.) More often, we misassess alternatives by overlooking critical alternatives. Assessing alternatives is one area in which ethics can improve business performance (as discussed in Chapter Four).

Once we have surveyed the alternatives, we must see what each alternative offers. There are two parts to this. One part is to see what we can say *factually* about each alternative. In other words, in order to reach a decision, we need to form a view concerning what is likely to happen if we adopt each alternative. Once we are clear about this, we must look at each of the projected outcomes and see what is in it for us. For our friends. For our employees, customers, competitors, and so on. Who should we consider?

In assessing outcomes, there are two salient questions: How much value do I see in each outcome, and what do I have to do to get the outcome I desire?

Ground Rules of Value. Answers to the first question reveal one kind of ground rule—ground rules of value. In reaching

a decision, we rate some outcomes as more desirable than others
—as more valuable.

For example, someone who chooses a career as a stock-
broker takes risks in pursuing wealth and independence (ground
rule: It is worth it to take risks in order to prosper and be free
of control). Someone else looking at the same career alternatives might decide to be a finance professor; she places a higher
value on security and on satisfying her curiosity about how
things work (ground rule: Once basic needs are met, it is important to discover the principles by which things work). The factual issues concerning career opportunities, abilities, and so
forth are certainly important. But once we have considered the
facts, what we count as desirable (valuable) and undesirable
(not valuable) orders the options.

Ground Rules of Evaluation. The second question is:
What do I have to do to get the desirable outcome? Answers to
this question reveal the second type of ground rule—ground
rules of evaluation. We often judge one option to be the most
desirable yet choose to pursue another because the first would
have required us to do things we just do not do. The point is
not that the option involves too much work, distasteful work,
or risks that we prefer to avoid; these issues relate to assessing
how desirable the option is. Rather, there are kinds of actions
that we will not take or do not want to take in order to obtain
even very desirable outcomes. We evaluate these actions as unacceptable in principle.

At one point, the chief executive of a major hotel chain
realized that the way to produce the outcome he judged to be
most desirable for the firm was to move into the casino business. He had no objection to people being in the casino busi
ness, but he did not believe in gambling or promoting gambling
himself. So he presented the casino option to his board as the
best option and resigned. The casino option violated his ground
rule: Gambling is not something I do, and I will not profit
from others doing what I will not do.

At the heart of every decision, and thus of every action
resulting from a decision, are ground rules expressing what we
value and what we will do to get what we value. To find your

ground rules, squeeze the factual assumptions out of your decisions; the ground rules are the residue that drives the decision. Practically, it is hard to separate one's factual assumptions from one's ground rules. But it can be done. My value-finding seminar asks participants, selected as organizational peers, to identify with relentless candor the patterns they find in each others' actions and decisions. If there is an atmosphere of genuine trust, the observations of others make it hard to bury one's ground rules under factual assumptions. It works because those who live with our ground rules figure them out more quickly than we do.

Organizations have the same kinds of ground rules. But just as it is hard to find responsibility in organizations, it is also hard to find the decisions and ground rules. Decisions of organizations are made by people and groups of people. The trick is to find out who makes them and then to pick through organizational diversions to see how decisions are made and evaluated. The following case study illustrates how a person who does not know and will not alter his ground rules established the ethics of a small organization.

Case: My Way or the Highway

David Farnswarth (fictional name), president of the small, successful venture-capital firm, D. F. Venture, did not know and would not change his ground rules; consequently, he was responsible for a series of firings, reorganizations, and personal frustrations that thwarted his firm's development.

Farnswarth was known for his enlightened concern for community well-being, for his willingness to seek win-win solutions to problems, and for his refreshingly lighthearted approach to business. He could be counted on for an honest opinion. Nevertheless, his firm suffered from a lack of expansion into areas unfamiliar to Farnswarth. The individuals who might have carried D. F. Venture into new areas either resigned or were fired.

Whenever Farnswarth's associates presented him with opportunities to expand into new areas, the discussion was lively and open at first. But at a critical point he would turn on them. He would challenge their expertise and insinuate that they were using the reputation and resources he had developed to carry the firm into dubious ventures. Farnswarth never backed down. Even if the person presenting the idea backed down, Farnswarth would later fire that person for an apparently unrelated reason.

Farnswarth acted on the ground rule: Cooperate with and help others, but only trust people you can control. For him, this was a ground rule of evaluation. He valued innovation and candor. He just failed to act consistently with these values. Thus his ground rules of value (favoring innovation and candor) conflicted with his ground rule of evaluation, which demanded that he be in control. Ground rules are often associated with factual assumptions; perhaps Farnswarth assumed that others were out to get him. Whether or not he made this assumption, his ground rule of evaluation was so entrenched that he would not admit assumptions conflicting with his ground rule in his decisions and actions.

Farnswarth succeeded despite his ground rule; he retained control of the small but successful D. F. Venture. Still, a business that had not changed for several years bored him.

Farnswarth had established his ethics as the ethics of D. F. Venture. Some members of the firm recognized that the ethics of D. F. Venture dictated that they would be richly rewarded for being aggressive and entrepreneurial *within Farnswarth's limits*. These limits were not exceeded. One associate who recognized this has been with the firm for four years and has prospered. Other associates recognized the ethics of the firm, confronted them, and got out. But most associates listened to Farnswarth's words, missed the ground rules, and suffered in confusion until they were fired or quit.

Farnswarth knew that his firm had problems. He judged the lack of growth and high turnover rate as unacceptable, and he hired a consultant to turn things around. The consultant pointed out to Farnswarth that these problems resulted from his dominating others when they tried to initiate new projects and that the cause was his need for total control.

Farnswarth set out to correct matters. Yet when his associates responded by starting new projects and building their reputations as venture capitalists, he became frightened and reverted to his defensive ground rule, demanding total control. To justify this, he began to maintain that anyone who seeks total control understands that power is the source of business success. "People who can control things," he came to say (meaning himself, of course, since others seldom challenged him), "are people who know how things really work." He judged that D. F. Venture's lack of growth proved that the company was so successful that new developments would have been anticlimactic.

Things have thus returned to normal at D. F. Venture. Farnswarth resists new ideas more than ever. He resolved the conflict between his ground rules of value and of evaluation in favor of his control-oriented ground rule. So far he has gotten away with this, but it remains to be seen how long D. F. Venture will prosper.

We have just seen how ignorance of ground rules can cause disorder. Many employees of D. F. Venture would have saved themselves grief by observing the ground rules operative in the firm. Farnswarth would also have been better off aware of them from the outset. Farnswarth has blood on his hands, in some cases that of close friends. It may be that he is now unwilling to change his ground rules because the cost of admitting his errors has become so high.

These downfalls are typical results of not understanding ethics. Managers who value their careers cannot afford to ignore ethics. Ignorance of ethics (ground rules) can thwart promotions, stifle entrepreneurial spirit, and generally frustrate career aspirations.

Ground Rules Can Make or Break Your Career

Do your individual ethics match the ethics of your organization? If they do not and if you cannot or will not adjust, you may be exiled to corporate oblivion, given a job that is more a sinecure than an opportunity.

This happens all too often to women executives.

Yes, corporate ethics does block the careers of women

executives. At the entry level, women executives are treated more or less as equals. This occurs not only because of socially enforced affirmative action but also because the starting positions held by women executives are too insignificant to threaten top-level male executives.

As women climb the corporate ladder, they find themselves running into an unwritten corporate rule: No woman shall hold operating power. For example, in banks this means that women are generally not given significant portfolio-managing power; in manufacturing businesses it means that women are not given line authority to manage "seasoned" male managers. Thus women on the verge of being promoted into an operational position find themselves being promoted out of line management and into human resources, public relations, or prestigious-sounding but sterile staff positions. If this sounds dubious, look around. How many women do you find in public relations, financial evaluation, or market research positions? Women are in positions to recommend but not to implement policy.

Women exiled into public relations, human resources, and other nonthreatening positions find it hard to make it back into the mainstream. "Sure she's bright, but can she handle line responsibility without having had experience in the branches, assembly lines, and so on?"

The female executive has been stymied by the corporate ground rule: Thou shalt not grant women operating power. This rule is backed by other ground rules. For example, high-level male executives often operate on the ground rule: Take what you can get or the other guy will take it. But female executives often operate on the conflicting ground rule: If I always have to be trampling somebody to get ahead, it is not worth it. This conflict in ground rules puts the female executive at a considerable disadvantage, particularly in organizations in which women operating on a "nontrampling" ground rule are perceived to be weak or lacking in ambition.

The options available to the female executive are to change her male superiors' ground rules; to change her own ground rules; to accept the limitations imposed on her career by operating on her own ground rules (in other words, to accept her position as a management outcast); or to exit from the organization.

Many confident female executives, when confronted with this ethical stone wall, take the highway and search for a corporation that promotes women into operational positions. Such organizations are not easy to find. Often the female executive gets what she wants initially, only to hit the ethical stone wall again. The option of changing one's own ground rules looks more attractive. But the more common option is to move to or start a small organization of like-minded people. Thus, a lot of talent is lost to major corporations.

The Issue of Control

If an organization's ground rules thwart the careers of people who would otherwise be valuable assets to it, why does the organization not shift its ground rules? The issue boils down to why ethics is so often an instrument for control rather than an instrument for making the best use of resources. I touched on this issue in looking at agreement-racket ethics. To understand the relationship of ethics to control, we need to look more closely now at how agreement-racket ethics works in organizations and to examine the elements of a non-agreement-racket ethics.

We must explore two attitudes towards ethics. The first, agreement-racket ethics, states that ethics represents the dark underside of our personalities. The second, autonomous ethics, states that ethics evolves from the highest part of our souls and expresses the best in us.

Agreement-Racket Ethics. Some psychologists argue that a central function of ethics is to gain control over others (Skinner, 1965). An example: When parents want to control their small children, it is fairly simple. They observe their children and punish or reward them in accordance with the parents' wishes. Yet this system's effectiveness is short-lived, for as the children grow, their domain of activity extends beyond the domain of observation and of reward or punishment. To counter this, parents begin their children's ethical education, introduc-

ing them to such words as *good, bad, right,* and *wrong.* Parents
let their children know that they should feel guilty when they
transgress the limits defined by these words. Children should
feel ashamed when they do something bad and proud when
they do something good. Parents reward their children for dis-
playing these attitudes.

In this way, parents work out a remote-control system
whereby their children punish and reward themselves. When a
child comes home, a parent merely has to push buttons on the
control: "Have you been good or have you been bad?" Parents
strengthen their control over their children's behavior by adding Santa Claus and God to the picture. Now, in addition to
their parents' remote control, the children feel that everything
they do is also being watched by Santa or God. There is always
someone judging their actions.

There is one flaw in the game. Instead of recognizing the
ethics game for what it is, parents buy into it. Thus they have
the same feelings of guilt and pride to control them. In fact, the
ethics game would not work if parents understood its true nature. It is hard to be that cynical in dealing with your own kids.

This agreement-racket picture of ethics includes groups.
The premise is that groups need to control their members. By
planting the seeds of guilt, groups and group leaders can control
their members by guilt manipulation. This essentially describes
the plight of the serfs in the Middle Ages; manipulated by family, church, and state, they were made to feel guilty if they
transgressed the feudal lord's property rights. Similarly, slaves
were made to feel guilty if they failed to perform well for their
masters. These control systems collapsed of their own weight—
after hundreds of years.

If you accept the belief that ethics is a tool of control
perpetuated by parents, groups, organizations, and society—and
if you believe that society is composed mainly of average people, with but a few substandard and excellent ones—then it is
reasonable to assume that the majority of average people create
rules to control the substandard ones and to exploit the excellent ones.

Society exploits achievers by saying: "Your achievements

are not a product of your abilities. You owe it to the common good to give away the products of your efforts." In other words, "Do not step out of line, do not embarrass underachievers, and do give us enough of your spoils to keep us off your back." Is this not the ultimate master-slave relationship? Everyone becomes a slave to the rules. And the thought leaders, the heroes and the entrepreneurs, are enslaved by the ethics of the masses (Nietzsche, [1887] 1967).

There is more than a grain of truth in this view of ethics as a tool to control and, specifically, to limit others. But there is another side.

Autonomous Ethics. Autonomous ethics views ethics as the product of reason combined with a person's sympathetic and empathetic capacities. According to this view, people have the ability to sympathize with others. To sympathize with others is to observe when they are well-off and to experience satisfaction that they are. It is also to observe when they are not well-off and to experience dissatisfaction that they are not. Sympathy is distinct from empathy. *Empathy* is the ability to experience the world as other people in other circumstances experience it. The capacities to feel sympathy and empathy constitute the emotional base of autonomous ethics.

There is no question that we have these capacities and that they are central to ethics. Indeed, the fact that we have these capacities is useful when we use ethics to control others. "Don't you see how what you're doing makes your father (coworkers) feel?"

Reason enters the picture. We naturally have sympathy and empathy for those who seem most like us; conversely, we tend to lack these responses the more distant or different someone seems from us. A brutal demonstration of this fact is that even though a combat-hardened soldier finds it hard to kill someone face to face, with hands or a knife, it is easy to press a button that drops a bomb on hundreds. This fact lies behind the only really effective method I have heard of to check the threat of nuclear war. The method is to have the heads of state of the United States and the Soviet Union exchange children or, alternatively, to install "the button" in their spouses. Of course, this method rests on the possibly dubious assumption that these leaders care more for their families than for anonymous citizens of the other's country.

Reason notices our tendency to discount the interests of those removed from us in our perception. Reason says, "If I had been born in Ethiopia, of a different race or gender or were born in the future, I would value my interests under those circumstances as much as I now do." Reason reminds us that children born in other parts of the world did not choose not to be born to you or your neighbors. It reminds us that whether people are killed with a knife or a bomb, they are equally dead. Reason counteracts our tendency to discount the interest of those who simply seem to be unlike us; it invites us to extend the reach of our sympathy and empathy.

Reason faces difficult obstacles. Technology has extended the effective range of our actions. Thus we can kill with intercontinental bombs, feed with contributions, maim future generations with chemicals (whose effects may last for hundreds of years), and destroy someone's credit with a computer terminal. But our capacities for sympathy and empathy remain fixed, and reason fights to extend them to distant places, different races, future generations, and people represented by numbers.

One expression of autonomous ethics is rebellion against the ethics of control. We see this in the rebellions of India against Britain; blacks against separatism; taxpayers against the welfare state; women against sexism; middle managers against the latest top-down management fad; and Sears, Roebuck & Co. against affirmative action run amok. Society in the very process of education plants the seed of self-reasoning that can undermine the ethics of control and foster autonomous ethics.

Unfortunately, we do not see enough autonomous ethics today. We do not see that reasoned criticism of the ethics of our organizations and institutions which is the cornerstone of autonomous ethics.

Corporations (and other organizations) should foster an environment of ethical debate so the corporation can learn and grow on the basis of its internal diversity. Any organization that champions the free marketplace of ideas as products should also honor the marketplace of ideas as ideas. Yet a conflict festers within corporations, especially as they grow larger and more cumbersome to manage. The conflict consists of trying to encourage the entrepreneurial spirit of autonomy and independence while at the same time needing to control people who act at a great distance from management with great responsibility.

Most managers resolve the conflict in favor of control. Control in the early days of industry meant reward systems, methods of observation and measurement to literally watch and control employees. But employees chafed under these restrictions. A new ethics of control emerged, packaged under many names. The latest name is *In Search of Excellence* and this new ethics emphasizes teamwork. Employees are now made to feel guilty if they neglect their duty to the team, if they violate the norms of the corporation (family).

But what does autonomous ethics say? What are its ground rules? (This is the main topic of Chapters Three through Eight.) One ground rule sure to be an element of such an ethics is to allow criticism within an organization in order to expose control systems masquerading as ethics.

Enough about the philosophy of ethics. Let us translate these philosophical thoughts into organizational life to enable you to take control of your relationship to organizational ground rules.

Determining the Ground Rules

If you hope to avoid being stonewalled by organizational ground rules, you must know what the ground rules are. The best way to find out is to cut through the rhetoric and analyze the corporation's actions.

To find the true ground rules, analyze a recent decision of your organization. Reverse engineer the decision. Ask what alternatives the organization considered in arriving at the decision. Then ask what data the organization looked at with respect to these alternatives. How did the decision makers evaluate the alternatives and data to reach the decision? By asking these questions, you begin to uncover the organization's ground rules.

It is equally important to determine your own ground rules. If you do not know your own ground rules, how can you know if there is an organization-individual fit? When determining your own ground rules, be relentlessly honest. Reverse engineer from your actions back to your decisions, your assessment of alternatives, your consideration of data, and finally your value and evaluation ground rules. Do not start with your beliefs about your values, principles, and so forth. Ask: Do I use one set of ground rules at one time and another set at another time? Is there a reason for this inconsistency? Are the ground rules I act upon and evaluate by the ones I really want?

Once you have evaluated your ground rules and the organization's ground rules, take a piece of paper and draw a line down it. List your ground rules on one side and the organization's on the other. You may be surprised to see a big gap emerge. You may also be surprised at the kind of gap that emerges.

If you discover gaps between the two sets of ground rules, you have several courses of action. You may try to change your ground rules or the organization's ground rules. You may decide to change jobs in order to find a situation in which your ground rules better fit the ground rules of the organization. Or you may decide to tolerate the differences. Since you are never going to have a perfect individual-organizational fit (unless you are an ethical chameleon), you have to tolerate some differences. Tolerating differences may foster your growth as a manager. It is possible that the organization is right and that you are wrong about some things.

This chapter concludes with two case studies and an exercise. The exercise assesses your ground rules and the fit between your ground rules and those of your organization. The first case study shows the pitfalls of an ethics of control.

Case: The Missing Tube

One feature of the ethics of Big Machines (fictional name), a feature common to strong-ethics companies, is rigidity. Big Machines adheres to an excellently conceived and implemented code of worldwide conduct. Because Big Machines takes this code seriously, its worldwide operations remain largely untouched by scandal.

Big Machines, unsure whether it was ingraining the code in its employees, hired a consultant to review its training program. One case used in the program particularly interested the consultant. The case noted that pilferage was a costly and growing problem, and it included a series of memos directing managers to crack down by warning employees, by explaining the economics of the problem, and by conducting checks, including spot inspections of employee lunch boxes.

During one spot inspection, a $0.25 tube of engine oil was found in the lunch pail of a machinist who had worked for Big Machines for over thirty years and was near retirement. The machinist explained that he needed it to oil his furnace. "I couldn't stop at the store on the way home," he said, "and I didn't think it mattered."

It mattered. According to the training manual, the right solution to the case is to fire the machinist. The manual emphasized that it is not the size of a theft that matters.

The incident reveals an evaluation ground rule for Big Machines. Known for its high level of concern for employees, the company expects absolute loyalty in return. Yet the incident also reveals that Big Machines is rigid and self-righteous about its ground rules. Its "We're ethical, we make the rules" attitude is partly responsible for the uncharacteristic labor problems that Big Machines has faced in recent years. (Pressure from foreign competitors, particularly the Japanese, must also be considered.)

By adhering to its ground rules with slavish rigidity, Big Machines has defeated the purpose of its ethical posture. For many years, Big Machines attributed its excellent labor relations to its code of ethics. This strict code ensured employees that management was ethical and aboveboard—in short, good guys to deal with.

Yet this rigid code backfired on Big Machines at the worst possible time. Just when the Japanese began invading its markets and Big Machines needed to have its team together, labor problems developed. Overly strict adherence to the code (as shown by the oil tube incident) did not convey mutual respect to employees. Instead, it made management appear inflexible, and it conveyed an attitude of moral superiority—of managers looking down at employees, teaching them the true meaning of honesty.

Big Machines demonstrated the pitfalls of using ethics as a tool of control. The following case study shows how a manager who fostered an ethics of autonomy slipped when she undercut her own ground rules.

Case: People Beat the System

S. L. is president of Western Management (fictional name), a hotel-office-building development and management company. S. L. knows her business, but she bristles at the accepted way of doing things. She sees the projects of Western as experiments in a new business philosophy. She would rather experiment, find out for herself what does and does not work, and take her lumps in the process. She works odd hours, seeks advice in odd quarters, and prides herself on being an individualist.

S. L. recently developed an office building near Western's first property, a business hotel. The hotel offered a casual environment and individualized service. S. L. called upon a friend to help her plan the new project. S. L. wanted to apply the principles of the successful hotel to the new project. The advisor was to help her clarify and state the principles. To analyze the hotel's operations, the advisor interviewed S. L. and the hotel's employees. He discovered a trouble spot, the front desk. Front-desk service was best described as slipshod, not individualized.

The front desk is a notorious thorn in the side of hotel managers, for it handles both the sales and the operations (billing) functions, and front-desk employees are not highly paid; thus, it is hard to achieve a balance of acceptable sales and operations performance.

When the advisor reported the problem, S. L. became angry. She said that she was aware of the problem but was interested in more important things. She added that she had recently hired P. J., a young woman who had studied hotel management, to improve the front-desk operations.

Within weeks, P. J. made progress. She implemented procedures more rigid than those governing other hotel functions. Everyone was happy except S. L., who worried that the procedures would destroy the spirit of the hotel. Although the advisor chided S. L. to let P. J. have a chance, S. L. insisted that P. J. was wrong.

The hotel's other supervisors liked what P. J. was doing and tightened procedures in their areas. Employees began to criticize S. L. for preaching individualism while running the hotel by the book. Morale suffered and revenues declined.

S. L. finally fired P. J., helping her relocate to a more tightly managed chain. The front desk again became a vexing, inefficient operation, but the staff cheered up, the good spirit improved business, and guests again joked about this quirky but lovable hotel.

S. L.'s ground rules of value gave more emphasis to employee autonomy than to operational efficiency. The hotel's ground rules accurately reflected S. L.'s. When P. J. then shifted the ground rules and other supervisors followed her lead, the hotel thus had two sets of conflicting ground rules. The predictable results were uncertainty among the employees about what really mattered and a corresponding decline in performance.

S. L., having observed the shift toward control-oriented ground rules, dispensed with them and restored order to the hotel. P. J., who did not realize the importance of the hotel's autonomous ground rules, met with failure.

The two case studies have emphasized the practical importance of knowing your own and your organization's ground rules. They have also underscored the potential hazards of gaps between your ground rules and those of the organization. The following exercise will help you identify your own and your organization's ground rules and the gaps between them.

Exercise: Into the Gap

This exercise may strike you as simplistic. But it works. Do not try for correct answers; try for candid answers. Do the exercise "by the book." You will then be in a better position to write the book on ground rules.

Identify Your Ground Rules. Make a list of the values that you think are most important for you to exemplify as a manager. Draw a line and make a list of ways of doing things as a manager that you think are exemplary, and a list of things you think managers should never do. Take these lists to work with you for a day or two, and make some structured observations. Note the following points: How often are the things that I do motivated by the values on my list? How many of my co-workers would identify these as my leading values? When do my actions exemplify ways I should act as a manager? How often do I do things that I regard as unacceptable for a manager?

Do this exercise in an observational frame of mind. Do not evaluate your observations. View yourself as an impartial consultant hired to observe your actions. Keep a record of your list and observations.

If you do this exercise candidly, you have a start on identifying your ground rules. You can tell if you are proceeding with candor by seeing whether you find yourself doing things you regard as unacceptable. If you are not finding any, you are not doing the exercise. Believe it or not, twelve unacceptables per day is a minimal candid response—unless you are a lot more ethical than the managers I know, including me.

Identify Your Organization's Ground Rules. The purpose of the next phase of this exercise is to look at the ground rules of the organization in which you work. Review your list of personal ground rules and the observations you made at work. Now repeat the first phase of the exercise—this time asking the questions about the organization rather than about yourself. What does your organization value? What actions does the organization regard as exemplary for managers? What actions does the organization feel that managers should avoid at all times? Make lists for these categories and take them to work. Observe whether or not what you see fits what you wrote down. Do this as if you were a consultant hired to determine whether the organization has successfully implemented its values and desired modes of operation.

Examine the Gaps. Compare the list of your ground rules with the list for the organization. Do some assessment at this point: Where are the largest gaps between your ground rules and those of the organization? Where do you think that you can adapt to the organization's ground rules? Where do you think that you cannot or should not adapt? Are the irresolvable differences important? Can you move the organization in your direction on any of these points?

What is this ground rule assessment likely to turn up? Of course, it depends. When I do this exercise with midlevel managers sent to a workshop by their companies, I find the following results: There is fairly good agreement between individuals and the firm on values. Disagreements tend to focus on autonomy (the individual places more value on it than the firm does) and innovation (the individuals feel they value it more than the firm does). In terms of evaluation ground rules, there are wider disagreements; these focus on the complaint that performance measures do not match stated company objectives, that the firm asks for results but does not care how they are achieved, and that the firm does not allow minorities and women to achieve their potential.

When I do this exercise with top-level managers, the responses differ. They find a larger gap between their values and those of the firm. They complain that they cannot do much about it. In particular, they feel that they place much higher value on performance, results, and self-direction than do those below them. At the level of evaluation ground rules, disagreements focus on concern for the good of the firm (they feel those down the line are careerist and indifferent to the overall picture), deception (they want to know what is going on, but get only candy-coated information), and lack of follow-up on good ideas. But this sort of data is of little value to you. You need to assess the ground-rule gap between yourself and your organization in terms appropriate to both.

Individuals and organizations have ground rules determining what they value and how they act. Some authors even claim that corporations have a conscience over and above those of the individuals in the corporation (Goodpastor and Mathews, 1982). But one need not conjure an ethereal spirit of the organization to allow that organizations have distinctive ground rules.

A cry heard in all organizations is "I'd be ethical if they'd let me" or "No one could act ethically in this place." This mystery about how everyone would act ethically if only someone or something would allow them to is central to ethics and management. The question raised is *who is responsible* for what happens in organizations? We will tackle this critical question. For now, let me say that too many people take the stand that they are victims of the organization's ground rules. This is an easy stance to assume. Of course, people who work in a bureaucracy tend to have an ethics typical of bureaucracies, and people who work in entrepreneurial firms tend to have an ethics typical of entrepreneurial firms, but this does not prove that organizations dictate a person's ethics. Instead, people usually either choose the organization that fits their ethics or choose to adapt rather than taking the more challenging path of trying to change the organization.

In short, we must examine the theme of the individual versus the organization. This issue is at the heart of hard management problems. Individuals cannot exempt themselves from responsibility by hiding behind the shield of so-called corporate ethics. We need to approach this issue by bringing further tools of ethical analysis into play, by sharpening our ability to reverse engineer actions to determine ground rules, and ultimately by looking at what it takes for organizations to implement and succeed through autonomous ethics.

3

Breaking the Gridlock
of Competing Interests

It seemed to me, and still does, that the system of
American business often produces wrong, immoral
and irresponsible decisions, even though the personal morality of the people running the businesses
is often above reproach.
   —*John Z. DeLorean, quoted by J. Patrick Wright,*
      On a Clear Day You Can See General Motors

The first question to ask about the ethics or management
of any organization is "Who is responsible here?" If each of us
answered this question candidly, the answer would be a nearly
unanimous "Not me." Sometimes the chief executive officer
(CEO) says, "I am." Ritual requires CEOs to say this, but few
CEOs believe that they can do much about most serious problems. They disavow responsibility because they believe, quite
reasonably, that most of the key variables are beyond their control.

I have asked countless managers if they act as ethically as
they would like to, and the answer, again, has been a unanimous
no. The answer is followed by "They don't let me" or "You
can't act ethically here" or "I would if they would." Even CEOs
candidly admit that their performance does not match their
ethical expectations. They cite the competitive situation, the

difficulty of changing their organizations, fellow managers, and the board of directors—fair excuses all.

When there are gaps between our ethics and the ethics of organizations, we judge ourselves as being more ethical than the organizations for which we work. This may be true. There may be something about organizations that makes them less ethical than the individuals who manage and work in them. But we also judge ourselves to be more ethical than others in the organization. Is there something about organizations that makes everyone in them, excepting ourselves, unethical? Asking this question raises an equally disturbing one: Are we the ones judged to be unethical by everyone else? Did we not just admit that we are not as ethical as we would like to be in our organizational lives?

It seems that we cannot act as ethically as we would like to and that no one is really to blame for this. It is as if there is a conspiracy to act unethically but no ringleader.

We all know that the problem with organizations is that no one accepts responsibility for anything ("Give me your boss!"), and no one will lead in being ethical ("I'll be ethical when you are"). How can this have come about?

In Chapter Two we looked at some ways to find and address the inevitable gaps between the ethics of individuals and the ethics of organizations. These suggestions were intended to take some heat off managers who would like to act more ethically than their work environments seem to permit.

We now turn to the more fundamental question: What is it about individuals and organizations that makes organizations less ethical, or less responsible, than the individuals who comprise them? Another way of asking this question is: What is it about organizations that makes individuals act less ethically than they say they would like to? In short, why does bad ethics drive out good ethics in organizations?

Our purpose is not to make a bold theoretical advance. It is to try to find out who is responsible for this situation and, more importantly, how it can be changed. To do this, it is necessary to break the gridlock of competing interests that arises in every organization and to examine how the very idea of justice helps support interest gridlock. (This chapter illustrates the perils of interest gridlock by examining how a failure to break the gridlock undercut one of America's basic industries, the steel industry.)

Bad Ethics Drives Out Good Ethics

Perhaps the ethically depressing, responsibility-dissipating character of organizations is an accident. Perhaps it is caused by something in the way in which organizations originate and develop. There is precedent in "the problem of the commons" for the accidental development of a situation in which irresponsible and unethical conduct is inevitable.

Garrett Hardin, a population biologist, argues compellingly that the problem of the commons is central to many of our most pressing policy issues (1977). Here is the problem in its historical form: A group of herdsmen keep their cattle on a common pasture—the commons. Each herdsman has the right to graze his herd on the commons, and the group shares the minimal cost of maintaining the pasture. (The costs are those of keeping other herdsmen and predatory animals out of the commons.) This is a workable arrangement as long as war, disease, and natural calamities restrict the number of herdsmen and cattle.

Things get better. Social stability reduces war, disease is controlled, and technology lessens the effects of natural calamities. Each herdsman can add to his herd, and each, being self-interested, seeks to improve his lot. What does rationality dictate? If a herdsman adds an animal to his herd, he receives the full benefit of the animal. The animal must eat, but the cost of feeding the animal is small since the herdsmen share the cost of maintaining the common pasture; the cost to the individual herdsman is the true cost divided by the number of herdsmen who use the commons. Each herdsman's individual interest is served by expanding his herd as rapidly as he can. The inevitable outcome? The pasture becomes crowded and overgrazed.

Eventually, the commons is destroyed and everyone loses. Who is responsible? Everyone and no one. Each herdsman acted rationally and without ill will. The group made no decision. Group irresponsibility resulted as if by accident.

I am not diverting your attention to agricultural ethics. The problem of the commons is alive and well in contemporary business. Consider a hypothetical example.

Clean-Chem (fictional name) is located along the Algonquin River. When Clean-Chem first located along the river in 1955, the river was clean. While Clean-Chem dumped wastes in the river, the river's natural replenishing processes dissipated the wastes and kept the river clean. Other chemical manufacturers followed Clean-Chem to the banks of the Algonquin. In time, the level of wastes in the river exceeded the river's ability to purify itself. Now a disaster is imminent on two fronts. First, the river is so polluted that it may never again sustain life, no matter what measures are taken. This not only raises an ecological issue, but the river has become so unpleasant that no one wants to work near it. Second, various agencies are threatening to institute antipollution regulations so strict that neither Clean-Chem nor the other companies can afford to comply.

Clean-Chem had wanted to limit its dumping of wastes into the river for almost a decade. But it did not. If Clean-Chem had decided to limit its waste dumping, it would have had to pay more to process the wastes. This would have entailed higher prices and loss of market share to competitors who continued dumping in the river. Clean-Chem tried to convince the other manufacturers to curtail dumping, but it was never able to convince all the manufacturers at a given time. Unless Clean-Chem had convinced everyone to stop at one time, no one could have afforded to stop dumping.

The river is a common resource. Those who use it gain a competitive advantage over those who do not. Consequently, the river is critically injured, and harsh regulations threaten to put all the manufacturers out of business.

In the commons, bad ethics drives out good ethics. In this example, there is a "solution" to the problem. Bring in the government to punish those who do not voluntarily refrain from dumping. This reestablishes competitive parity at a higher ethical level. But the competitive parity is at an economic level that may equally bankrupt all the firms without saving the river. Furthermore, this hypothetical example is unrealistically simple, for the companies located along the Algonquin may have to compete with firms in other areas or countries where dumping is still unrestricted. The example is hypothetical, but our polluted common resources and inflated regulatory bureaucracy are not.

Grazing the Corporate Pasture

The problem of the commons also exists within organizations, diluting responsibility and forcing ever lower ethical standards. Members of an organization often regard it as a common pasture. An organization, particularly a large one, need not be very successful to generate this perception. When employees and managers see the organization as having a large pool of resources that one must try to command for one's purposes, the organization essentially becomes a commons. The overall performance of the organization diminishes in importance because overall performance is distant from the day-to-day battles one fights to get more than the other guy.

I ask the managers I meet in seminars and consulting to identify commons problems in their firms. It is not hard. A middle manager with the Airframe Corporation (fictional name) described the following situation:

> The manufacturing process I oversee involves drills, drill bits, and drill bit supports. The bit supports are a small item used to make the drill bit function more steadily and safely. We used to hand out a certain number to each drill operator at the beginning of the shift, but the operators complained that they sometimes ran out. Then we tried an inventory system, but this wasted time because the operators had to stop and fill out requisitions to get more bits.
>
> We decided just to put the number of sup-

ports required on a usual shift into a bin, allowing the operators to take them as needed. It was a disaster. Some operators took more supports than they needed at the beginning of a shift. Other operators, seeing the bin emptying, also took more supports than they needed and began hoarding them. We were handing out twice as many supports as we ever handed out on the worst shift. Further, we found the supports stashed everywhere. Some workers would even take them home to be sure they had enough for the next day. An inexpensive part became a major burden.

When we tried to reinstitute the former system, we met with surprising resistance. Operators felt they had a right to supports on demand and were outraged that we didn't trust them.

This is a typical commons problem. The operators are, for the most part, acting from the best motives. They want to get the job done efficiently. Some are less responsible than others. The more responsible operators are forced to act irresponsibly so as not to be at a disadvantage. A sense of rights develops around the common resource, without a correlated sense of responsibility.

A prime area of commons problems is the battle over office space. When it is possible to obtain space, we take more than we need. We know the time will come when we are asked to surrender space. But we become accustomed to the space, and we demand more and more as we fill the space we have.

The real battle of the commons in most organizations is the budget. When I ask managers to identify commons, nearly all of them cite the budget process as the critical commons in their firms.

The budget is a hard measure of how much the firm values what we do. If we feel that we have an important function, it is rational for us to seek increased support for that function and increased pay for ourselves and our staffs. More important, we all know that if we do not seek a bigger budget, we will end up with a smaller budget; indeed, we may find ourselves unable to operate, especially if costs rise in hard-to-predict ways. The budget is a commons because each of us approaches it rationally in an effort to get what we can for our area. Although we realize that attacking the budget has a negative impact on the firm, none of us can unilaterally change the process. This is a real gridlock of interests. We assume that someone else is responsible for seeing that the process does not go mad. But the people we imagine doing this are in a poor information position to tell what is really needed down the line. So we inflate our needs, protest the size of whatever budget we get, and decry the foolishness of top management when it cuts needed items from our budgets. In the best case, the budget process is a time-consuming mess. In the worst case, the budget commons is depleted.

Organization members graze the organization-pasture— whether it is space, budget, or drill bit supports—in pursuit of their interests. As long as the organization-pasture can support the hungry herd, all is well; management may even brag about a competitive spirit. The collective irrationality becomes obvious only when the organization-pasture is critically overgrazed. At this stage, organizations sometimes exhibit symptoms of collective irrationality. Disclaimers of responsibility can be heard from all quarters: "It's not our fault. Foreign competitors have cheap labor, governmental protection, industrial policy, and more days of sunshine."

I ask managers what commons problems affect their organizations. Ask yourself this question. Once you have identified the budget, common staff (researchers, for example), space, nonbudgeted office supplies, and other obvious commons, press on. You are likely to identify many of the key problems that make your life difficult and your organization unprofitable. Here is one of the critical lessons that thinking ethics teaches us about management:

Lesson: If you want to find the critical problems affecting your organization, ask what commons exist in the organization.

The Issue of Justice

What happens when we try to reorganize a commons so the individual's pursuit of self-interest does not lead to collective breakdown? The issue that comes up is justice. Any proposal to modify the terms of access to the commons is viewed as unjust by those who expect unimpeded access. On the one hand, rationing access to the commons on the basis of herd size will raise cries of injustice on the part of those who have small herds. On the other hand, if usage is taxed, those with large herds will contend that they are unjustly penalized for success.

Attempting to reorganize the budget commons yields an analogous result. If access to the budget is based on past performance, those who have had tough assignments will complain that they are being unjustly punished for having taken on hard tasks. If access to the budget is zero-based, those with records of accomplishment will complain that their past efforts are being unjustly ignored. If you have had significant budget responsibility, you know these complaints will not be polite protests. They will be a virtually unanimous roar. And these complaints have a lot of validity.

The problem is that the participants in a commons come to view their terms of access to the commons as rights. This by itself would not be a problem if responsibilities were associated with these rights. By its nature, however, this is not the case in a commons. When it comes time to reduce or eliminate rights, each party loses a right for having done nothing particularly wrong. For instance, when the right to procreate was slightly crimped by reduced income-tax dependency allowances, there were screams of "You've changed the rules in the middle of the game!" These were screams of injustice.

No ethical term frightens managers more than *justice*. One rationalization of this says that the business of business is not justice; justice is the business of government. But this is neither accurate nor fair.

It is true that justice is not the business of a particular firm or industry. The exceptions are firms that make some aspect of justice their business. For example, Control Data Corporation has a strategy of looking for social problems it can solve profitably. Some firms specialize in administering affirmative action programs or in providing health care services to the indigent (McAuto, Inc.). But most businesses are directly concerned with justice only as a matter of internal operation. Businesses must be concerned with fair employment practices, just promotion and merit procedures, and impartial distribution of corporate resources (distribution by reason, not by favoritism).

Business does uniquely contribute to the promotion of justice. This contribution takes the form of providing opportunities for all sectors of society through job creation, income increases, and financial support of governments. Business even allows you to create your own justice by starting a firm. Many legal and illegal immigrants have taken this route when government was busy discriminating against them. It is arguable that business contributes more to justice in these ways than do the many programs and agencies whose avowed purpose is justice.

The problem with business's contributions to justice is that the stated purpose is not promoting justice. If you happen to get wealthy promoting justice through business, you are more likely to produce envy of what you have earned than respect for what you have given. For these reasons, managers seldom speak the language of justice. After all, unlike bureaucrats, managers do not justify their existence in terms of how well they promote justice. So the consensus is that business should be concerned with justice *in addition to* being concerned with business. If business is to get credit for its contributions to justice and ward off attacks on its indifference to justice, it must learn the language of justice. Unfortunately, this language is at odds with itself.

Justice, like most ethical words, means different things to different people. One ambiguity exploited to undermine business is that between just *distribution* and just *process.* In contemporary society and political institutions, justice has come to mean just distribution.

Some see a footrace and say that it is unjust that only one person or team wins. They have a point. The winner may have won through no fault of his own, but by virtue of a good genetic background. The winner may have had more time to train because of corporate sponsorship or personal wealth. Or perhaps the parents of the winner instilled an exceptional competitive spirit and sense of pride in the winner. And there is always an element of pure luck. These factors can be considered unjust because they are not evenly distributed among competitors and because the competitors did not earn them. From this line of reasoning, some conclude that redistributing the winner's prize to other participants (or nonparticipants) is only just.

I am of course parodying the redistributionists' sense of justice. The analogy between a footrace and the distribution of life's necessities and luxuries can be pushed too far. But the problem in contemporary American society is that it is not pushed far enough. We are increasingly averse to competition. When we resent the Japanese winning a few trade battles and respond with import quotas, we ask to have the winner's ribbon handed to us when the Japanese crossed the finish line first.

Distributive justice is an *outcome* concept. It looks at how society's goods have been distributed and calls it fair or unfair. There are many standards for rating an outcome as fair or unfair. One of the most famous is Karl Marx's: "From each according to ability; to each according to need." There are many other standards, including those murkily implicit in our income-tax system.

Procedural justice is a *process* concept. Procedural justice rates an outcome as fair provided that the process leading to it was fair. In the footrace analogy, procedural justice says that the outcome of the race is fair if the race proceeded according to understood or agreed-upon rules. With respect to economic goods, procedural justice is concerned with the process by which goods are distributed rather than with the outcome of the distribution. Procedural justice asks, "Did this outcome arise from fair competition?" not "Is this distribution too uneven to be fair?"

While distributive justice has its roots in ethics' ecclesiastical era, procedural justice has its roots in Locke's social contract ethics. Thus the idea behind procedural justice is that the rules of justice are those rules that the participants in a foot-race, organization, or society would agree on as conditions of competing. Implicit in this approach is the American idea that fair competition is a good way to allocate resources.

Differences between the two concepts of justice show up clearly in affirmative action programs. Both concepts of justice favor affirmative action, but in different forms. The California State Board of Regents adopted a distributive approach. In the mid 1970s they mandated that the ethnic composition of the faculties of California's state colleges and universities match the ethnic composition of the state population. They were uncon-cerned about whether this distribution of jobs matched prefer-ences or abilities or violated standing contracts. They addressed only the outcome.

The procedural approach to affirmative action focuses on the fairness of the employment and promotion processes. This approach fits the American sense of justice better than the dis-tributional approach does. This approach to affirmative action prescribes strong actions. No one considers the outcome of a race fair if some competitors use performance-enhancing drugs or if some competitors' legs are broken before the race. Simi-larly, if competitors for economic goods are handicapped by poor education, past discrimination, present prejudice, or other factors, then fair competition must be restored. But this ap-proach does not presume that unequal distribution is, ipso facto, unfair.

But we have now learned enough about justice to see how commons undermine responsibility and how issues of justice cement commons gridlock. Let us examine an industry brought to its knees by such problems—the steel industry.

Big Steel's Big Steal

The decline of the steel industry since World War II and its troubled labor-management relations are a painful but edu-cational example of how hard it is to break a commons problem and restore responsibility. I admit to a jaundiced view, for my family was divided between labor and management in U.S.

Steel; my father was a white-collar worker for the company, and his brother was a founding official of the United Steelworkers of America (USW). The insightful and fair discussion of the history of the steel industry presented in Paul Lawrence and Davis Dyer's *Renewing American Industry* (1983) has tempered my view. Robert Reich offers a very critical but insightful picture of the industry in *The Next American Frontier* (1983).

Through most of its history, the steel industry symbolized the industrial might of the United States. The steel industry dominated world markets and was essential to our success in World War II. In 1962 President Kennedy, convinced that rising prices in the steel industry were driving inflation upward, summoned the force of the presidency to obtain a rollback of price increases. U.S. Steel and the other major steel producers were accurately perceived as worthy foes for the president of the United States. The steel industry today is a frightened pussycat compared to the industrial lion of the recent past.

Neither management nor organized labor in the steel industry gets much respect these days. The public views the steelworkers as a greedy special-interest group that has demanded outrageous wages and destroyed the competitiveness of the industry. Business scholars scratch their heads and their statistics, trying to understand why anyone ever thought a steelworkers' union was a decent idea. They forget the hard-to-quantify insults, intrusions, lockouts, and strikebreaking activities. In fourteen years I have never taught a student who vigorously defended the USW or any other union. (Of course, few students plan to work for a union.) The press sees no connection between the courageous struggles of Solidarity against Poland's puppet government and the struggles of organized labor in the United States. The steelworkers appear rigid, uncooperative, and self-defeating even in the hardest of times. They oppose both technical and management innovations, fearing that the union will be undercut and jobs lost. The interests of the union leadership are thought to be closer to those of top management than to those of the rank and file.

Management fares no better. The consensus is that one should study steel industry management only to learn how not to manage. Managers are indicted for being slow to adopt technical innovations, for paying dividends instead of modernizing plants, and for excessive inbreeding. Steel industry management consistently underestimated foreign competitors, finally responding by seeking government protection. When the federal government offered protection to allow the industry to modernize, management squandered the opportunity by continuing to emphasize dividends and high compensation for themselves. This led in turn to more pleas for protection, again followed by no constructive management action. Management was obsessed with breaking the USW, even when this was patently counterproductive. Antiunion activity is one of the few areas in which steel industry management has been innovative. The capstone of industry management has been to milk the steel industry as a cash cow to finance diversification into unrelated businesses, as strikingly symbolized by U.S. Steel's purchase of Marathon Oil.

Management and labor in the steel industry treated the industry and its major firms as commons. They pursued their own interests, ignored the overall viability of the industry, and assumed the major firms were inexhaustible resources. Both sides enjoyed a long stretch of prosperity, followed by a slowly recognized period of decline. Their common efforts, rather than having been directed toward maintaining and developing the resources of the industry-commons, have been limited to keeping outsiders off the industry-commons. Each party correctly held the other parties responsible. It would have been unjust for the steelworkers to have cut back their demands when management's salaries and stockholders' dividends were rapidly rising. It would have been unjust for management to have cut its salaries or to cut dividends when this would only lead to the claim that more was available to support already inflated wages. Notice that these claims are claims of distributive justice. No one bent to break this gridlock of interests.

There are two important lessons here for managers:

Lesson: If you want to find the critical problems affecting your industry, ask what commons exist in the industry.

Commons problems operate at the level of entire industries as effectively as they do within firms.

Lesson: The critical symptom of a commons problem in a firm or industry is that issues of distributive justice prevent the solution of problems of mutual interest.

When members of a firm or industry cite issues of justice as an excuse for self-defeating conduct, you have a locked-in commons problem.

I offer a harsh assessment of steel industry labor and management. Both sides settled into patterns of industry-destructive thinking and acting. It was not always so. Consider the following statement on employee participation:

> Management's assumption of sole responsibility for productive efficiency actually prevents the attainment of maximum output. The participation of organized workers in management provides an outlet for their creative desires, as it is essentially a creative and cooperative undertaking. Union-management cooperation to reduce costs, eliminate wastes, increase productive efficiency, and improve quality represents a practical program that provides workers with effective direct participation in the creative phases of management. Union-management cooperation tends to make management more efficient and unions more cost-conscious, thereby improving the competitive position of a business enterprise and increasing the earnings of both workers and owners. [Lawrence and Dyer, pp. 70-71.]

This idealistic statement is not from a current book on Japanese management or excellent companies. It is from a 1942 manifesto of the Steelworkers Organizing Committee. Reading this statement now, one thinks it propaganda. It was not. It was an expression of optimism and hope. However, the time of these ideas had not arrived in 1942. Labor did not take its own

insights seriously and concentrated on wage and benefit increases. Management took a hard line. Bitter strikes predictably
resulted.

In the golden era of steel, managers had to innovate to
stay in business. Lawrence and Dyer, commenting on Andrew
Carnegie, the manager, say, "While it would be ludicrous to hail
him [Carnegie] as an enlightened employer . . . , Carnegie publicly supported the workers' right to unionize. His relentless
drive to reduce costs led him to many confrontations with the
work force. . . . Nevertheless, among his peers, Carnegie stood
out as an innovator in labor relations. . . . The Carnegie mills led
the nation in moving from twelve-hour shifts to three eight-hour
shifts, although this plan was opposed by labor. . . . At a higher
level, Carnegie used incentive plans and the prospect of partner-
ships to motivate his managers and increase their involvement in
the company" (1983, pp. 60-61). Carnegie implemented new
technologies in his plants. He centralized management, pursued
vertical integration, and diversified products. Carnegie was hardly alone as an innovator in the early, intensely competitive days
of steel. Indeed, steel industry management was a model for
American management through the era guided by the thinking
of Alfred P. Sloan (former chairman of General Motors).

The Superstitious-Learning Hypothesis. How did these
optimistic beginnings for management and labor deteriorate
into a situation in which both sides compete to exploit the industry commons? One plausible explanation is the superstitious-
learning hypothesis. *Superstitious learning* occurs when unrelated
factors are associated in a person's thinking through a nondis-
criminating reward pattern. For instance, a person who flies on
only one airline and always arrives safely may associate safe flying with that airline alone, even though other airlines are
equally safe.

According to the superstitious-learning hypothesis, management and labor did a lot of superstitious learning prior to,
during, and immediately following World War II. Prior to the
war, the industry had reduced competition among major producers through government-condoned price-fixing. Based on the

accomplishments of past management, the industry held a strong edge over foreign competitors. Management was rewarded for continuing the patterns of the past. During the war, the industry prospered; authoritarian, control-oriented management was again reinforced. The war's end left American steel without serious foreign competition. Thus management succeeded by doing what it had always done, having learned that this was the right way to manage. Labor learned that management would not yield on issues of participation or quality of work life. But labor could always win more wages and benefits.

This knowledge has only been tested recently by serious foreign competition—and found wanting. Once something is learned, it is hard to unlearn it. Unlearning requires admitting that one was wrong. We often prefer being wrong to admitting error.

The superstitious-learning explanation of the steel industry's decline rings true. Essentially, participants in the industry superstitiously learned to regard the industry and its major producers as commons. Labor "knew" that no matter how much it took from the industry-commons, there was plenty left. Evidence for this view was abundant. Strike or no strike, management's salaries escalated constantly and dividends moved ever higher. Occasionally, management would reduce the work force or threaten to relocate a plant to punish the union. No worry. Things always returned to normal. The leading concern was how to get your fair share of the commons. Attention focused on distributional justice. Shares were grudgingly conceded.

Management "knew" that labor was a commons. Any worker was expendable. There were always more workers waiting in the wings. This attitude spread to other elements of the firm. Since one could count on solid profits year after year, why not grant oneself ever increasing compensation? Criticism could always be warded off by increasing the dividends. Stockholders were happy to buy into the picture of the industry as a commons. To avoid appearing profligate, management took a hard line with labor. When the government granted protection, everyone queued up to get as much advantage from it as one could. Labor would certainly ask for more; shareholders expected increasing dividends. No worry. There was always plenty of pasture left.

Return to the herdsmen and their common pasture. What happens when the pasture is crowded to capacity and disaster is imminent? The herdsmen may call a meeting to decide on some formula for limiting access to the pasture. They are not likely to reach agreement. Each has superstitiously learned that it is his *right* to increase his herd at will. Any restriction of that right will be viewed as unjust. The best hope is to tax the use of the commons based on herd size. This, too, may fail. Those with large herds may use their economic advantage to force out small herdsmen. Or, if the small herdsmen are greater in number, they may use their political advantage to force a subsidy from those with larger herds. We thus have disorganized competition backed by an ethics of free (irresponsible) use.

The Ratchet Effect. Ethics changes slowly, especially when reinforced by superstitious learning. The likely outcome? Each herdsman will see disaster coming, figuring that only one in a hundred animals will survive. This produces a high incentive to increase your herd rapidly. The larger your herd, the larger is one hundredth of your herd and the better your chances of surviving. Movement toward disaster is hastened. Population biologists call this a ratchet effect. Most of the herd perishes. The game starts again.

Lesson: If you allow commons to persist in your firm or industry, the likely outcome is a ratchet effect that will destroy the common resource.

By the mid 1960s, labor and management in the steel industry knew they were destroying their commons. Two options were available: Agree to a mutually beneficial plan to preserve the commons, or rush to the ratchet and hope your side fares as well as possible.

The former option was not wholly ignored. In 1973 labor and management adopted the Experimental Negotiating Agreement (ENA). The purpose of ENA was to ban strikes in return for guaranteed wage increases. Neither labor nor management could have endured a prolonged strike in 1973. But the learned adversarial history of labor-management relations was a powerful force. Under ENA, wages rose faster than productivity, jobs were lost, and management hastened to diversify out of steel.

Labor and management continued marching toward the ratchet, with ENA solidifying the outcome. Neither side was responsible for this. Labor can cite management's incompetence and ill will. Management can cite greed, opposition to innovation, and ill will on the part of labor. Both are right.

The hypothesis that participants in the steel industry regarded the industry and its major firms as commons is painfully borne out by the conduct and thinking of the participants. Recognizing this does not yield a solution to the industry's problems. Labor and management have learned their superstitious lessons well. I offer a prediction and a lesson. The prediction: Major firms will continue their ratchetlike plunge. The lesson: Just as good ethics and good management go together, so bad ethics and bad management reinforce each other.

Uncommons Sense

This leaves us with several puzzling questions. How do participants in an industry come to regard the industry and particular firms as commons? Are conditions in the steel industry unique, or does the commons hypothesis explain the epidemic of irresponsibility in organizations across industries and types of organizations? Once a commons situation arises in an industry or firm, is there any going back short of a ratchet effect?

The only apparent way out of commons gridlock is for someone (typically a government) to introduce some factor to realign the interests in the commons. This is intended to produce an outcome that someone (typically the intervening government) views as better than the ratchet. This approach may or may not work. Either way, there is no responsibility in it, for the truly responsible parties who have created the commons can now blame someone else for their problems. This someone else, as a nonparticipant in the industry, lacks the information needed for sound management. When the intervenor fails, someone must be blamed. Since labor has more votes than management and is, at any rate, the underdog, management is elected the goat. Management is in a tough spot, given that it deserves a good half of the blame it receives.

Each of us believes that if we had been key players in the steel industry, we would have, or at least might have, done better. Part of this is the arrogance of hindsight. Part of it is the ethical superiority of the uninvolved. We believe that we would not have played the game with the sole objective of ending up with the biggest herd. But it is hard to believe that a mysterious force kept people as smart or ethical as us out of the steel industry. We are driven to the view that who is involved in a commons makes no difference.

Why You Make No Difference

Viewing problems as commons problems is the dark side of viewing problems as economic problems. In economics, the self-interests of individuals are inexorably blended by the market into a desirable outcome for all concerned. In the commons, the self-interests of individuals are inexorably blended by the commons into a disastrous outcome for all concerned. The difference is in whether or not self-interest has an inexhaustible resource to consume in the blending process.

In both types of explanation, the choices and values of individuals are inconsequential, canceling each other out in the process of positive or negative blending. Since responsibility presupposes that our choices matter, neither approach leaves any room for responsibility. This is the ultimate division of labor in which individuals become *morally interchangeable*. The better these approaches explain things, the less room there is for our choices to count. The better the explanation, the bigger the booby prize.

The commons model explains how the question "Who is responsible?" can legitimately be answered "No one." It explains the lack of responsibility in organizations (and industries) so well that it leaves little room to let responsibility back in. Yet we must let responsibility back in if organizations are to function ethically and effectively. The ethical tools we shall learn about help us find the leverage points in commons problems. But we must also find some force to apply to these leverage points. Responsibility is the only effective force because it breaks the commons gridlock of interests. We must *create* responsibility. The concept of creativity is so worn and exploited that we can barely recall its true meaning: to bring forth from nothing. Bringing responsibility forth from nothing is the only way to bring it back into our organizations.

Case: Divide and Conquer

I have emphasized that managers fear issues of justice and that this fear helps cement commons in place. What happens when managers overcome this fear? This case explores one strategy for employing justice to deal with public constituencies and shows one way of using justice to break a commons gridlock. Once managers begin addressing issues of justice, they have one of the essential tools for beating the commons. In the following, a company willing to take justice seriously achieves a result which was otherwise unachievable and which is still unachievable for most firms in similar situations.

For two years, Big State Bell (fictional name) has unsuccessfully sought a major rate increase. It has argued with the utility commission that while labor costs have risen steadily, the rate structure has remained constant. If given the rate hike, Big State has assured the commission, it can hold the line on further rate increases for at least two years. These arguments have been cooly received by the utility commission. Big State recently received a substantial rate increase to cover the costs of modernizing its equipment. At that time, Big State made no mention of increased labor costs. If it had, the commission might have rejected the modernization program.

The commission feels, given Big State's track record, that if it approves the present request, Big State will "need" another rate increase before this one even hits the monthly bill. The line has to be drawn, and the commission draws it here.

Big State's management is desperate. A rate increase is absolutely necessary, but the managers know the utility commission's attitude is justified.

A strategy that Big State tried earlier in the hearings had failed. In lieu of a general rate increase, it had proposed charging for specific services, especially information calls. The utility commission said no, arguing that this would sneak the rate increase in the back door, torturing the consumer with a thousand small miseries instead of one clean punch. Big State promptly abandoned the approach, yet the idea keeps resurfacing.

At a Big State management meeting, Bill, an offbeat thinker, asks why the idea will not die. A vice-president stresses that the public must see Big State as a provider of specific services rather than as a provider of a commodity (telephone service). Bill disagrees.

"It's a question of justice," he says.

Blank stares greet him.

"Most of our customers don't deserve a rate hike, only a few do. You know the type of customer. They're so lazy that they call the operator for directions to the bathroom. They deserve a rate hike."

Bill argues that the current distribution of charges is unfair. It penalizes the majority of responsible customers and subsidizes irresponsible customers, who ride the system free. In short, current practices make information services a commons.

The other managers come around to Bill's viewpoint. Big State launches an advertising campaign. It blasts the lazy slob who is unwilling to open the phone book and rudely eats up the operator's time. Then it shows a responsible customer opening a large bill and asking, "Why?"

Big State drops all its other arguments to the commission and focuses on the issue of fairness to responsible customers. To underscore its sincerity, Big State offers to lower the basic charges slightly in return for the right to charge for specific services, including information calls.

This new rate plan wins prompt approval. Big State's revenues increase to the level they would have reached with a general rate increase.

Big State's management achieved its revenue objective by framing its request in terms of justice rather than strictly in terms of economics. By raising the issue of justice, it divided its consumers (who traditionally oppose rate increases) into two groups having diverse interests. Both economics (the needed rate increase) and justice (the rate decrease for responsible customers) were served. Because many consumer-oriented issues are presented in terms of business versus the consumer, framing such issues in terms of justice helps reveal the false aggregation of truly diverse consumer interests.

Big State's case reveals a strategy that managers can use in some cases to break a commons gridlock.

Lesson: If there are more responsible than irresponsible users of a commons, manage the commons by separating the interests of these groups.

This strategy will not work with all commons, for it is often impossible to divide the users of a commons into responsible and irresponsible users, and sometimes the irresponsible users outnumber the responsible ones. In either event, we would have no choice but to seek ways of creating responsibility in commons.

Since managers instinctively expect to lose battles over issues of justice, they seldom express positions in terms of justice. Thus ethics-blind management deprives itself of a valuable tool in many adversarial processes.

4

Knowing Who Really Counts
in Difficult Decisions

An act has no ethical quality whatever unless it be
chosen out of several all equally possible.
—*William James,* The Principles of Psychology

Managers today manage interests as much or more than
they manage people and assets. Internally, the workplace is a
tangled web of conflicting interests vying for scarce resources
and diverting attention from the tasks at hand. Externally, managers must try to balance the interests of stockholders, regulators, the media, customers, suppliers, organized public interest
groups, informal interest groups, lenders, foreign governments,
criminal elements, and a seemingly endless list of outside constituencies (Mason and Mitroff, 1981). The problem of the commons clearly demonstrates that failing to manage conflicting interests can destroy firms or entire industries. But the problem
of managing interests is a day-to-day fact of life for managers,
whether or not these interests form a commons.

Managing interests is an area in which ethics can be of
great use to managers. Although many experts tell managers to
be aware of interests and to manage them, they say little about
how to do either (Davis and Frederick, 1984). The basic issue in
ethics is and always has been dealing with conflicts of interest.
In addition to the concept of ethics as ground rules and the
model of the commons problem, I provide three ethical models,

or tools, to use in tackling hard management problems. These models are called end-point ethics, rule ethics, and the social contract model. The model that applies most directly to identifying and managing interests is end-point ethics. This chapter will show how we can use end-point ethics to refine our process for reverse engineering decisions to uncover ground rules, to help managers determine whose interests count in complex decisions, and to provide a strategy for resolving issues of justice.

Whose End?

If you want to know just one ethical model, know end-point ethics. It is the ethical model of establishment thinkers and the ethical basis of capitalism. It can be used to extend our reverse-engineering process, and it provides a way for decision makers to pull outside perspectives into organizational decision making. End-point ethics also unlocks the mystery of why we do so little but talk so much about managing for the long run. In fact, I believe that end-point ethics contains the insight needed to make strategy emerge from hiding in notebook binders and drive firms. End-point ethics states: *A person, organization, or society should do what promotes the greatest balance of good over harm.*

But whose good and whose harm counts? This is a fundamental question in ethics and in all complex management decisions. Let us see how ethics has historically addressed this question.

It Starts with Hedonism

End-point ethics started life as *hedonism,* a philosophy that tells each person, "Do that which brings you yourself the most pleasure and the least pain." In fact, when people speak critically (or jealously) of the "me generation," they are speaking about hedonism. (I criticize the current generation not for being hedonists, but for underachieving as hedonists. Does anyone imagine that accounting classes are the path to hedonic pleasure?)

A fundamental criticism of hedonism is that there is more to life than seeking pleasure. Psychologist Jose Delgado invented a device I call the pleasurometer. An individual can use this device to stimulate the brain, producing pleasure in any amount at will. Delgado says that "studies in human subjects with implanted electrodes have demonstrated that electrical stimulation of the depth of the brain can induce pleasurable manifestations, as evidenced by the spontaneous reports of the patients, their facial expressions, and the desire to repeat the experience" (1969, pp. 142-143). In other words, subjects keep pushing the button of the pleasurometer until they are exhausted. If hedonism were correct, the meaning of life would be owning a pleasurometer.

It was this narrow viewpoint of hedonism that made later thinkers reject it. They felt life involved more than just seeking pleasure and invented *egoism,* which directs each of us to "Do that which brings you yourself the greatest balance of good over harm." In egoism, good and harm include more than pleasure and pain.

Egoism still focuses on one individual (yourself) and still nurtures the philosophy of looking out for number one. Many business executives and academics think looking out for number one *is* the ethics of capitalism. Business critics and other promoters of the business-is-unethical lie are quite happy to go along with this belief. But this belief perverts the basis of capitalism. Because the belief that business rests on egoism is so widespread and pernicious, we need to relearn something from capitalism's father, Adam Smith.

If anyone invented capitalism (the market economy), it would be Adam Smith. Smith, a University of Glasgow professor not of business or economics but of moral philosophy, is best known for *The Wealth of Nations* (1776). In it he preaches that it is far better to make pins with co-workers than to make them alone—hence, the division of labor. But Smith's great book, *Theory of Moral Sentiments* (1759), emphasizes the roles of sympathy and impartiality in *individual* moral judgment. While *Theory of Moral Sentiments* is dated, its ideas are profound and still enlightening.

Smith was smart. He knew that even if everyone read and

agreed with *Theory of Moral Sentiments,* it would not produce the coordinated action essential to a workable, decent society. He recognized that self-interest is a powerful counterforce to sympathy and that no book would change that. *The Wealth of Nations* attacks the problem of how self-interested individuals can live together in a way that they would, on *sympathetic reflection,* judge to serve their common interests. Smith accepted self-interest, turning it to the common good. Like Buckminster Fuller, he accepted the idea, "Don't oppose forces; use them."

The common good is the supreme goal in Smith's view. He would have rejected capitalism if convinced that another system better served the common good. Self-interest is a force to reckon with in promoting the common good, but it should not be enshrined as the ethics of capitalism. Even the supply-side capitalist philosopher, George Gilder (1981), argues for the market on the grounds that it promotes the common good, while noting that egoistic capitalism quickly declines into socialism.

In the 1800s arose another end-point ethics, *utilitarianism,* which echoed Adam Smith's concern for the common good. In Chapter One, I noted utilitarianism's role in making ethical room for the industrial revolution and for capitalism. In its mature version, as stated by John Stuart Mill, utilitarianism offered a radical critique of the existing Victorian ethics of privilege. Utilitarianism states: *A person, organization, or society should do that which promotes the greatest balance of good over harm for everyone.*

With utilitarianism, end-point ethics comes full circle from hedonism. Like egoism, utilitarianism includes more in good and harm than pleasure and pain. Utilitarianism differs from both hedonism and egoism in considering the consequence of actions not only for oneself but for *everyone affected.*

Cost-benefit analysis and risk-benefit analysis are modern variations on the utilitarian theme. The relationships among utilitarianism, cost-benefit analysis, and risk-benefit analysis are not complicated, no matter how esoteric these models appear in classes on quantitative methods in business.

Cost-benefit analysis is no more or less than utilitarianism with the word *benefit* substituted for the less fashionable word *good* and the word *cost* substituted for the less fashionable word *harm*. It is typically thought that a cost-benefit analysis should result in a numerical assessment of whether the benefits of a course of action exceed the costs; thus, much effort goes into expressing costs and benefits in numerical, typically monetary, terms. This satisfies our obsession with quantitative measures, however inappropriate they may be. It also supplies an excuse when an action certified by cost-benefit analysis comes out a loser: the costs and benefits were improperly converted into numerical terms.

Risk-benefit analysis is a variant of cost-benefit analysis which takes account of the fact that risks should be considered as costs and weighed against benefits.

Applying End-Point Ethics

Since utilitarianism is the only currently viable form of end-point ethics, I simply refer to utilitarianism as end-point ethics from now on. It is not obvious how to apply end-point ethics in actual decision making. It is not clear who *everyone* is, or if the direction to consider everyone is intended seriously. Everyone is a lot of people. And what counts as good and harm? How do you balance good against harm?

Let us begin with an artificially formal three-step end-point decision process and then apply this process to a complex decision concerning banking strategy. This example will wash the excess starch out of our overpressed process.

Identify the Stakeholders. The process begins by addressing the issue of whom we should consider in decision making. End-point ethics says, "Everyone." But it is not possible to think about literally everyone in formulating an employment policy or marketing strategy. As important as the Eskimos are, they have little to do with policies for promoting accountants or with strategies for marketing bikinis. *Everyone* is thus usually understood as *everyone affected* or *everyone seriously affected.* This is a bit more sensible than plain *everyone,* but not very helpful.

Is everyone affected by our decisions affected in the same way? And who is to say what is a *serious* effect? In short, everyone affected and everyone seriously affected are large, heterogeneous groups. The best way to get a grip on whom to consider is in terms of *stakeholder groups*. Ask yourself, "Who has an identifiable stake (or interest) in the outcome of this decision?" and "What is their stake (interest)?" In this way, you can formulate a list of critical stakeholder groups and assess the consequences of decisions for each group.

Identifying stakeholder groups is a difficult process. In a seminar with American managers involved in international trade, I asked participants to identify the stakeholders in a decision concerning whether or not to bribe foreign officials. (Such bribes are now illegal. I discuss international bribery in Chapter Six.) While almost everyone identified shareholders, regulatory agencies, stateside employees and managers, and foreign officials, no one identified one important stakeholder group—citizens of foreign countries who must live with corrupt officials. We have already seen one example of how distinguishing stakeholder groups aids decision making. In the Big State Bell case, management succeeded by recognizing that responsible consumers and irresponsible consumers are distinct stakeholder groups.

The first step of our end-point decision process is to identify what stakeholder groups are critically affected by a decision and how they are affected.

Lesson: In any complex decision, start by identifying the significantly affected stakeholder groups.

(For more on identifying stakeholder groups in decision making, see Mason and Mitroff, 1981.)

Survey the Alternatives. End-point ethics says to choose that action which promotes the greatest balance of good over harm for everyone. Greatest compared to what? If there is but one possible course of action (*not acting* is a course of action in this sense), then that course of action is the best by default. For end-point decision making to apply, there must be more than one course of action. Then we can say that we should choose that action which promotes the balance of good over harm better than any alternative action does.

The second step of our decision process is to identify alternative courses of action. The direction, "Identify the alternatives open to you and the firm," is too broad to be practical (there are countless alternatives) and too vague to be helpful (plausible, innovative alternatives are hard to come by). How do you rule out the countless frivolous or implausible alternatives? And how do you identify the critical but nonobvious alternatives that may lead to optimal results?

Our decision process adds substance to the unethical end-point directive to consider the alternatives. The second step is elaborated as follows:

Lesson: In any complex decision, identify the alternatives you believe to be most plausible. Then look at the alternatives that each stakeholder group would identify as plausible.

This can be an armchair exercise, based on your sense of the stakeholder groups. But if it is practical for you to do so, you should seek the direct input of key stakeholder groups. There are two advantages to surveying the key stakeholders. (When I suggest surveying the stakeholders, I do not recommend a paper-and-pencil survey. The chances of candid responses on critical issues are small unless you demonstrate your interest in stakeholder input through your presence.) First, you may find that the alternatives you regard as optimal meet strong resistance in stakeholder groups needed to implement the decision. It is better to learn about such resistance in the decision-making process than in the market. Second, those who have a different stake in your decision than you do may see important alternatives that you have overlooked.

Information Democracy, Decision-Making Authority. Once you have identified the stakeholders and surveyed the alternatives, you must decide which of the alternatives to choose. The end-point model directs, "Choose that alternative which leads to the greatest balance of good over harm for everyone." Easy to say; hard to do.

Who is to say what is a good outcome and what harm

could be done? There are two approaches to this question: democracy and authority. Democracy recommends the path of least resistance; it says: "Ask what each stakeholder group considers a good outcome and a harmful one. Choose the outcome that maximizes the balance of good over harm, all stakeholder groups considered." Authority says: "It is the manager's responsibility to decide which outcomes to seek (good) and which outcomes to avoid (harm). So decide." The best approach is first to ask what the stakeholder groups see as good and as harmful outcomes and then use your authority. For the manager, stakeholder groups are not created equal. Although the manager needs to know what the stakeholder groups perceive as constituting their good and harm, the manager's responsibilities to the various stakeholder groups differ.

Lesson: When surveying alternatives prior to making a decision, assume that all stakeholder groups are created equal. When deciding, prioritize stakeholder groups in terms of your responsibilities to each group.

The manager who uses *decision-making authority* backed by *information democracy,* as we recommend, is left with a lot of information and a decision to make. Now that you know the stakeholder groups you are dealing with, the options available, and how the affected groups perceive the options, the decision *process* is exhausted. But how is the manager to know if the final decision is sound? There is no process that tells you what to do at the existential moment of choice. Responsibility begins where process, or method, ends. Responsibility is the glue in our chest of ethical tools, to be added once we have the full set of tools (see Chapter Eight).

The Shortcomings of Cost-Benefit and Risk-Benefit Analyses

How does our end-point decision process compare with cost-benefit analysis and risk-benefit analysis? Although these forms of analysis are based on end-point ethics, the end-point decision process is richer than they are. To begin with, the cost-

and risk-benefit analyses do not distinguish among stakeholder groups; all groups are falsely homogenized in an overall summing of benefits and costs (risks). Further, cost- and risk-benefit analyses issue an answer irrespective of whether the relevant alternatives have been identified; they accept the alternatives as *givens* and assess a balance of benefit over harm for each. Finally, they inaccurately assume that assessment of benefits and costs is constant across stakeholder groups.

Both Mel and Big State Bell failed when they used cost-benefit analysis. Mel failed because this analysis, by homogenizing the stakeholders, missed the winning issue of justice to the townies. Big State Bell failed because cost-benefit analysis did not reflect the strength of interest of some stakeholders (consumers and their representatives on the commission) and because it lumped critical stakeholders (responsible and irresponsible consumers) together. Both Mel and Big State Bell reversed their failures by considering new alternatives and distinct stakeholder groups.

Lesson: Unless you are certain that stakeholder interests are homogeneous, use an end-point decision process rather than cost- or risk-benefit analysis.

In cost- and risk-benefit analyses, decision making conforms to the requirements of method. In order to have the univocal numerical measures that make us comfortable, we sacrifice key dimensions of sound decision making.

Case: The Ostrich Syndrome

Ms. McB. the decision maker in this case, faces a strategic decision of broad ethical and economic impact. While Ms. McB. is an end-point thinker, her thinking does not match step by step the procedure outlined above. Actual decisions never follow structured procedures. Let us track her decision through its steps and compare it to the end-point procedure in order to see where this procedure would help or hinder Ms. McB.

Ms. McB. is the chief executive officer of Central National Bank (fictional name), a midsize regional bank ($7.5 billion in deposits). She is talking with a consultant who has completed a study for her. Ms. McB. commissioned the study because Central National's markets are being invaded by competitors offering new services, better rates, and aggressive marketing. Central National continues to survive mainly because of its size. It has been the Queen Mary amid a bunch of tugboats. Moreover, Central National was for many years the first and only bank in many of the markets it serves.

But now its competitors are pushing Central National into a harbor mined with low-cost, high-margin specialty banks, and national financial institutions are testing Central National's strength. Ms. McB. is the only one who seems to see the danger. Her ostrichlike managers, softened by years of easy success, refuse to see their markets being siphoned off by a variety of competitors. Ms. McB. therefore called in an outside consultant to discuss the options open to Central National.

The consultant begins by laying out the aggressive option for Ms. McB.

Consultant: This option takes guts. Basically, it calls for Central National to plunge in and try to dominate a broad spectrum of this area's financial services markets.

Ms. McB.:   Well, we have to make *some* move.

Consultant: With the aggressive option, you'll be making lots of moves. Let me summarize it for you. First, Central National should enter the real estate market. You should acquire a computerized real estate brokerage. That would give you a whole new market for mortgages, escrow services, and insurance products. It would also give you potential new customers for traditional services.

Ms. McB.:   That move alone would give half of my board members heart attacks.

Consultant: Then they'll love the next two ideas. The aggressive option would launch Central National into venture capital. Right now, there's precious little venture capital activity in this market. You could provide a much-needed service.

Ms. McB.:   Real estate and venture capital. What else?

Consultant: One more item. Most banks underplay research
                 and development. So establish a financial research
                 lab. Study how to apply new technologies to
                 bank services. Find the right idea and you'll bury
                 the competition.

Ms. McB.:   What about the passive option?

Consultant: The passive option. Basically, it's circle the wag-
                 ons and hope the Indians go away. They won't.
                 But by sticking to your knitting, two things will
                 happen. First, you'll be able to concentrate on
                 your current customer base.

Ms. McB.:   And second?

Consultant: Here's the punch line. The main hope in the pas-
                 sive option is that Central National can hold off
                 the competition long enough to be acquired on
                 favorable terms by a larger financial institution
                 seeking a foothold in this region.

Up to this point, Ms. McB.'s attention is focused strictly
on defining the alternatives. While specifying the alternatives is
a step in our decision-making process, it is a second step that
rides piggyback on identifying the stakeholder groups. Has Ms.
McB. missed options as a result of not having first surveyed the
stakeholders? She needs to consider the residents of the state in
which Central National operates and their elected representatives. Considering these groups might suggest a political strategy, such as erecting legislative barriers to delay further intru-
sion by out-of-state institutions. Also, by considering out-of-
state financial institutions only as a competitor group, Ms. McB.
may be overlooking the possibility that some out-of-state institutions are better viewed as nonacquiring partners.

Strolling through Central National's headquarters, Ms.
McB. glances at the managers. She realizes that the aggressive
option would shock them. The strategy would demand an incredible infusion of new talent and a strong dose of psychiatric
care for those waiting for retirement.

The passive option, she knows, would certainly cause
Central National's management less uncertainty in the short

term. In addition, the passive option recognizes that Central National's chances of success in pursuing a bold strategy may be small. And, despite the recent contraction of its market share, Central National is still the big boy on the block.

In the long run, of course, the passive option would neither revitalize Central National nor allow it to survive; Central National would become a used car, needing only to look good until someone acquired it. If she made Central National a target of acquisition, she would have to hide this plan from key managers, the public, and perhaps her own board. Yet a favorable acquisition would benefit the stockholders, those managers who have a significant equity position in Central National, and even Central National's customers and lower-level employees.

Ms. McB. considers the benefits and costs of the aggressive option. In the best case, Central National would dominate the area's financial markets and drastically increase its profits. Although some current Central National employees would lose their jobs, many new employees would come on board and be richly rewarded. Further, Central National might become an important national force in banking. Ms. McB. sees the flaw in this rosy scenario: It probably would not work out in time to prevent disaster. The risk of the aggressive option scares her. She cannot imagine turning this sluggish brontosaurus into a saber-toothed tiger. While craving the excitement of the aggressive option, she dreads total failure.

The passive option? She knows she can implement it. The biggest problem would be convincing Central National's employees, stockholders, directors, and customers that she was steering Central National along the path of survival. On the plus side, the passive option would improve the bank's performance immediately, if not strikingly, by abandoning all pretensions to a bold strategy. There would be no need to fire a lot of people, and if someone acquired Central National, the stockholders might receive a premium on their holdings.

The down side of the passive option? Even with tighter controls and a conservative strategy, Central National's position might continue to deteriorate, perhaps rapidly. This could lead to an acquisition of Central National on unfavorable terms.

Ms. McB. and her fellow managers would come off as slow-thinking goats.

Finally, an intangible but important factor is that she would have lost an exciting challenge. She would face boring days, mundane problems, and mundane managers.

Ms. McB. has now brought many of the key stakeholder groups into the picture. She is to be commended for casting her net widely. For example, she has considered not only those present employees who may favor the passive option for reasons of personal security but also those people who, under the aggressive option, would become employees. She has also considered stockholders, directors, and, to a lesser degree, customers. Implicitly, she has considered how each group would perceive the good and the harm of each option, and she has correctly included herself as a stakeholder.

But even while Ms. McB. cast her stakeholder net widely, she confined herself to armchair assessment. She might be surprised by the willingness of some old-timers to back the aggressive option. The present strategic decision is more important than most marketing decisions at Central National. Ms. McB. would consider it irresponsible to make those marketing decisions entirely on speculation. Does Ms. McB. pay a price?

Ms. McB. picks the passive option. She cannot justify picking the aggressive option because its chances of success are too small. This is probably a sound business decision from the perspective of those having an immediate financial stake in Central National; from a broader market perspective, its soundness is less clear. While the failure of Central National is undesirable, the financial services industry will gain little from Ms. McB.'s selection of the passive option. This choice gives priority to present employees over the new employees that Central National might hire. Further, it virtually ensures that Central National will be acquired by—and its customers served by—an outside financial institution.

The Intangible Fallacy

Let us see how we might challenge Ms. McB.'s choice from the perspective of our end-point decision process.

A strength of the end-point decision process is that it highlights issues concerning affected constituencies that the decision-maker might otherwise overlook. Here we can fault Ms. McB. for granting customers only a peripheral role in her decision. Her inattention to this stakeholder group may account for her having overlooked legislative options for fending off competition. Still, it is unlikely that her consideration of this option would have changed the direction of her decision.

A weakness of most end-point decision processes (cost- and risk-benefit analyses) is the *intangible fallacy*—the mistake of assessing outcomes by a measurable standard even though intangible outcomes are equally important. Our own end-point decision process is structured to short-circuit this problem by emphasizing that outcomes be assessed from the perspectives of stakeholder groups.

Thus, although Ms. McB. is an end-point thinker, she is open to the charge of bias toward the measureable at the expense of the valuable. This bias was aided and abetted by the short shrift she gave to stakeholder perceptions of good and harm.

Ms. McB.'s decision critically depended on her assessment of what count as good and harmful outcomes. The fact that she was unwilling to risk significant financial loss to try the audacious strategy shows that she valued immediate economic consequences more than the experience, learning, and satisfaction of taking on a challenge. Ms. McB.'s priorities probably reflect her accurate sense that she is responsible for and has agreed to focus on economic results.

Interestingly, her sense of responsibility is irrelevant in terms of all end-point decision models, including cost-benefit analysis and risk-benefit analysis. For these models are concerned with *what* outcomes you produce—not *how* you produce them. Indeed, the very fact that these decision models ignore how results are produced leads many decision makers to prefer the rule ethics model (discussed in Chapter Six).

Examining Ms. McB.'s decision further, we can question whether the predictability of the passive option justifies foregoing the opportunity to do something. There are hidden pitfalls in the passive option and hidden opportunities in the aggressive option. Moreover, the passive option may fail simply because there is little in it to inspire anybody. Lack of inspiration and interest lead to inattention and poor service. And Central National is already dispirited and losing ground. The very audacity of the aggressive option is inspirational. The aggressive option could really be sold. Some of the bank's woolly mammoths might show a few zebra stripes. Some risk can be taken out of the aggressive option by paring it down to size; a pared-down version should offer some reasonable chance of success. We cannot fault Ms. McB.'s final decision so much as the fact that she did not give the aggressive option a full hearing.

Lesson: When weighing the pros and cons of alternatives, do not undervalue intangible consequences simply because they are intangible.

What Is in It for Us?

End-point ethics is a good ethical tool for the decision maker. The prescription is simple: Start with the consequences. Begin by considering the consequences of what you do for those affected. *Decision models are valuable more for the questions they pose than for the answers they generate.* The end-point model directs the thinking manager to ask: Who is significantly affected by this decision, and what is the impact of the decision as perceived by each of these groups?

The issue is this: As best you can assess the probabilities, what course of action will produce the optimal balance of good over harm for those concerned? Keep in mind that part of your decision involves taking a stand on what this good or harm is. Applying this decision-making tool assures you that you have included one important ethical theme in your decision making—concern for the general good. It also improves the quality of your decision making in strict business terms by forcing you to consider the full range of individuals who have a say over whether or not your decision succeeds.

There are two further areas in which our end-point decision process supports good business decision making: justice and strategy. (We will turn to strategy in Chapter Five.) End-point thinking can help with issues of justice by focusing a group's attention on the result it is trying to produce, rather than on the internal issues of rights, justice, or turf that constrict all organizations.

Another way that the end-point model helps with issues of justice is by converting them to issues of a different kind—to issues of fair transaction. For example, if you operate a steel mill that pollutes an adjacent farmer's land, you can address the issues in two ways: You can let the farmer seek recourse in the regulatory bureaucracy and then try to beat him there, or you can try to maximize the overall benefits by compensating him for his loss. The overall balance of good and harm is served if paying him is cheaper than building a towering smokestack and if he is as well off as he was before you became his neighbor. People tend to vote their interests; if they do, the fair transaction approach will work.

Lesson: Convert recalcitrant issues of justice to issues of overall benefit by avoiding the costs of conflict and intervention.

To get a better look at how end-point models help resolve issues of justice and contribute to sound decision making, we look at a British company, Jaguar Cars PLC, which has experienced a remarkable turnaround. Jaguar's managers blended ethical and economic thinking to beat one of the hardest problems faced by managers in recent years—how to denationalize a company, reduce labor costs, and restore labor peace in Great Britain.

Case: Jaguar PLC

In 1980 Jaguar Cars was a troubled company. The company was losing between £2 million and £3 million per month. Jaguar had been absorbed by British Leyland in 1968 and nationalized along with British Leyland in 1975. Charles Dellheim notes, "By 1980 Jaguar cars had become synonymous with a lack of quality and reliability" (1984, p. 1). And yet by 1984 Jaguar was a profitable private firm, independent from British Leyland and the British government and on the way to reestablishing its reputation for quality and style. Ethics figures in this turnaround at several points. We concentrate on the role of end-point thinking.

When Sir Michael Edwardes became head of British Leyland in 1980, he initiated a process of decentralization. Edwardes recognized that diversity of and conflict among stakeholder interests was more important than economies of scale. Jaguar stakeholder groups perceived themselves as unfairly treated within British Leyland. They felt that their craftsmanship and tradition of excellence actually made them targets of discrimination. They responded with low morale and poor performance. So among Edwardes's first decentralization moves was the reestablishment of Jaguar Ltd. as an autonomous division of British Leyland.

This resolved one set of stakeholder conflicts—between Jaguar and British Leyland interest groups—by separating the groups. But this was not enough to restore Jaguar's health, for Jaguar, like many old-line British industrial firms, was viewed as a commons both by its labor and its management. Both Edwardes and John Egan, whom Edwardes appointed managing director of Jaguar in April 1980, felt that labor consumed too large a piece of the Jaguar pie. Instead of pursuing an exclusively adversarial approach, they relentlessly confronted both labor and management on the issue of the overall well-being and viability of Jaguar. They convinced both labor and management that each side would maximize its own benefits if it pursued a fair transaction approach rather than a conflict or outside intervention approach. They argued that the costs to the firm of conflict or outside intervention (government control) outweighed the benefits to particular groups at particular times. As a result, Jaguar was able to reduce its work force (benefiting management and the company), to improve working conditions (benefiting labor and the company), to reward Jaguar employees for their unique skills (benefiting Jaguar's craftsmen and the company), and otherwise to maximize benefits to both the company and key stakeholder groups within it. In 1984 Jaguar completely separated from British Leyland and emerged as the private Jaguar PLC.

There is no question that this turnaround depended on the unique skills of Edwardes and Egan. But other fine managers had failed where Edwardes and Egan, with their instinctive application of end-point decision making to unclog interests, succeeded. There is more to the story, for it is not easy to convince a divided company to think in terms of overall benefits. And it is not easy to sustain this way of thinking even if it is once achieved at the brink of collapse. The rest of the story is in Chapter Seven.

End-point ethics gives us a tool for analyzing business decisions. The value of this tool is that it gives us a systematic way to pull outside constituencies into our managerial decision making and to get an accurate sense of how decisions affect their interests. In short, it directs the thinking manager to ask not only who counts in key decisions but also how they count, and it provides a structure for pursuing these questions.

Another important area in which end-point thinking benefits business is strategy. What I have to say about strategy is central to correcting the sorry state of strategy in contemporary business; thus, I treat this topic at length in Chapter Five. The issue is how much managers should think about the long run. The consensus is "much more." But that is not what ethics says.

5

Why Managing
for the Long Run
Is the Wrong Strategy

In the long run we are all dead.
                              —*John Maynard Keynes*

A Pandora's box of economic ills assaults our industries.
The brick heavy enough to close the box is said to be long-run
thinking. From every quarter, managers are urged to think long-
run. This advice has been repeated so often in so many forms
that it seems heretical to dispute it.

One sermon preaches that long-run thinking will improve
a firm's ethical conduct and social responsibility: "Good ethics
may not be good business in the short run, but good ethics is
good business over the long run." John Diebold succinctly states
this viewpoint: "We deal too often in the short term, whether
in the techniques with which we analyze problems, the terms of
political office, or our stock market evaluations of earnings, or
financial analyses that emphasize discounted cash flow. . . .
Short-term decisions may make sense for the individual manager
or politician or investor, but they are bad for our society"
(1982, p. 88). This idea is repeated again and again in almost
every discussion of the ethics and social responsibility of busi-

ness (Davis and Frederick, 1984; Steiner and Steiner, 1985; Steckmest, 1982).

Another sermon contends that American businesses, particularly those in the smokestack industries, are losing their competitive edge because management emphasizes short-term financial results over long-term development. Francis Steckmest and the Business Roundtable note: "An increasing number of observers have suggested that a general preoccupation by corporate management with short-range profit goals, for whatever reason, hampers long-term planning and investment, with adverse effects not only on the vitality of their companies and their shareholders' interests but on United States technological innovation, productivity, and ability to compete with foreign companies" (1982, p. 29). This theme is repeated in recent influential books by Robert Reich (1983), William Ouchi (1984), and Paul Lawrence and Davis Dyer (1983), among many others.

No one is challenging what should be challenged—the consensus that managers should focus on the long run. There has been debate over the *causes* of the short-run emphasis and on possible *remedies*. Typically cited causes include tax policies that encourage short holding periods for stocks, pension fund ownership of significant equity positions, and business education that teaches managers to attend to short-term financial results while giving scant attention to the nuts and bolts of running a company. Favorite remedies include instituting a publicly debated national industrial policy, purging business colleges of accountants, changing the tax system, overhauling management compensation programs, and promptly visiting Japan. These recommended dramatic and potentially disastrous actions are backed by little evidence or clear thinking.

I claim that ethics helps managers gain new perspectives on recalcitrant issues and entrenched beliefs. I will now use endpoint ethics to look at why emphasizing the long run is ethically and strategically the wrong answer to the wrong question. The message in this chapter is essentially a negative one, but knowing what does not work is the necessary first step to discovering what does.

Short-Run Shortcomings

What are the supposed shortcomings (pun intended) of the manager who emphasizes short-term results at the expense of the long run?

Supposedly, short-run managers often dodge the consequences of their managerial actions. These managers ensure that their units perform well just long enough to guarantee their raises and promotions, hopefully into another unit or company. These managers ignore the long-term good of the company or its constituencies if this does not affect their quarterly or annual evaluation. As Reich says: "Managers who anticipate a short tenure with their firm unsurprisingly have little interest in long-term solutions to its basic problems. Their goal is to make the firm (and themselves) look as good as possible in the immediate future" (1983, p. 164). In fact, these managers may harm the long-run interests of the company if doing so advances their interests (when the piper is paid, someone else pays). Short-run managers care little about research and development or employee satisfaction and retention unless these are their explicit responsibilities. These managers avoid costs by shifting them to other divisions or outside the firm. These managers do not address industrywide problems or social issues even if the company can act more effectively than other companies, interest groups, or agencies. Even short-run managers will take an interest in long-term results and social responsibility if these are necessary to being positively perceived and evaluated, but these managers will do *no more* than they deem necessary for advancement.

These managers, although unsavory, are quite familiar. The ethic, or basic operating philosophy, of short-run managers is to do exactly what advances their interests. These managers are egoism personified. If they are not busy pleasing one of us, and if they cannot mask their egoism by pretending to have a team spirit, we dislike them. If they are fellow employees, we view them as hurting the company and society and as imposing hardships on the rest of us. We should not be too hard on such characters, for we see someone like them in the bathroom mirror most mornings. But would we not all be better off if these managers were more concerned about what happens to company, group, and society in the long run? And does end-point ethics not mandate that these managers give more attention to the long-term consequences of their acts in the interests of the greatest good of the greatest number? Perhaps.

Case: Elliot's Brilliant Career

Six years ago Ron was assigned to head Amtech's small computer division. Amtech (fictional name) was an established force in the minicomputer market but had no products in the small computer market. Ron worked hard to make the company's small computer efforts a success. Among his accomplishments, he convinced corporate management, first, that it must take a long-term perspective on developing products for and penetrating the small computer market, and, second, that it would have to accept a lower per-unit profit to penetrate and hold its position against large competitors in the small computer market. Ron had done a superb job, and Amtech was well-positioned for steady, profitable growth in specific small computer market niches, including quality portable computers and multipurpose modems.

Ron acted partly out of necessity. On studying the small computer market, he realized that Amtech would not be able to develop products that would be competitive in this market in the time it took the company to develop new minicomputers. Further, Ron also realized that the company would have to expect lower per-unit profits to fund the continuing research and development necessary to stay competitive in the small computer market and to allow the all important dealers a large enough margin to want to carry a small company's product line. (In the minicomputer market, Amtech sold through its own sales force, and had no dealers' network.) As a result of his success in the small computer division, Ron was scheduled for promotion to a corporate-level job overseeing research and development for both mini and small computers.

Ron's replacement as head of the small computer division,

Elliot, was considered a "whiz kid" at Amtech. Elliot expressed merely polite interest in Ron's approach to the small computer market, but, he no sooner took over the division, than he advised corporate management that it need not accept lower per-unit profits in the small computer market than it expected in minicomputers. Further, he documented so-called sloppy management practices, particularly the retention of an excessive number of research engineers and "dealer caddies." Elliot promptly fired many of the engineers and "dealer caddies" as part of a stringent cost-cutting program. Per-unit profits shot up so quickly that Elliot was promoted to a new corporate position, whereupon Ron's accomplishments were reexamined and his career advancement halted.

The new head of the small computer division maintained Elliot's level of financial performance for a while, but then he began to write memos reminiscent of Ron's earlier messages on the distinct character of the small computer market. He, too, was replaced, but Amtech's small computer division earned a bad name with dealers and customers and never fully recovered.

Elliot is a typical example of the short-run manager. Moral perfectionists might also fault Ron for not having made an issue of Elliot's merely polite interest in current practices in the small computer division. Elliot's replacement was also a short-run manager, or more accurately, a short-term manager, by the grace of Elliot. *Ethically,* Elliot displayed all the warts of the short-runner. He fired employees who reasonably expected to be continued, he permanently hurt the company's performance in the small computer market, and he seriously injured the careers of Ron and of Elliot's successor. *Strategically,* Elliot was a disaster, undoing Ron's well-thought-out and well-executed plan for success in small computers. Business and society surely would be better off without the likes of short-running Elliot.

But everything is not as it appears. It is easy to agree on Elliot's faults. It is not so clear that Elliot's faults arose from his short-run approach to management. Before diagnosing the disease of Elliot and his ilk, we need to be clear about the comparative merits of long-run and short-run perspectives. (See also Culbert and McDonough, 1980.)

The Long Run Is Now

It is as American as apple pie to live for the long run. Living for the long run is part of both puritanism and the work ethic. Here is how it works. When you are a kid, you cannot do what you want. You are told that if you work hard, you can do what you want when you grow up. You grow up. If you are reasonably lucky, you go to college. There you major in something uninteresting because there are no jobs in the interesting fields. You need a good job to get what you want, including Mr. or Mrs. Right and a flock of little Right children. You get the job and Mrs. or Mr. Right. You need to work hard to keep Right with you, support the little Rights, and avoid misery in your old age. (You are smart enough not to count on Social Security.) Retirement? Look back on the good old days when you were young and did what you wanted.

Cynical, but accurate. All of us think we can break the cycle ("This is true for them, but I have a plan!") sometime in the future. Seeing the price of playing the long-run game, students in our universities say that they do not want to grow up to be like their parents (who once dreaded working in a steel mill or washing diapers). The kids say this while playing the long-run game for all it is worth.

Eastern thinkers, including the spiritual forebears of the model Japanese manager (supposedly a long-run but actually a short-run manager), take a different view. They view life as a successive series of moments just like the present moment, commonly known as *now*. Life is now, now, and now, and so on. A long run is good if it is a series of nows that includes a preponderance of good nows over bad nows, with no very long runs of successive bad nows (see Kapleau, 1967). I argue in Chapter Eight that understanding this basic philosophical orientation of our Far Eastern competitors is more important than understanding their management techniques.

This Eastern view entirely agrees with end-point ethics. A benefit or harm now equals a benefit or harm later. (The later benefit may be less likely to accrue, but it is not less valuable per se.) End-point ethics treats every time equally. It is foolish to trade a few good moments now for a lot of lousy moments later. It is equally foolish to trade a lot of lousy moments now for a few good moments later. Neither *now* nor *then* can be rationally emphasized at the expense of the other in a sane life or a sound corporate strategy.

What do these thoughts mean in practical terms? They mean that managers should analyze the irrational bias toward the future that is being foisted on them. A substantive future benefit may not be worth the high present costs of obtaining it. A substantial reinvestment of present earnings to produce a small or uncertain increase in future earnings is a loser. A substantial reinvestment of present earnings to produce an equally substantial increase in future earnings is a dead draw. At the level of rational assessment of costs and benefits, the long-run pitch is wide of the mark. For those who think that our competitors from the Orient respect the long run and that they know something that we do not, what they know is that *then* is no different from *now*. That just happens to produce good long-run results.

Diagnosing Elliot's Disease

The short-run Elliots of the world certainly pose a problem, but the problem is not to get Elliot to care about the long run. Look at this in terms of ethics.

Ethical conduct has two components: good character coupled with good judgment. Good character needs good judgment in order to produce consistent ethical conduct. The managers of the prebankruptcy Braniff Airlines were people of good character. But their judgment was bad, so they violated obligations to passengers, employees, stockholders, and creditors. The conduct of these managers was ethical in the sense that their motives were not malefic. But their conduct was definitely not ethical in the sense of keeping their word and meeting their obligations to passengers, employees, stockholders, and creditors.

Good judgment without good character also fails to produce ethical conduct. Albert Speer, architect of the Nazi war machine, had excellent judgment. In his memoire, *Spandau,* he attributes his poor ethical conduct to poor character (Speer, 1976). He is right.

Poor ethical conduct leads us to look for flaws in character or judgment. Individuals of good character and judgment have a better-than-even chance of acting ethically.

Elliot's problems are problems of character. Would Elliot's conduct improve if he were more interested in the long run? No. I observed earlier that it would be easy to elevate Elliot's interest in the long run. Tell him that his success or failure depends on helping the long-run interests of Amtech, and measure his performance accordingly.

Say that Elliot is interested in the long run. What does he do? He argues for long-term goals requiring an immediate increase of resources for his area. He argues for goals, which will be achieved in any case, to minimize his chances of failure. But Elliot wants goals that will bring him notoriety when he claims credit for having achieved them. He will play "set the goals" by the same rules he played "get the goals." Once goals are set (as Elliot wishes or otherwise), he will advertise his commitment to them. When he misallocates resources to enhance his career, he will argue that he is working for some future objective. He will diminish the accomplishments of competitors in the firm by saying that they obtained short-term results at the expense of long-range objectives. His ethical shortcomings, with their correlated strategic and operational costs, have little to do with his short-run perspective. If Elliot worked for me (I would rather he did not), I would prefer that he keep his eyes on short-run goals. With these, I may be able to monitor his performance and contain the damage.

If the short-run manager is unethical, we trace this to poor character or poor judgment. If the problem is poor character, we hardly want this manager shaping the future of the firm; he will do so along self-serving lines, waste resources, and deceive us along the way. If the problem is poor judgment, we again want the manager to keep his hands off the firm's future; a manager demonstrating poor judgment regarding present conditions will be even wider of the mark in assessing less tangible future contingencies and options. Both ethics and strategy advise that we keep the attention of managers who do not meet our standards firmly fixed on the short run.

What about "good" managers? Do managers of good character and good judgment sometimes undermine a firm's ethics or performance because they overemphasize the short run? Begin by asking whether a manager who acts counter to the ethics or long-run interests of the firm in order to satisfy short-term goals really merits being classified as a good manager. This is probably an unrealistic, harsh attitude. Even good managers seek personal survival and success and respond to the short-term demands of supervisors and outside constituencies (such as institutional investors who demand their 15 percent real return on investment or trade their blocks of shares).

Consider the assistant professor who publishes dozens of articles to get tenure because his university's evaluation system is more sensitive to the number of publications than to their quality. The professor's research is largely inconsequential; he loses the opportunity and initiative to do good work, and he develops no long-term research program to guide his career. It is not that the professor enjoys writing inconsequential articles— he must if he is to survive and look forward to better days. Surely, universities should find ways to encourage long-term quality research rather than promoting a glut of unread, unreadable journal articles.

Curiously, the case of the "good" manager (or professor) turns out to be like Elliot's. If the university emphasizes long-term research, our assistant professor will turn even the smallest ideas into "major" research projects. The system will expect and reward this, and the professor will go along. *The truth is simply that the manager, or any other member of an organization, should have neither a long-term nor a short-term perspective.*

Lesson: In weighing the present versus the future benefits and costs of an action, remember that short-term consequences are exactly as valuable as future consequences—and typically a lot more predictable.

One's temporal perspective should *fit* what one is doing, the problems in the environment, and the resources available over time.

The problems of short-run managers are not problems of restructuring systems in order to encourage a shift in their time frame. They are problems of individuals who adjust to whatever system is in place and play for a win. The problem is one of integrity. In one sense, the professor does lack integrity. But the kind of integrity he lacks is a kind that we all lack to some degree. His lack of integrity is *responsive* to a perceived lack of integrity in the system that evaluates him.

This suggests that we could elevate individual integrity by improving our evaluation systems. But integrity cannot be manufactured by shifting time frames, reward structures, or anything else we know about. Uncomfortable though it is to admit, the issue also is not one of bad managers versus good managers.

This is not to say that our current short-term reward systems are optimal.

Lesson: Reward systems, like the time perspectives of individual managers, should be neither short-term nor long-term. They should fit the business; its environment, problems, and resources.

We have inadvertently shortened the time perspective of reward systems in response to our advancing capacity to measure each manager's and unit's performance (see Chapter Nine). Another driving force is the short-term investment perspective of institutional investors, especially pension funds.

But these factors may not be at the heart of the evaluation problem. As Keniche Ohmae, Director of McKinsey and Company's Tokyo office, has emphasized, Japanese managers produce long-run success even though they are evaluated on very short-term criteria. The "secret" is that the short-term criteria are realistic and exceedable (Ohmae, 1982). If you meet your reasonable short-term objectives, you can invest your remaining time and resources pretty much as you please. In short, Japanese managers are mainly rewarded with autonomy for meeting their short-term objectives. This gives Japanese managers who have the desire to try something a high incentive to exceed short-term goals and get on with their pet projects. But autonomy is the most jealously guarded of rewards in most American corporations.

Consider the experience of a flight systems manager I recently consulted to. He, too, is measured on short-term criteria, but unless he sets his negotiated goals very high, he is viewed as a slacker. So he sets them about as high as his peers do—much too high. Senior management then makes financial and production projections based on these inflated objectives, and the system goes crazy. (It is time for the managers who overcommitted to take their lumps.) My friend could not indulge a long-term project if he were dying to, and he is. He does not seek long-term goals that would preclude his project as effectively as the present system does. He seeks a rational short-term mode of operation.

Lesson: Set short-term goals that are realistic, and reward managers who meet these goals with the opportunity to set and pursue long-term goals for themselves.

Ethical and business rationality must be restored to reward systems. But our systems fit our irresponsible and irrational response patterns as much as our response patterns fit the systems. The flight systems evaluation procedure under which the manager labors evolved for good reasons. Reward systems are designed in response to irrational and irresponsible conduct, which they in turn promote. This problem is analogous to the problem of the commons: As long as we view ourselves as rationally self-interested individuals playing against the reward system, there is no chance of responsible conduct. One of our fundamental objectives as we proceed is to find a view of ourselves that allows for genuine responsibility.

Making Strategy Work

If any component of management is long-run-oriented, it is strategy. According to Alfred Chandler (1962), strategy determines long-term goals and allocates the resources necessary to achieve these goals. What is the supposed value of strategy? There are many tales of organizations succeeding without or despite a strategy. Thomas Peters, coauthor (with Robert Waterman, Jr.) of *In Search of Excellence* (1982), likes to tell the story of how Honda, wishing to unload some mini motorbikes they could not sell in the United States, hit upon the legendary "You meet the nicest people on a Honda" theme. Then there is the story of how Sony, sticking with radios when strategy dictated a rapid march in the opposite direction, hit upon the Walkman. Stories of companies succeeding by pursuit of a thought-out strategy, on the other hand, are hard to come by.

The supposed value of strategy is that it aligns people and resources around goals advantageous to the firm.

Most strategies live their entire lives in notebook binders, where it is quite difficult for them to align people and resources. These strategies have little effect. But why are strategies buried in notebooks? Is it, as is often assumed, because managers are obsessed with the present and ignore the long run? One of the hardest problems of management is figuring out why organizations are so strategy-resistant.

I often work as a strategy consultant; however, I spend little time working on strategy with clients. This experience is common among strategic planning consultants. For a map to be useful, it must show an X to mark your present location. The most accurate and detailed map in the world will not keep you from getting lost if you do not know your present location. So strategic planning begins with an assessment of where the organization is: Is it aligned with the goals it presently has?

Consulting law states that the more top management wants a new strategy, the more the firm is out of alignment with or unaware of its present goals. Few organizations out of alignment with their present goals will profit from having more goals and different goals. Just as the manager who wants to improve ethics should try being ethical for one day on a simple issue (for example, telling the truth), so the manager concerned with strategy should align his or her organization's people and resources behind present goals for at least a few days before filling the strategy notebooks.

Strategy fails because managers are *not sufficiently concerned with the present.* The manager who aligns his organiza-

tion with a set of present goals will have little trouble finding a
workable strategy. Workable strategies flow naturally from
what a firm presently cares about and is good at.

*Lesson: If your firm needs a new strategy, check whether it is
aligned with its present goals. If it is not, you need to discover
what the present problem is before adopting more goals not to
be aligned with.*

Managers concerned with ethics and strategy should concentrate on now rather than then. If an organization is ethical
now—and now—and for the most of its nows, it is guaranteed an
ethical long run.

This does not mean that managers should ignore the future consequences of what they do. As end-point ethics makes
clear, the future consequences of actions are just as important
as, but no more important than, the immediate consequences.
To be ethical and strategic now is to weigh future consequences
accurately.

Suppose the present ethics of the organization is poor or
the present strategy is unsound or nonexistent. It is best to
understand how the organization got into this condition and
correct those problems before inculcating a new and probably
equally poor ethics or unsound strategy. When the thinking
manager sees that an organization is acting unethically or failing strategically, he or she asks: What is the present source of
this unethical or nonaligned conduct? The thinking manager
keeps asking until there is a clear answer, and then turns his or
her attention to the future.

Beyond End-Point Ethics

End-point ethics provides us with a tool for analyzing
business decisions. It gives us a systematic way to pull outside
constituencies into our managerial decision making and to get
an accurate sense of how our decisions affect their interests.
End-point ethics is concerned with consequences, but it actually undercuts the current wisdom that managers should give
more attention to the long run. For end-point ethics weighs the

consequences equally, irrespective of when they occur. But we have learned more about what does not work—and that is very valuable knowledge—than we have about what to do to make things work better. End-point ethics has not given us the specific insights into what to do about our reward systems, and ourselves, to eliminate the irresponsibility that we falsely diagnose as dodging the long run. And it has not told us what to do about strategy, here and now, in order to produce alignment. Our next ethical tools, rule ethics and the social contract model, deepen our understanding of the day-to-day workings of organizations, of the rules by which we now decide and act, and of how unethical, nonaligned conduct becomes entrenched. These tools will give us a working base from which to initiate change.

Exercise: Test Your Integrity

I have argued that the fundamental issue in achieving ethical conduct in organizations is integrity. Where do you stand on this issue? The following exercise is designed to allow you to do a self-assessment.

In my training programs on ethics for managers, I suggest to participants that they surely do not want unethical managers determining the present or future ethics of their firms. The participants then try an experiment (try it!) to determine whether they themselves are qualified to discuss and influence the ethics of their organizations. The experiment is this: Go one full work day without saying anything that you think is false, partly false, misleading, or otherwise likely to misinform or underinform. If you cannot tell the truth as best you know it for one full day, then management ethics, including debates about the long run versus the short run, exceeds your qualifications.

Perhaps, you argue, the test is too stringent. Being truthful for a day is not that easy, and sometimes—not often—it is not even right. Suppose the truth is too painful for someone to bear? My study indicates that what you do not want to tell someone (in an evaluation meeting, for example) is precisely what that person would most like you to say; chances are that it is your own skin you are trying to protect. At least try erring on the side of candor.

The point of the test is not to force you to be recklessly truthful. We are such habitual shapers of the truth (to our own ends) that there is little chance of this happening. Everyone who has seriously attempted this test has found it extremely difficult.

The point of the test is that the problem of ethics is not a lack of concern for the future, but a problem about being ethical *now*. If you want to alter the ethics of your firm, the only place to start is now. And I am willing to bet that managers who come *close* to passing this truth test for a few consecutive days do a pretty good job of weighing present versus future interests in their strategic thinking as well.

6

Resolving Conflicts
Between Business Ethics
and Public Ethics

All law is universal, but about some things it is not
possible to make a universal statement which shall
be correct.   —*Aristotle,* Nicomachean Ethics

Conflict is a fact of life in business, but not all conflicts
are conflicts of interest. Many of the most difficult issues in
business involve conflicts of rules rather than, or in addition to,
conflicts of interest. The discussions of ground rules in previous
chapters have focused on the conflicts between the ground rules
of individuals and of the organizations in which they work, a
type of conflict that can directly injure the individual and less
directly injure the organization. In this chapter we focus on a
different type of conflict of rules—that between the rules of organizations and the rules of different societies and cultures.

One of the clearest examples of such a conflict is that between the bribe-prohibitive ethics of most American corporations and the bribe-demanding climate of many countries in
which these corporations operate. Because this conflict sharply
raises so many of the facets of rule conflicts, I will examine it in
depth. But similar conflicts arise over different safety standards
here and abroad (ours are more stringent), different trade prac-

tices (our arms-length business-government relationship versus the hands-on practices of other countries), different environmental standards (standards vary among regions within the United States and between countries), different attitudes towards nepotism, and different attitudes towards religion in the workplace.

To address conflicts of rules, this chapter adds another tool—rule ethics—to our ethical toolbox. Rule ethics will help us look at organizational actions and decisions and see the potential rule conflicts they raise. We will also look at ways in which ethical rules are intentionally misinterpreted to the detriment of business. The chapter's case study of international bribery illustrates these points. The chapter concludes with a preliminary look at one variety of rule ethics—social contract ethics—which is especially useful not only for resolving conflicts among rules but also for producing the kind of lasting ethical changes in organizations that I have outlined in earlier chapters.

Rule Ethics

Rule ethics is simplicity itself. Rule ethics states: A person or organization *should do* what is required by valid ethical principles; further, a person or organization *should refrain from doing* anything contrary to valid ethical principles.

In short, rule ethics says that some actions are *obligatory* and some are *prohibited*. Actions that are neither obligatory nor prohibited are *permissible*. If you promise to repay a debt before a certain date, then you have an obligation to do so. On the other hand, you are prohibited from selling your children to raise money to pay your debt. You are not obligated to repay the debt before it is due, but you are permitted to do so.

Rule ethics offers a reassuring categorization of right and wrong. An action is right if it is obligatory, or at least permissible; otherwise, the action is wrong. At long last, some clear ground to stand on! Rule ethics is appealing to those who admire structure and legalism. This happy picture fades only when one asks to see the list of valid ethical principles separating right from wrong.

I noted in Chapter One that the roots of rule ethics are ancient. Every religion proclaims a set of rules, such as the Ten Commandments, which embodies that religion's understanding of right and wrong. (The terms *rule* and *principle* are interchangeable in ethics.) Thus, one rule frequently cited by rule ethicists is the Golden Rule: Do unto others as you would have others do unto you. Nonreligious ideologies also have sets of ethical rules; a predominant one is the Marxist maxim: From each according to ability; to each according to need. The fact that the religions and ideologies of the world are far from agreeing about right and wrong underscores one feature of rule ethics: Unlike end-point ethics, rule ethics does not *by itself* answer any ethical questions.

It is tough to follow the rules if you are not told what the rules are. Further, you need rules specific enough not to leave everything open to interpretation. Thus, rule ethics must have a firm set of rules, or principles, in order to provide a genuine ethical perspective. There is no *one* rule ethics; instead, there is a whole array of rule ethics corresponding to the many ethical codes adopted in the history of mankind—and that is a problem.

Whether or not a person believes that there is one true ethical code (supporters of rule ethics usually think there is), one thing an ethical model should do is to help us resolve conflicts among differing ethical perspectives. But rule ethics seems to offer little help in resolving conflicts. It is not very helpful to be told, "This is how it is according to my code, so line up!"

Supporters of rule ethics have responded to this problem. Defenders of religious versions of rule ethics try to resolve conflicts by insisting that their god(s) told them such and so and by trying to convert you. If that does not work, there is always holy war. If Marxists cannot convince you by appealing to their concept of justice, they annex and reeducate you. As long as the rule ethicist's fundamental appeal is to faith, force, the "pure light of reason" (Kant, [1785] 1981) it is hard to establish even a starting place for discussion.

There is a lesson to learn from the very problems that rule ethics has in resolving ethical conflicts. One reason that it is hard to resolve conflicts within rule ethics is that rule ethics pulls these conflicts to the surface, where the differences really show. We build on this feature of rule ethics in looking at the role of ethical codes in decision making and action.

Applying Rule Ethics in Decisions

What is the relationship between rule ethics and ground rules? If a person's or organization's ethics is no more or less than the ground rules of the person or organization, it would seem that we have no alternative to being rule ethicists. If you have ethics, you have ground rules, and those ground rules would seem to be your own rule ethics. But we are not so easily compelled to be rule ethicists.

Recall our reverse-engineering process for uncovering the ground rules of a person or organization. We look beneath actions for decisions and beneath decisions for ground rules. What we find at the core of a decision, once we uncover the alternatives and data considered, are ground rules of value (what is desirable) and ground rules of evaluation, or operation (what are acceptable ways of pursuing what is desirable).

As the result of this reverse engineering, you may find that your (or an organization's) ethics is end-point ethics. In this case, you, or the organization, have essentially one ground rule of value and operation: Seek to maximize the balance of benefits over harms, and operate in ways that do the same. Your ethics may also be end-point ethics even if you find that you have several distinct ground rules. In order to determine whether these ground rules are a form of end-point or of rule ethics, you must now ask: Do these rules serve as the basis of my (or the organization's) decisions and actions because they promote the greatest balance of benefit over harm? If the answer is yes, the ground rules are still a form of end-point ethics. If the answer is no, the ground rules are genuinely a form of rule ethics.

Suppose you find through the reverse-engineering process that your or an organization's ground rules are a form of rule ethics. This leaves the question of what particular rule ethics you or the organization subscribe to. Knowing the specific code by which you and others act can help you better foresee what actions you and others are likely to take and to find approaches to problems that satisfy the ground rules of all involved.

The way to assess the rule ethics of a person or organization is to build on the stakeholder approach introduced in Chapter Four in connection with the end-point decision process. In any key decision, first identify the key groups having a significant stake in the decision. Then correlate with each group the ethical code—the specific rule ethics—of that group. This helps you spot those points of resistance to your decision that would not be uncovered simply by specifying the interests of each group.

Lesson: If you are dealing with groups (particularly public interest groups) whose actions cannot be foreseen or understood in terms of their reasonable interests, determine the specific rule ethics of the groups. Their actions can be better foreseen and understood in terms of their ethical codes than their interests.

For example, if you are dealing with environmental groups, zoning boards, or the media, knowing the ethical codes (and I do not mean formal codes) of these groups will help you anticipate their responses to your initiatives. These groups often act in ways not easily viewed as self-interested; thus it is difficult to grasp the ethics of these groups in end-point terms. But just as Mel, Diesel Engines Inc., and Big State Bell managed a city council, the Congress, and a utility commission successfully by knowing their opponent's ethics, so you can manage relations with external groups by learning their basic ethical rules.

Exercise: Try Their Ethics

The following exercise shows how to foresee and understand the actions of groups whom your decisions affect by anticipating how they would act in terms of their rule-ethical codes.

Look at a pending decision facing your organization. First list the groups that have a critical stake in the decision. Work hard to identify every group. The common failure is missing critical groups rather than identifying too many critical groups. Try to write down the ethical code of each critical stakeholder group. Remember to identify the actual ground rules, not the professed ground rules.

Now take on an advocacy stance on behalf of each group. Use that group's ethics to argue that the decision likely to be made is unethical. Keep trying until you make a case that you could proudly present on behalf of that group in a public forum.

If you have done a good job with this exercise, you have gone a long way toward escaping the no-ethics box of management thinking. You have also done a good job of forecasting. If you proceed with the decision, you are very likely to find the various groups raising the same arguments that you already raised on their behalf. You now know where they are coming from and what ground to meet them on.

Lesson: The way to truly grasp the ethics of the people and organizations with whom you interact is to take their position and to argue as effectively as you can from their premises to their conclusions.

One area in which a lack of understanding of conflicting ethical viewpoints is a daily hazard is international business. American executives often go to great lengths to understand the economic and technical conditions that prevail in a foreign market only to fail because they did not understand the local ethics. One reason for this is that the ethical differences often seem so great that there is little hope of understanding the local ethics. But the prize is for those who succeed in finding enough common ground to allow for action that satisfies both one's own ethics and the local ethical viewpoint. Roger Fisher and William Ury base their "principled negotiation" process on essentially this rule-ethical point (1981, pp. 17-40). In the following case, a manager who sought common ethical ground rather than concentrating on differences was able to create and sustain an important competitive advantage.

Case: Trust Across Cultures

This case illustrates how finding common ethical ground can establish and stabilize good business relations across cultures. In the case, Mr. Jackson (fictional name) rose above the regular rules of business (including his business), which insist on written contracts and documentation as a basis for service. Instead, Mr. Jackson met the customer more than halfway and did business in the way the customer expected—based on undocumented trust. This opened a market for Mr. Jackson and allowed him to hold it.

Mr. Jackson owns one of the most successful Caterpillar Tractor dealerships in the United States. He has succeeded by buffering his U.S. business from ups and downs through extensive participation in international markets. Here, Jackson illustrates why he has been so successful in international markets:

> In the early days of the dealership, I received an inquiry from Southeast Asia concerning an earthmoving machine. The fellow could only afford a very old, partly rebuilt machine, which I sold him. A few weeks after the machine was delivered, I received a panicked phone call from the guy. He said the machine broke down in the middle of a field. He was so busy telling me that he was going out of business and that he would come to the United States and kill me that I couldn't get a word in edgewise. I had no contractual obligation to repair this machine. It was sold as is. In fact, I had no contract at all with the guy, since we handled the entire deal by telephone. I finally found out where the machine was and had it repaired immediately. The fellow called me in shocked disbelief that he had been treated fairly, without a contract, *by an American.* He became a key source of my Southeast Asian business. We still move very little paper on business in that part of the world.

It is now over twenty years since the original incident. Mr. Jackson's dealership prospers in markets that his competitors regard as literally impenetrable. Mr. Jackson, aware that different people act from different ground rules, regularly teaches his representatives the art of finding an ethical common ground firm enough to provide a basis for doing business.

Lesson: When dealing with people or organizations having ethical rules widely divergent from your own, reverse engineer their actions with an eye to finding rules that provide an ethical common ground—and ignore the divergent rules as far as possible.

Ethical Exceptions

One feature of ethical rules is so often overlooked and contributes so much to the misunderstanding of ethics and to the ethical indictment of business that I single it out for special attention. Ethical rules may be one of two distinct kinds—*categorical* or *prima facie.* Categorical rules allow absolutely no exceptions, but prima facie rules do.

Most ethical rules are not categorical. For example, the rule that one should keep promises has clear exceptions; in fact, sound ethics *requires* that this rule sometimes be broken. Suppose I promise to sell the rights to a patent to a friend. After making the promise, I learn that he is selling new technologies to the Soviet Union for military uses. He probably befriended me for no other reason than to find out what I know about missile guidance systems. I conclude that my "friend" wants to buy my patent to help the Soviets build an offensive missile. I am obligated to break my promise to him and, if possible, to sell him a very misleading fake patent.

The rules that one should keep promises and tell the truth are not categorical. They are prima facie rules. These rules can, and sometimes must, be violated in favor of more pressing obligations, such as the obligation to help others avoid military domination. Prima facie rules have the form: *Other things being equal,* one should keep promises, tell the truth, obey the law, and so on. The problem, then, is determining when other things are equal.

Review your ground rules and decide if there are any that you will not violate under any circumstances. If there are, these are your categorical ground rules and they take priority over all other rules. Very few managers will find that they have any categorical ground rules. The world of the manager is very complex, and circumstances often require that one think twice be-

fore rigidly adhering to any rule. Think of H. Ross Perot's decision to rescue his Electronic Data Systems (EDS) employees
held hostage in Iran. Perot had to violate many rules, including
rules to respect our laws and the laws and customs of other
countries, in order to make an ethical decision.

A common and effective strategy for attacking business
on ethical grounds is to indict all business, a specific firm, or an
executive for violating a commonly accepted ethical rule. The
trick is that although the rule is commonly accepted (do not lie,
bribe, violate the law, or such), it is a prima facie rule that
sometimes *must* be violated to uphold ethics. And the complex
circumstances of international business tend to produce just
such situations that do not conform to simple maxims. Businesses and executives typically respond to such attacks in economic, legal, or other defensive terms, whereby they appear to
concede that they acted unethically. But once you realize that
violating an ethical rule may be ethical, or even ethically required, you can take a positive stand without conceding ethics
to the critic.

*Lesson: If you are criticized for violating an ethical rule, de-
termine whether the rule is a categorical or a prima facie rule.
If it is a prima facie rule, meet the criticism by citing the ethical
rules you upheld by violating the rule at issue.*

We see in the following case study how the strategy of
confusing prima facie and categorical ethical rules was used effectively to attack business. We bring all of the ethical tools we
have assembled to bear in analyzing this case and in forming a
considered assessment of the ethics of bribery.

Case: International Bribery

According to a Louis Harris survey ("Antibribery Act...,"
1983), most Americans condemn businesses for bribing officials
of foreign governments. The conviction that bribery is wrong is
based on rule ethics. Paying bribes violates ethical rules, or principles, such as the rules that one should not lie (as one surely
must in covering up bribes) and that one should not cheat (tak-

ing advantage of honest competitors). But the issue of bribery is not as ethically clear-cut as this observation suggests. And many businesses and some government officials know there is something suspicious about this easy indictment of a once common business practice.

The issue of bribery in U.S. policy is a conflict among ethical views. The health of American businesses that engage in international trade, and thus the overall health of our economy, depends on resolving this conflict. It is clear that the American public and most American businesses abhor bribery of domestic government officials and, by extension, of foreign government officials. The issue of bribing foreign officials came to a head in the aftermath of Watergate. Many of the corporate slush funds used to finance the Watergate skulduggery existed primarily to provide funds to bribe foreign officials in order to gain or facilitate business. Battered by the public outrage about ethics in the superheated environment of the time, Congress did the only honorable thing—it regulated business and left itself untouched.

On December 20, 1977, President Carter signed into law S. 305, the Foreign Corrupt Practices Act (FCPA). This act makes it a crime for American corporations to offer or provide payments to officials of foreign governments in order to obtain or retain business. Violators of the FCPA, both corporations and managers, face severe penalties. A company may be fined up to $1 million, while its officers who directly participate in violations of the act *or have reason to know of such violations* face up to five years in prison and/or $10,000 in fines. The FCPA establishes extraordinarily stringent record-keeping requirements for publicly held corporations to ensure that the proscribed payments, or knowledge of them, are not concealed.

The primary motivation for the FCPA was neither economic nor legal. The motivation was ethical and political. First, the ethical motivation: The public and Congress disapproved of corporations bribing foreign government officials. This disapproval was based on our strong prohibition of bribes to our own officials and on the easy assumption that other governments work as ours does. The political motivation mixed the desire to comply with the popular antibribery sentiment, the sense that attacking big business is politically advantageous, and the need to divert public attention from congressional misdeeds. Given the important role of ethics in motivating the FCPA and the serious economic consequences of this law, we must ask whether ethical disapproval of international bribery makes sense.

Are They Bribes? We first ask whether or not the pro-scribed payments really are bribes. The willingness of the public to see these payments as bribes shows how business is losing the battle over ethics. A good case can be made that in many cases the payments were extortion payments extracted from American corporations by corrupt foreign officials.

Carl Kotchian, President of Lockheed Aircraft Corporation during the period of the notorious Lockheed bribes to Japanese government officials, begins his memoir of the bribery scandal by saying, "My initiation into the chill realities of extortion, Japanese style, began in 1972" (1977, pp. 6–12). Kotchian makes a convincing case that Lockheed had already won the competition on behalf of its Tristar passenger plane when he was informed that he would either have to pay "pledges" to high officials of the Japanese government or lose the sale. Kotchian strongly resisted paying the pledges, but they were absolutely demanded.

Whether or not Kotchian should have complied (we are obliged to resist extortion if possible), the payments in question do not look like bribes. However, with so many dubious payments made in every part of the world, it is overwhelmingly likely that some American companies paid genuine bribes to foreign officials. The head of the legal department of a major oil company once showed me a list he developed to advise company representatives new to the Middle East about the customary levels of bribes in each country. The next question is whether such payments are ethical.

The View from End-Point Ethics. Opposition to international bribery cannot be based on end-point ethics, which gives many kinds of secret payments and bribes a clean bill of ethical health. Suppose the Lockheed payments were out-and-out bribes. Using end-point ethics, we weigh the benefits against the harms of the payments to determine whether the payments were ethical.

The benefits are clear. The most important was selling the

Tristar. This benefited Lockheed management and stockholders, as well as Lockheed employees who would have lost their jobs without this sale. Kotchian offers the following assessment of Lockheed's stake in the Japanese market: "Lockheed had nowhere *else* to go but Japan. . . . The bleak situation all but dictated a strong push for sales in the biggest untapped market left —Japan. This push, if successful, might well bring in revenues upwards of $400 million. Such a cash flow would go a long way toward helping to restore Lockheed's fiscal health, and it would, of course, save the jobs of thousands of the firm's employees" (1977, p. 7). Kotchian's statement is accurate. Further benefits of Lockheed's payments included the savings to American taxpayers from the revenues generated by this business and from the unemployment benefits avoided. Finally, All Nipon Airlines benefited in acquiring what was, at the time, an outstanding airplane.

There are three harms associated with secret payments to officials of foreign governments. First and foremost, these payments help corrupt officials maintain their positions, to the detriment of their local constituents. Second, the cost of the payments must be passed along to consumers. Third, the payments may in some cases lead to the presence of inferior, possibly dangerous products on the market. In the Lockheed case, however, and in most reported cases of bribery by American companies, all three harms were absent or minimal.

If Lockheed had not paid the officials in question, it is clear that somebody else would have paid them. The Japanese people were not made worse off. Their position was arguably improved, since the Tristar is a superior plane. On balance, there were substantive and otherwise unobtainable benefits to the Lockheed payments. There were few harms, and these harms could not have been avoided by Lockheed's refusal to pay.

The end-point view issues a favorable verdict on the Lockheed payments and on analogous payments and bribes made by other American corporations. This does not mean that all such payments are ethical in terms of the end-point view. It means that such payments are ethical if the product is good, the payment is demanded, and others will pay if a particular firm does not. There are hardly grounds here for a blanket condemnation of bribes.

End-point ethics does not explain our blanket disapproval of international bribery. Although bribes may in fact promote our individual or collective best interests, we nevertheless oppose bribes because they violate our fundamental ethical principles. Thus, our grounds for condemning bribes must be sought in rule ethics.

The View from Rule Ethics. The ethical codes of most American citizens and managers include this rule: "No person or organization should offer or pay a bribe or other secret payment to any legitimate government official." Even if the ethical codes of some countries tolerate bribery, ours clearly does not. The code of conduct for employees of the Electronic Data Systems Corporation concisely summarizes the view typical of American business: "A determination that a payment or practice is not forbidden by law does not conclude the analysis. . . . It is always appropriate to make further inquiry. . . . Could you do business with someone who acts the way you do? The answer must be YES." While some of us do not live up to the standard embodied in this code, it is nevertheless clearly a part of our ethics.

The fact that our ethics prohibits bribery does *not* close the case against bribes paid to foreign officials. Understanding the reasons for this is essential if we are to intelligently apply any code of ethics and to meet biased ethical attacks.

The rules proscribing bribes and other secret payments are prima facie rules having many exceptions. American pilots flying relief missions into Cambodia regularly bribed Cambodian officials to be permitted to unload critically needed food and medical supplies. It would have been morally degenerate for these pilots to have refused to pay bribes because this violated their ethical codes. Countless children would have died. In terms of rule ethics, the issue of paying foreign government officials boils down to this question: Do American businesses have obligations that override our ethical prohibition of bribery?

Let's take a final look at the Lockheed case. Kotchian states that he felt obliged to Lockheed employees to promote their job security. Kotchian also had an obligation to Lockheed stockholders to earn a reasonable return on their investments. A less specific obligation on Kotchian was to promote economic well-being in the United States through the economic success of Lockheed. If these factors do not seem significant enough to override a general prohibition of bribery, you probably did not put in twenty years of service at Lockheed or have a significant portion of your retirement fund committed to Lockheed stock.

Rule ethics, which appeared simply to prohibit bribes at the outset, is not that simple at all. Kotchian's obligations to promote the well-being of Lockheed's employees and investors weighed heavily against the obligation not to pay bribes. Rule ethics, despite any prohibition of bribery it may include, allows no blanket condemnation of payments like Lockheed's.

A rule-ethical assessment of the FCPA is also not unequivocally supportive. While the FCPA reduces under-the-table payments to foreign officials by U.S. firms, it increases the number made by foreign firms, and it forces managers to violate obligations to employees and investors. If we assume that the federal government is obliged to promote the interests of U.S. business and labor, then the FCPA requires that the federal government violate some of its obligations. Some versions of rule ethics include a principle of tolerance, requiring that we respect the ethical views of others even when they disagree with our own. But the FCPA requires that this principle be violated with respect to any country whose ethics permits officials to accept bribes. While the final reckoning of these conflicting obligations is unclear, it cannot result in an unequivocal endorsement of the FCPA. At best, the FCPA is an ethically motivated piece of legislation in search of ethical motivation.

Given the great costs that the FCPA imposes upon business and labor, as well as the lack of a clear ethical purpose for imposing these costs, it is depressing that we passed this law with little discussion of the ethical issues. Once a piece of legislation that purports to have the backing of ethics is put forward, it is hard to prevent passage. Once the law is passed, it is nearly impossible to rescind.

Lesson: Once legislation that is supposedly ethically motivated is passed, it is almost impossible to rescind. The time to partici-pate forcefully in discussion of ethically motivated legislation is before it is passed, no matter how difficult this appears to be at the time.

The FCPA is the Prohibition of our time. There have been repeated attempts to modify the stringent accounting pro-visions of the FCPA. The intent of these efforts is to gut the law without repealing it. Executives and legislators have the courage to speak on behalf of gutting the law, but they fear arguing for repeal. A Louis Harris poll revealed that 78 percent of U.S. executives view the law as a serious impediment to doing busi-ness in countries where bribery is an accepted practice and that 68 percent favor gutting the law. Only a few endorse outright repeal ("Antibribery Act . . . ," 1983). Yet off-the-record inter-views with executives of multinational corporations reveal al-most universal scorn for the FCPA. In short, we painted our-selves into an ethical corner by passing the FCPA without thoroughly considering its ethical implications. (These issues are discussed in Pastin and Hooker, 1985, pp. 169–177.)

The Ties That Bind

We conclude our survey of rule ethical tools by intro-ducing social contract ethics. Social contract ethics is a form of rule ethics because it looks beyond the consequences of actions in assessing their merits. We take a quick look at social contract ethics here. Because the social contract model is so important to understanding several important issues, including the relation-ship of ethics to organizational culture and the emerging form of new organizations, we devote an entire chapter (Chapter Seven) to it.

Social contract ethics sees the ethical rules we live by as products of an implicit contract. Social contract ethics empha-sizes that social contracts are *not* explicitly negotiated, although they are subject to intentional change. Social contracts are carried by the cultures of the groups, organizations, and society to which we belong. The social contract is an implicit agreement about the basic principles, or ethics, of the group. Our ethical discussions probe the adequacy of our contracts and the possibility of changing them.

In Chapter Seven we offer a detailed picture of how to apply social contract ethics. The basic method is to understand the standing contracts in an organization and then to consider how the proposed actions will affect the contract. If the contract is unilaterally shifted to the disadvantage of a particular group, or if this is the perception of the group, that group will take action (or inaction) to restore the perceived balance. Since contracts within organizations are typically shifted to the disadvantage of middle managers, this group often lobbies strenuously and effectively against change. We look at a participatory management program stalled over the social contract and at organizations that succeeded against very long odds by giving persistent attention to the contract.

Independent Thinking Is the Scarce Resource

When managers address ethics, they often think in terms of rule ethics as expressed in formal ethical codes or codes of conduct. When I receive something labeled *code of ethics* from an organization I belong to or work for, I promptly throw it out, or I initial it illegibly if absolutely required. My intelligence and integrity are insulted, ethics is associated with legalism and bureaucracy, and a lot of wastebaskets need emptying. No one earns the right to control anyone's ethics by employing them or by holding higher organizational office. Executives who promulgate such a code endorse the idea that ethical rules are categorical. They and their organizations appear foolish and without integrity when the inevitable exceptions occur.

The scarce resource in ethics is independent thinking—not rule compliance. Codes constrict thinking and reinforce the myth that the heart of ethics is compliance.

Lesson: To gain anything by having a code of ethics, management must relentlessly emphasize that codes are merely guide-

*lines, that the rules have exceptions, and that the essence of eth-
ics is independent thinking and questioning.*

   This sort of responsible implementation of a code of ethics is virtually untested. My search of thousands of pages of
management journals uncovered no evidence that codes of ethics
have a positive effect on conduct.

Know the Rules

   The thinking manager can learn by considering rule ethics, particularly in its application to international bribery. End-
point ethics asks: What is in this course of action for me and for
others who are affected? Rule ethics asks: What set of rules are
we playing by and who set the rules? This latter question forces
managers to see their actions as instances of a code that they
must either reinforce or oppose. Because ethical positions resist
change, it is important to clearly grasp the accepted ethical
code. Changing an organization is a long-term project. It requires that the manager be aware that he or she is trying to
bring about a fundamental and lasting change and that he or she
work consistently toward this change on every front.

   Managers who turn their attention to the ethics of an organization will find conflicts among different sets of rules in
different groups within the organization and more conflicts
within each rule set. Because ethical rules are deeply felt and
difficult to modify, attempted shifts should be framed in terms
of the accepted code or codes as far as possible. For instance,
once it is admitted that there is an ethical obligation to promote
equity, one can argue for a balance of this obligation against
other equally important obligations, such as honoring commitments to long-term employees and rewarding performance. A
shift toward an ethics of performance may gradually result.

   In public forums, it is particularly important to distinguish between prima facie obligations, which include almost
everything under the title of ethics, and categorical obligations.
When business is attacked on ethical grounds, a standard strategy is to take a prima facie obligation and pretend that it is a
categorical obligation. Thus, critics might cite the obligation

not to bribe, other things being equal, or the obligation to provide equal pay for equal work, other things being equal, while
ignoring obligations to employees and stockholders (bribery) or
local pay standards (equal pay). Violators can then be characterized as unethical monsters. If one acknowledges the obligation
without emphasizing its prima facie nature, one appears to
plead for an exemption from ethics.

　　We have now looked at two ethical models, end-point
ethics and rule ethics. Should we cynically embrace both, opt-
ing for one or the other as suits our interests? Several studies
show that this is the first response of students in business ethics
courses. Well, it just cannot be true that one should promote
the common good and that one should obey a given code irrespective of whether it promotes the common good. Choice is
necessary.

　　We have also gathered questions raised by the two ethical
models. We need not choose among questions. The thinking
manager recognizes both kinds of questions as essential to
thinking outside the no-ethics box. In the following two chapters, we move toward a unified approach that includes all the
questions in a practical ethics for managers.

7

Why Organizations Should Have Weak Cultures and Strong Ethics

Customs are made for customary circumstances
and customary characters.
                        – *John Stuart Mill,* On Liberty

Managers are in search of something. They jump on the bandwagons of theory Z, situational leadership, matrix management, the McKinsey-Waterman-Peters seven-S model, various culture-change programs, and almost everything else offered to them. Managers are like children in a video arcade armed with an unlimited supply of quarters gratis the stockholders. But this is not just a reckless binge. Managers correctly sense that there is something unworkable about the way they have learned to manage. To their credit, they experiment. But the experiments are costly and frustrating. There is a real risk that managers will "learn" that no models work—that thinking about management does not pay. This would not be an unwarranted conclusion, given the rapid and expensive pace of management fad, rejection of fad, new management fad . . . (Kilmann, 1984).

This chapter focuses on organizational culture. We focus on culture for several reasons. Culture certainly qualifies as a management fad. Today, admitting "I ain't got no culture" is

127

like admitting "I can't read"; you only make those around you think that you have lost interest in management. *Culture* has become part of the standard lexicon of management. By now, many managers suspect that organizational culture is just a fad. A *Fortune* article entitled "The Corporate Culture Vultures" (Uttal, 1983) warns against consultants hawking culture change. But many excellent, thoughtful managers remain interested in culture.

Organizational culture has struck a deep and resonant chord in just those managers who are not typically taken in by the latest fads. They sense that there is something correct about concern for meaning, symbols, myths, or whatever it is that constitutes an organizational culture. This instinct is sound even if organizational culture is the wrong vehicle for it.

Even though ethics and culture are closely related, the infatuation with culture does not extend to ethics. One reason is that those promoting organizational culture are now competing in a small but quite profitable industry—organizational culture consulting. Introducing ethics into the discussion is perceived as not at all likely to help sales. And those who sell culture, like the managers who buy it, have allowed themselves to become illiterate in the language of ethics. So they ignore it. But the truth is that ethical ground rules are the heart of organizational cultures. In fact, if ethics is the heart of organizational culture, then the myths, symbols, rituals, ideologies, and customs—the elements of culture on which the organizational culture movement focuses—are the fat around the heart, strangling it and destroying its vitality.

My thesis is simple. Ethics is not only the heart of organizational culture, it is also the fulcrum in culture for producing change. Since ethics is the fulcrum for changing culture, changing culture without ethics is akin to changing a tire without a jack. I argue that the *adaptive organization* seeks strong ethics and weak culture. This combination of strong ethics and weak culture is achievable, and this chapter offers several examples in which this combination has produced both ethical and economic effectiveness.

To understand the relation of ethics to culture, we need

our final ethical model—social contract ethics. Social contract ethics explains what it takes to achieve strong ethics in organizations. It also figures centrally in understanding the new form of organization—the organization by agreement—that is emerging in the information and biotechnology industries of today and tomorrow. Finally, the social contract model will help us understand not only why corporate tragedies are becoming an ever more pervasive fact of management life but also how to manage them.

Getting Culture

Let us begin with a quick overview of culture: *Webster's New Collegiate Dictionary* defines it as "the integrated pattern of human behavior that includes thought, speech, action, and artifacts and depends on man's capacity for learning and transmitting knowledge to succeeding generations." This tells us that the culture of an organization is an information system for preserving and transmitting knowledge, beliefs, myths, and attitudes.

Marvin Bower defines culture as "the way we do things around here" (1966, p. 23). (Both definitions are cited in Deal and Kennedy, 1982, p. 4.) In other words, culture addresses *how* things are done as much as *what* is done.

The definition I prefer says that culture is all the "historically created designs for living, explicit and implicit, rational, irrational, and nonrational, which exist at any given time as potential guides to the behavior of men" (Kluckhohn and Kelly, 1945, p. 97). Cultures are conservative, judging the future by the past, and often irrational.

The question the definitions raise is: Why would any organization want a strong culture? A strong culture puts basic beliefs, attitudes, and ways of doing things beyond question. But unquestionables must be questioned for an organization to be quick on its feet, strategic, and just plain smart. Because cultures are rooted in tradition, they reflect what *has* worked, not what *will* work. Can anyone doubt that AT&T's problems in adapting to a competitive environment are partly due to its strong bureaucratic culture? If a culture is an information system, who says whether it preserves and transmits the right information for adaptation and success?

Organizational cultures contribute to corporate tragedies. How? Tragedies are tragedies partly because they are not foreseen as likely or possible. When I asked a group of executives why they did not anticipate tragedies, they responded that tragedies are not predictable and so not worth thinking about. Much that is unpredictable—and tragedies cannot be predicted in a specific form (who, when, where)—can be foreseen. The possibility can be considered and anticipated, if only in general terms. Even if tragedies are unpredictable in specific terms, it is predictable that most major corporations will someday face a tragedy and that certain industries will see specific types of tragedies.

If there is a small chance of a tragedy afflicting each particular firm in an industry, there is a good chance that some firm in the industry will see the tragedy. And tragedies that afflict one firm redound on the whole industry. Someone will kill a lot of people by poisoning an open food bin (flour, fruit, candy) in a supermarket. All supermarket chains will suffer, and those which rely on fresh items to distinguish themselves from competitors will suffer more than others. The chance of a particular nuclear power plant experiencing a meltdown are quite small, but there will be a meltdown in the United States in the next twenty years. The industry knows this. When the meltdown occurs, it will affect all nuclear operators. Biotechnologies are very safe, but they will generate a tragedy. There are no tragedy-proof technologies. When there is a tragedy, biotechnology may end as abruptly as nuclear power technology has in the United States.

These are not startling revelations, but fairly obvious facts. Managers do not think about them because in the cultures of most corporations, these facts are literally unthinkable. The facts that might stir managers to foresee tragedies are among the beliefs and assumptions that corporate cultures remove from the domain of consideration. The idea that someone might tamper with Tylenol packages was beyond consideration for

McNeil Laboratories. The culture would not tolerate this idea. When a consultant urged McNeil to think this through, years before the disaster, he was accused of creating problems. Cultures contribute to tragedies by prohibiting consideration of them. This is not to say that McNeil could have prevented the Tylenol murders. It is to say they had the opportunity to think through their response to this tragedy before it was upon them.

Cultures are, by consensus, hard to change. The stronger the culture, the harder it is to change. And most established organizations have strong, if not attractive or "appropriate," cultures. Passenger railroads had strong cultural traditions (poor service, disregard for passengers). Most chose to perish rather than change. The steel industry is afflicted by a strong adversarial and antientrepreneurial culture. Only new steel companies, such as Nucor, have escaped this debilitating cultural trap.

Finally, culture is process-oriented rather than result-oriented. Who cares if the process is right if you do not get the desired results? There is little consolation in knowing you ran the plays right if you lose the game. In the next chapter I discuss the amazing Eagle team within Data General. The team blew every play, ignored the culture, and won the game.

The complaint about organizational cultures is that they change too slowly. But the complaint about ethics is that it is changing too fast. ("What happened to the work ethic of integrity, honesty, and hard work?") This is puzzling since the ethics of an organization comprises the basic ground rules by which it operates. What is the relation of ethics to culture? Are there *strong-ethics, weak-culture* companies? There are, and these companies have the best prospects for sustained success, unimpeded by tragedy. Before we look at such companies, let me sharpen the picture of the ethics-culture connection.

The Ethics-Culture Connection

Ethics is closer to the surface of a culture than are other components (myths, ideologies, and aesthetics). I observed earlier that we use ethics to ensure that others agree with us on the basics and to lock out those whose ideas or values threaten us.

When an organization enforces its ethics, its principles come to the surface. When the every-man-for-himself ethics of an organization forces out a female executive, she sees one strand of the organization's ethics clearly. When the boss said, "Pastin, you're too aggressive," I learned that the ethics of my organization said, "Don't make waves."

Ethics has another role. Ethics is the forum in which societies, groups, and organizations argue fundamental changes in their bylaws (ground rules). American society is torn by ethical debate on abortion. Large segments of society seek a change to a more permissive ethics of abortion. Other segments seek a return to a past ethics (they would be among those who say that ethics changes too quickly). Criticism is as much a part of ethics as enforcement is. You can ignore criticism of your aesthetic ("You call that music?"), your ideology ("You can't be serious about voting for him?"), and even your personality ("You lack drive!"). But if someone criticizes your ethics, take note.

Ethical criticism is not offered lightly and is not to be taken lightly. If you disregard ethical criticism by the group you belong to, you state your willingness to exit the group. You are saying that you regard the organization so lightly that you do not even care about its ground rules.

For a culture to persist and serve those who work and play in it, the culture must *learn.* It must allow challenges to its basic principles in a setting that tolerates some change without threatening to undo the culture. Thus, culture promotes discussion of issues in ethical terms and mandates that these discussions are serious. This is functional in that it provides an opportunity for a culture to change while keeping what is valuable in the culture intact. It is dysfunctional in that it remands vital issues to the court of interminable discussion, well out of the line of action. Since the discussion is held in the culture's living room, fundamental change is inhibited. It is like discussing modernism on the steps of the Parthenon.

The moral of the story for managers?

Lesson: If you want to change the culture of your organization, start discussing ethics.

But do you want to and will it work? The answer is a qualified yes. We shall look first at an organization that initially tried to change its culture without using ethics to do so. (When I say that the organization, Motorola, initially attempted a culture change without using ethics, I do not mean that Motorola is unethical; Motorola is a high-ethics company. I mean that Motorola did not look at culture change in ethical terms until it ran into problems.)

Case: Good Deal, Bad Deal

Motorola was one of the first major corporations in the United States to see the advantages of participatory management. The company committed significant resources to creating a company-wide culture of participation. Motorola began by fostering participation at the level of workers and their supervisors. Workers liked it or, at least, accepted it. Once supervisors got used to putting in the time (a lot) required to foster participation, the performance of their units improved. So did the supervisors' compensation. The program stalled at middle management.

What halted the program at middle management? The philosophy "This too will pass" is entrenched at this level in most large organizations. Experienced managers know that other programs have been tried and that one survives by producing results, no matter what gizmo the boys at the top are playing with this month. Motorola's middle managers "knew" this wisdom and acted accordingly.

Unlike the workers' jobs, the middle managers' jobs were unprotected by union contracts or the mimicking of union contracts in nonunion companies. In theory, two compensations make this a fair deal: Middle managers have the opportunity to make more money and rise to higher rank, and they have the freedom and security of being able to move laterally to an equivalent or better position in another company. Motorola's participation program threatened both compensations.

The middle managers continued to be evaluated by the numbers. It is almost impossible to quantify good participation.

Shouldn't middle managers be able to translate good participation into good numbers? Good participators should not receive two rewards for the same conduct, as they would if good participation and good numbers were separately rewarded.

The problem: Motorola's middle managers were already "stretched out." Time spent on participation would detract from the numbers for the foreseeable future. There was also a sense of hypocrisy. Middle managers were expected to listen to every suggestion offered by line workers. But they felt that they were not equally listened to by those above. They knew too well that numbers were still the game and, moreover, that top management would not yield one iota of its power to give middle managers more say over top-level decisions.

Surely, you say, the middle managers who did not like the new culture could leave. Not so easy. The participation program required that the managers concentrate less on their own areas of specialization and become more familiar with other areas. The managers thus moved from area to area, spending more time "learning the company" and less time developing skills related to their training. They became more specialized as Motorolans and less specialized in finance or engineering. This lowered their market value.

Motorola's move to a culture of participation met resistance because of ethics. The relevant concept is that of the social contract: The shift to a participatory culture produced a correlated shift in the social contract between the company and the middle managers. The program to change the culture did not reckon with the shift in the social contract. The middle managers did not like the result.

Most culture changes are thwarted by middle managers. Middle managers are the lubricant in these changes. When a contract is violated in a one-sided way, there is a response. Since middle managers cannot start a protest movement or go on strike, they respond quietly. They slow the program down, talk about its silliness, and create an atmosphere of unworkability. Underhanded but effective. Cultural changes seldom work. When they do, they are inordinately expensive. Exploiting the social contract, even inadvertently, has a price.

Lesson: Whenever a significant organizational change is perceived to disadvantage one group, that group will take action or inaction to restore perceived fairness.

Motorola's top management caught this problem in time. Top management realized that one of the firm's ground rules stated that all that really matters are the numbers. So they created ways of quantifying participatory success at the middle management level. They also realized that you cannot have a ground rule emphasizing the value of listening to those beneath you unless you, too, listen to those beneath you. Motorola's top managers now bend over backward to listen to managers and employees at every level.

Motorola's top management restored fairness to the social contract, and it has worked. Motorola has dealt much more effectively with the downturn in the semiconductor industry than its U.S. competitors have, and it is positioned to move ahead when the market picks up. It has held on to critical employees by living up to a fair social contract.

Culture by Contract

Social contract ethics illuminates the problems of change in organizational culture. Whenever you attempt to change the culture of an organization, you shift the underlying social contract of the organization. Even if the changes in the social contract were entirely fair, the process would be upsetting, since it creates uncertainty about the ground rules by which organization members live. They do not know if the contract shifts will be fair. And we have seen that the changes can be quite unfair to some groups, particularly middle managers.

We need to look more closely at social contract ethics before applying this model to achieve organizational change without the pitfalls of culture. This model points the way to a new form of organization capable of meeting the needs of new forms of industry.

In Chapter Six we observed that social contracts are *not* explicitly negotiated. Social contracts are carried by the cultures of the groups, organizations, and society to which we belong. While cultures carry social contracts, there is little correlation between the strength of a culture and the strength of the contract it carries. (Bodies carry brains, but there is little correlation between the strength of the body and the strength of the brain.) The social contract is an implicit agreement about the ground rules of the group. Organizational social contracts establish ground rules relating to rewards, conditions of employment, and performance expectations.

Every organization is a web of implicit contracts. Every time we enter a new organization, we also enter this web of contracts. How do we tell if these contracts are sound? Social contract ethics offers a standard: A contract is sound if the parties to the contract would enter the contract *freely* and *fairly*.

Since social contracts are not explicitly negotiated, social contract ethics asks what parties *would* agree to in a hypothetical negotiation. Obviously, there is plenty of room for debate over what someone would agree to. The only acid test is an actual negotiation. But even if the basic contracts we live by will not be part of an actual negotiation, social contract ethics helps us judge whether to support standing contracts or to seek their change or demise.

A contract has no standing unless the involved parties entered it, or would enter it, freely. *Freely* is open to interpretation. If I hold a gun to your head, you may freely agree to pay me $10,000 for one copy of this book. Your agreement was free in that it was not an involuntary reflex, such as twitching with fear. You could have refused and faced the consequences. But no one would ethically criticize you for welching on this agreement.

It is for such reasons that employment by agreement fell into disrepute. Management used to argue that workers were not entitled to organize unions on the grounds that they were free to either enter into or not enter into an agreement to work for the company. David, however, was in no position to negotiate a fair deal with Goliath. Instead of blaming unfair *application* of employment by agreement and creating legal recourse, employment by agreement became the villain. As always, when a social contract is perceived by one group to be unfair, that group takes action (for better or worse) to restore perceived fairness. Unions were formed.

Social contract ethics addresses this point: Contracts must be both free and *fair*. A contract need not be fair in the sense that everyone fares equally well under it. A contract allows people to pursue interests cooperatively or competitively, *without expectation that each party will reap the same rewards*. The contract ensures that the involved parties understand the conditions of joint or competitive action and can not cry foul if the outcome is not what they hoped for.

A contract is *fair* if the parties to the contract would agree to the contract without knowing who they represented.

Here is another way of saying the same thing: A contract is fair if the parties would freely agree to the contract even if their roles might be switched upon enactment of the contract. In a labor negotiation, this means that a contract is fair if the negotiators would agree to it without knowing whether they would be assigned to labor or management upon ratification.

Lesson: If you want to find out if the existing contracts in your organization are perceived as unfair, assume the position of the other affected parties and ask how you would view the contract.

Lesson: If you want to find out if a change you would like to introduce shifts the social contract in ways that will be perceived as unfair, assume the position of the other affected groups and ask how you would view the contract.

There is a minor industry devoted to techniques for win win negotiations. (Consult your mailbox.) If you grasp the simple turnabout-is-fair-play idea of this paragraph, you know the secret.

Motorola's middle managers initially resisted the participation program because they believed that top management would not freely agree to work under it. The shift in the social contract created advantages for one side and disadvantages for another. This is the problem with culture changes. Culture changes shift the basic contracts by which the firm works. In bureaucratic organizations, the hint of change breeds resistance.

When the change disadvantages those who must implement it, the resistance is effective. Middle managers practice Gandhi's philosophy of passive resistance. If it worked against the British Empire, it will work against the personnel department. It does.

Organization by Agreement

While the social contract is an ethical idea, a handful of organization researchers have taken up its cause. These researchers view the relentless managerial search for something that works as a harbinger of a new form of organization, one to fit the changing nature of industry. And they see the social contract as the foundation of the new organization.

Michael Keeley states: "A traditional alternative to modeling social systems after goal-seeking, biological entities is to model them after *contracts*. From a contractual perspective, organizations are seen to be sets of agreements for satisfying diverse, individual interests" (1982, p. 147). And Jay Forrester writes: "In the new organization, an individual would negotiate, as a free individual, a continually changing structure of relationships with those with whom he exchanges goods and services. He would accept specific obligations as agreements of limited duration. As these are discharged, he would establish a new pattern of relationships as he finds more satisfying and rewarding situations" (1975, p. 95). Forrester argues that organizations must become networks of contracts negotiated against the background of a stable basic social contract. The organization with a fair *basic* contract supporting flexible *specific* contracts can adapt rapidly to changing external circumstances and new technologies. The basic lesson is:

Lesson: If you acknowledge organizational social contracts and measure them against standards of voluntariness and fairness, you can change the organization without fighting managers and employees.

The language of the contract model of organizations is misleading in one critical respect. If we think of organizations as networks of contracts, we might generate organizations that are as internally litigious as the external environment of organizations has become. Nothing could be worse. What matters in an organization is that people *agree* on the ground rules. Agreement does not suggest negotiation or litigation. Some agreements are entirely natural, requiring no actual or implicit negotiation. We agree with gravity, except when we fall down. In a healthy organization, the same is true; we are in agreement with it except when we fall down. And then both sides want to restore equilibrium. Thus, I shall speak of the *organization by agreement* rather than of the contract organization.

The idea of organization by agreement is important and deserving of implementation and testing. It may well be the emerging form of organization. Like all new organizational forms, once we have the idea, we find organizations that have used it all along. It is worth reviewing the experience of organizations that have tried managing by agreement.

We will now look at one firm, Cadbury Schweppes, which has lived and succeeded by agreement for over 150 years. We will then consider different types of firms (a stock brokerage and an automobile manufacturer) requiring different agreements to produce success.

Case: Cadbury's Anticulture

Suppose you manage a multinational corporation based in Great Britain. You compete in an industry in which labor costs are crucial, the labor force is unionized, and production technologies are changing rapidly. Your chances of success? Small. These are the exact circumstances under which Cadbury Schweppes has managed strong, sustained success.

Cadbury Schweppes has done so by attending to little more than basic agreements (ground rules). Cadbury Schweppes' main products are confections and soft drinks. It is an old company. The Cadbury line of the company started in 1824, when John Cadbury opened a tea-and-coffee shop in Birmingham. Jacob Schweppes founded the Schweppes line in 1783. The present company resulted from a merger of Cadbury and Schweppes in 1969. The merged company is dominated by its Cadbury lineage.

You would expect Cadbury Schweppes to have a strong

culture. The company has always been run more or less in accordance with the Quaker ethics of its Cadbury founders. A visit to corporate headquarters or to manufacturing facilities undercuts this expectation. There are few corporate symbols, none of the bells and whistles characteristic of strong-culture companies, and no need to do things "the Cadbury way." The corporate environment is free from ceremony.

While Cadbury Schweppes does not have a "strong culture," it has an evident corporate philosophy. The philosophy is simple: The individual is to be fully respected, and all significant decisions are participatory (at the least), ideally reached by consensus. Although this philosophy is now couched in business-school-speak, it would hold firm even if it did not fit management fashions.

This philosophy explains the lack of a strong culture. The individual is to sacrifice nothing except a commitment to work to the best of his or her abilities at Cadbury Schweppes. The culture of a Cadbury Schweppes operation fits the culture of the community in which it operates. Respect for individuals requires this. Sir Adrian Cadbury, chairman of the company, warns fellow directors against regarding the mandarin culture of the directors as a company culture.

Sir Adrian says, "One thing I'm totally clear about, whether we're talking about the structure of organization or whether we're talking about methods of involving people in the business, is that the way it's done must be related to the culture, the way people manage and expect to be managed in those countries" (Blodgett, 1983, p. 137). There is no exporting of theory J (Japan), theory Z (hybrid), or theory B (Britain) to every environment in this management philosophy.

Cadbury Schweppes pays excruciating attention to its basic agreements with managers, employees, suppliers, and customers. While this commitment to fair basic agreements has been expressed in a formal participation program since 1973, it has always been practiced. This manifests itself in countless meetings between top management and every level of manager and employee. During interviews, several employees stated that if a problem was unresolved on-site, they would "take it up with Sir Adrian" when they saw him next. Sir Adrian spends a lot of time on the road. In fact, he plans to limit the company's growth, which has been steady, in order to maintain this level of communication.

When management meets with employees, employees are given detailed candid information about the financial and operating issues. The thinking of management is offered, and the advice of all employees is sought. Advice is not sought in the suggestion-box mode. Employees are asked directly whether they agree with management and whether they have better ideas.

At one meeting, floor-level union officials chided top management for going too slowly in closing a dated facility and transferring operations to a more modern site requiring fewer employees. The atmosphere at such meetings is businesslike, with friendly banter and hard argument across ranks.

Cadbury Schweppes' management is not enamored of new trends in management. But it is no accident that Sir Adrian speaks of a new era, driven by new technologies, in which management-employee relations will be governed more by individualized contracts; he says that "you need flexibility in responding to the heightened desire of individuals to live their own kind of life. And that is likely to be reflected in the view that work needs to be adapted to what people expect out of life rather than the other way around. . . . If the employer contracts with you to get certain things done, you are no longer paid by time spent but for work done, and when you do it becomes very much your own decision" (Blodgett, 1983, pp. 141–142).

Despite its age, Cadbury Schweppes is an adaptive company. Since it can discuss its problems forthrightly, it can address them realistically. Because the basic agreements are fair, and expected to be fair, managers and employees speak up without fear. The company atmosphere is definitely interrogative. Everyone asks everyone hard questions. When managers at various levels were asked to discuss possible tragedies, there was none of the bristling and hedging apparent in virtually every corporation. Instead, forethought, confidence, and a willingness to think things through was evident. This is the best tragedy insurance you can get.

Different Strokes

Call it culture, contracts, or agreements, what Cadbury Schweppes does fits the recommendations of the culture pushers in some respects (participation; keep it simple). But the greater flexibility and adaptative capacity of the agreements-contract approach is evident in firms that fit few of the standard recipes.

R. L. Carol Inc. Consider R. L. Carol Inc. (fictional name), a small, extraordinarily successful stock brokerage. The company was founded by Ray Carol when he was already top producer in a large house. He objected to team-play hoopla, the necessity to sell a company-dictated product line, and the general lack of freedom. So he started his own firm based on a unique set of agreements.

Carol's agreement with his brokers is clear from the beginning. Their job is to sell successfully by any means they deem appropriate, within the limits of a very high ethics. Loyalty is actually discouraged; brokers are encouraged to find better offers elsewhere. The firm is confident that it is the best and that it can offer you the best deal if you deserve it. The outcome? Every broker is a star—and is payed full market value. If a broker makes it past the first two years, he or she will want to work at Carol forever. The reason? The basic agreement is fair, clean, and enables each individual to flourish in the way that is best for that individual. No loyalty is asked, brokers are essentially unmanaged, and there is no evaluation since you set your own pay through performance. Carol violates every rule of the culture-excellence-leadership movement and leads a high-ethics, no-culture, excellent firm.

R. L. Carol Inc. weathered a near tragedy in its early and most vulnerable days. At the time, the company placed a strong emphasis on resource-based investments. Subsequently, many brokers were stung (although not as badly as their clients) when such investments turned bad. But R. L. Carol Inc. had foreseen the problem and changed course in time. It did so because its brokers had argued for the change. They had been intensely critical of Ray Carol, attacking the heart of his investment philosophy. Consequently, the company took a course that was controversial but correct. R. L. Carol Inc. is a high-thought company because its basic agreements make it safe to question and disagree.

Jaguar PLC. Return to Britain. I study British companies because I know that if something works in the hostile British business environment, it has something going for it. Let us look again at the decline and revival of Jaguar Cars PLC. When I initially discussed this case in Chapter Four, I credited Sir Michael Edwardes, the managing director of British Leyland, and John Egan, the managing director of Jaguar Cars, with turning Jaguar Cars around. I said that they did this by refocusing the attention of Jaguar management and employees on the overall benefits of avoiding a conflict or outside intervention approach. How exactly did they do this? And how have they succeeded in maintaining this orientation?

When Edwardes took charge of British Leyland and Egan later took charge of Jaguar, they regarded the standing agreements governing labor-management relations as unfair to management. They violated a basic tenet of the culture movement by directly confronting labor with this issue and by holding the line. Both Edwardes and Egan made it clear that their aim was not to crush labor but to restore fairness to basic agreements. They were not beloved by labor. But in time their commitment to fairness in the negotiating process became apparent. Edwardes and Egan also started talking about quality, productivity, and economic performance. But their main emphasis was on ground rules that were fair.

Edwardes "Make my day!" commitment to tough-minded fairness made it possible for Egan to concentrate on Jaguar's production problems. But Egan, too, has made it clear that he will be fair to labor if labor is fair to management. Labor has begun to acknowledge Egan's commitment to fairness. Egan has worked hard to sell the idea that labor relations must be fair *over time* if the company is to survive and prosper. In short, standing on mutually fair ground rules, he has been able to argue mutual benefits. While Egan has been tough, he has also been available, interested in details, and clearly dedicated to the mutual prosperity of both labor and management. He has asked workers and managers a lot of questions. At first, they were surprised to be asked; now they, too, ask a lot of questions. Jaguar is becoming a high-information company.

Edwardes and Egan have succeeded by bringing a tough-minded fairness to management—one emphasizing the reciprocal character of basic ground rules and the mutual benefits to both sides of living by the rules. With a base of fair agreements, and the accompanying free flow of information, Jaguar will sustain its new winning ways.

R. L. Carol Inc. and Jaguar Cars practice management in ways not to be found in the culture-excellence-leadership movement. Like Cadbury Schweppes, they manage the basic ground rules, or agreements, above all else. Because the agreements are fair, even if adversarial (Jaguar) and competitive (Carol), they work. This approach points the way to the future. As more work is done away from the shop floor or desk, management by culture will not work, for it requires a lot of personal contact. But management by fair agreements requires minimal contact, and a fair deal is what we all seek. Companies that run by agreement can think about what the cultures of other companies make unthinkable. Managers and workers can think outside the box, and the agreement-based firm can adapt quickly and even think the possibility of tragedy through.

Lesson: As organizations allow more and more off-site work, managing culture will become less effective and managing agreements will become more effective. Because culture does not inhibit thinking in the agreement-based organization, it becomes possible to think through hard problems, including corporate tragedies.

Manage Agreements

The lesson is clear. Forget culture and think about fair agreements. Think about the basic agreements, or social contract, in your firm. Establish and stand by agreements that are good for you and the firm.

Be sure that you would work under the agreements (contract) voluntarily. The thinking manager will ask, "If I were to occupy the position of a lower-level manager or employee, would I accept this agreement?"

Can you find a good agreement for every situation? Of course not. That is why it is so important that the underlying agreements (social contract) be sound. If they are, you can quit handing out "atta boys" looking like "atta bozo" and get on with the job of managing.

8

Make-or-Break Factors
in Organizational Success:
Purpose, Responsibility,
Creativity

The only thing missing in the carrot-and-stick approach is the ass that goes between them.

—Anonymous

In previous chapters, we have puzzled over responsibility
—why there is so little in our organizations and how to let responsibility back in. We have puzzled over why managers play
against reward systems regardless of whether they are rewarded
for long-term, short-term, or midterm performance. And we
have puzzled over what basis for agreement exists in organizations in which different individuals seek different goals and the
organization seeks no goal in particular.

In this chapter, we look at three factors which managers
know are critical to success but which they give little attention to.
These factors are purpose, responsibility, and creativity. Managers
ignore these factors because there is no way to think about them
inside the no-ethics box. Because these factors cannot be studied with standard research tools, management researchers give
them even less attention. Yet these are the factors that make or
break managers as they tackle the truly hard problems.

146

We first look at purpose—how it can bind the organization together and give meaning to its activities. We then look at responsibility—how individuals can come naturally to act responsibly in their organizational life. Finally, we look at creativity—the life-force of any effective organization. Once we have mastered these three key factors, we will reconsider three problems: individual versus group responsibility, beating the organizational commons, and strategy and the long run.

Purpose Binds Organizations Together

People resort to old sayings because they are effective. One of the most effective is "You can't see the forest for the trees." As managers, that is how we approach most of our problems—one tree at a time—for we lack the perspective to see how cutting down or saving one tree will affect the whole forest.

That is the problem with the ethical toolchest I have provided. We know from end-point ethics that a person or organization should do what promotes the greatest balance of benefit over harm for all. We know from rule ethics that a person or organization should do what is required by valid ethical principles. And we know from social contract ethics that a person or organization should do what a fair, voluntary contract would mandate. Now we can analyze a problem in one of three ways: what approach will promote the greatest benefit over harm, what rules should I follow in making this decision, and what agreements should I live up to?

If we take the path of end-point ethics, we might say: "Let's cut down this tree, for cutting it will provide fuel for the townspeople. Moreover, selling the wood will give us money, and we'll spend the money to stimulate the economy." So we chop down the tree.

Then we come to another tree. This tree is a giant Sequoia pine and it is illegal to cut it down. Rule ethics gives us a simple decision: It is illegal to cut down this tree, so leave it standing.

Now the problem arises. We followed end-point ethics to cut down one tree and rule ethics to save another. We have solved two problems (dealt with two trees), but we are still in the middle of the forest, have little idea how our actions have affected the whole forest, and eventually may go crazy deciding on trees one by one. It seems like an endless project with no clear direction.

Then the head woodchopper gives an order. We are to cut down 50 percent of the trees in six months. So we follow that order. Wielding our axes, we chop down trees every day for three months straight. At the start of the fourth month, we stand bleary-eyed, looking at trees stretching endlessly in front of us, and do not care if we never see another tree. Even if the head woodchopper wants 50 percent of the forest cleared in six months, we do not want to do it.

What is lacking? We have always been told to set clear goals. What could be clearer than cutting down 50 percent of the trees in six months? But a faint suspicion lurks at the back of our minds. Even if we cut down 50 percent of the trees in this forest, chances are that we will merely be moved to another forest and told to cut down 50 percent of the trees there. We are reminded of Sysiphus pushing a boulder almost to the top of the hill only to have it roll down, push it up again, roll down, push it up again . . .

We are getting tired of goals.

We must discover what is lacking, what the fuel is that drives us to accomplish goals. We seek answers to a few basic questions: Why should I do a good job? Why should I care if this organization continues to exist? Why should I exemplify integrity in what I do? Why should our various publics tolerate and support our existence?

The most basic question of all, if answered honestly, could have resounding repercussions throughout the organization: Why does what I do matter?

It is hard to find a word that answers these questions. The answers are complex and strike at the very heart of an organization and our relationship to it. The best word I have found is *purpose*. What is lacking in the woodchopper example is purpose. Purpose need not be grandiose. You may simply want to be the best woodchopper ever. If that is your purpose, then you relish the endless chopping down of trees. When your task matches your purpose, you have a framework that helps to answer the questions posed above.

That brings us to what is missing from our ethical tool-chest—a framework determined by purpose. It is hard, if not impossible, to base a decision on rule ethics or end-point ethics or any other ethics unless you know your framing purpose and the framing purpose of the organization. Given a framing purpose, you can take a stand on how to decide and on how to give the sum of your decisions a semblance of unity. This not only gives coherence to your decision making; it also enables you to give direction to the actions of the organization.

It thus behooves us to examine purpose in more detail, for purpose is an important addition to our ethical toolchest—a needed addition if we are to make anything with our tools.

Distinguishing Between Purposes and Goals. There is a temptation to think of purposes and goals as one and the same thing. They are quite different. The confusion of these two different ingredients of decision making is the cause of much confusion in management. It is usually understood that goals are the intended output of strategic thinking; however, the role of goals in strategy has often been confused, as evidenced by inflated jargon (goals, superordinate goals, objectives, directions, driving forces, guiding beliefs) and by an ever lower confidence in strategic thinking. Let us begin distinguishing between goals and purposes by examining them in the context of strategy.

A *goal* is a more or less specific target toward which one aims.

A goal can be achieved, and it is exhausted if achieved. Suppose my firm sets the goal of having $5 million in sales by the end of 1990. The firm now has the opportunity of reaching that goal or not. If sales reach $5 million by the end of 1990, that exhausts the goal; new goals must be set. Stating a goal answers the questions: Why am I doing this? Where do I expect my company to be in one year? Five years? Goals are typically economic in form and include a target date (15 percent return on investment by 198X). Goals need not be economic and quantified (greatest market share), but noneconomic, nonquantified goals should translate into specific economic-temporal terms.

The ways in which superordinate goals contribute to organizational performance have recently received considerable attention. Waterman, Peters, and Phillips say that "By 'superordinate goals' we mean guiding concepts—a set of values and aspirations, often unwritten, that go beyond the conventional formal statements of corporate objectives. Superordinate goals are the fundamental ideas around which a business is built" (1980, p. 16). These authors are reaching for the concept of a purpose, as opposed to a goal. If an organization is built on goals and the goals are achieved or not achieved, then what? If we want more goals, where will they come from? Consultants? Management retreats? Organizations often avoid thinking about superordinate goals, or formulate unreachable or hopelessly vague goals, in order to avoid asking, "Then what?" The answer to the "Then what?" question is not, however, a bigger, more distant, or fuzzier goal. It is a purpose.

A *purpose* is a way of being or functioning viewed by an individual or organization as valuable in itself.

A purpose makes a value (as in a ground rule of value) specific or operational. If my purpose is to sell insurance aggressively and honestly, then this purpose makes the values of being aggressive and honest concrete for me.

While the concept of a purpose is hard to separate from the concept of a goal, a clear grasp of the differences between purposes and goals is essential to sound strategic thinking. If purposes and goals are not distinguished, the process of setting goals seems to require that goals be wished into existence from nothing. Goal implementation becomes difficult, since it is unclear where the goals came from and why anyone should care whether or not they are implemented. These points are clarified by considering cases of individual and organizational purposes.

Individual Purposes. Suppose you have the individual purpose of realizing your potential. It is your conviction that people could have no better purpose than to discover and develop their individual intellectual and personal abilities. If you are intelligent and curious, you might realize your potential by pursuing a challenging research problem. Say that you choose the goal of finding a cure for lung cancer within five years. Although this goal is specific, your background purpose—realizing yourself—resists specification in economic, temporal, or other terms. Contrasting this goal with your background purpose reveals some surprises.

For instance, you might consistently live up to your purpose over the next five years and not achieve your goal; you might set out to discover a cure for lung cancer and, instead, discover a cure for cerebral palsy. On the other hand, you might achieve your goal without living up to your purpose; if you discover a cure for lung cancer through a fluke (a child scribbles a formula and insists that you try it), you have not realized your intellectual potential. If your goals are not arbitrary, you have chosen them on the basis of purposes—but the connections between goals and purposes are not simple.

So far we have learned that goals can be made specific and that purposes cannot. Further, even though goals are set for purposes, goal achievement does not assure purpose satisfaction, and purpose satisfaction does not assure goal achievement.

Another difference between goals and purposes is that goals are exhausted at a specific time, whereas purposes are not. You may not discover a cure for lung cancer in the next five years. If you do, your goal is achieved and exhausted. If your goal is not achieved, you must adopt a revised goal (differing, say, only in target date) or abandon this line of action. The original goal no longer exists. Purposes persist. Even if you have satisfied a purpose up to a given time, the purpose is neither exhausted nor nonexistent. If you have fully exercised your intellectual abilities up to a given time, the purpose of realizing yourself is not exhausted.

Purposes are never completed; at a given time, they are either being lived up to or not. Achieving a particular goal does not diminish the value of further successes from the perspective of a purpose. For example, an intellectual achievement does not diminish the value of later achievements for someone having the purpose of realizing his or her intellectual abilities.

Purposes undergo transformation over time, but they are not lightly changed or abandoned. Since purposes define who you are, shifts in purpose threaten loss of identity.

Organizational Purposes. The above observations about

individual purposes and goals also apply to organizational purposes and goals. Citing company goals answers the questions: Where is the company headed, and when does it intend to be there? Citing company purposes answers the questions: Why is the existence of this firm worthwhile, and why should I perform this task or seek this company goal with maximum commitment?

If these questions seem philosophic, the need to address them is quite concrete. Purposes give a company a sense of who it is, where its goals come from, and why trying hard matters. Purposes provide continuity for an organization through its inevitable changes in goals, people, operations, structure, markets, and success.

Lesson: Goals change quickly and often need to. Purposes change slowly. To identify purposes in an organization, focus on that which is relatively constant over time and ask how specific goals relate to this.

No Change Without Purpose. An electronics manufacturer employed an outside consultant when its program of instituting a set of shared company values (or *purposes,* in our frankly ethical jargon) bogged down. The program had bogged down despite a strong commitment to it at the top, a supporting training program, a complementary reward structure, and a general sense that shared values would be good for all.

A study of the values of managers and employees two years into the program revealed three kinds of values: product values ("Given a quality product, everything else follows"), human values ("Committed, capable people are the source of success"), and economic values ("It all boils down to the return on net assets"). Low-level employees favored product values; top managers favored economic values; middle managers were "conflicted." Although the process of trying to establish values had heightened awareness of values in the company, discouragement was setting in.

The problems had deepened when the company adopted as its leading goal beating (or crushing) the foreign competition by 1985. This goal was highly publicized and a war-campaign atmosphere was consciously generated. But how do product quality, committed employees, and maximum return on net assets fit with beating the foreign competition by 1985? What really counts?

This company could not align itself with a goal because it ran its goals and purposes together. Each constituency in the company identified whatever matched its own values as the leading value of the company. There was no sense of a central purpose, no rationale for backing a particular purpose, and no sense that any of this truly mattered. It was unclear to employees and managers whether the company genuinely cared about shared values (purposes) or whether the values would be junked if something better served the goal of beating foreign competition. Perhaps shared values were just the latest weapon? This was a confused company, and the confusion showed. It showed in economic performance, product quality, and disgruntled employees.

Is the moral of the story that companies should skip purposes altogether in order to avoid such difficulties? Having no purpose is exactly as feasible as having no strategy. To have no strategy is to have the strategy of letting the company drift at the whim of external forces, internal politics, and chance. To have no purpose is to have the company stand for nothing. The zero option in strategy or purpose is not attractive.

There are powerful advantages in having clearly subscribed to purposes. I observed earlier that purposes provide the continuity that companies require if they are to succeed in the long run. A company that knows what it stands for can evaluate strategies, goals, and people. (This is the key to the recalcitrant problem of evaluating people in the face of changing goals and shifting perceptions of what matters.) Virtually every action of a manager or employee is discretionary. A company with clear purposes can expect a higher percentage of discretionary actions to be aligned with the interests of the company. If company purposes tie the company to an encompassing community, the purposes produce a higher level of motivation.

The true moral is that a company setting out to adopt,

create, or entrench a purpose must understand what it is up to. It must respect the differences between purposes and goals. To be sure, this alone will not produce a purposeful, value-driven company, but distinguishing what you stand for (purposes) and where you want to go (goals) is a precondition of success.

Lesson: Before you set goals for an organization, determine the underlying purpose. Only set goals that make sense in terms of the purpose.

Purpose solves the riddle of the long run. The riddle is that managing for the long run does not work unless you know where you stand now and why you are standing there. The organization that can manage for the future is the organization that has purpose now. Purpose can produce the present alignment requisite to adopting new goals; it gives you a framework for adopting goals that fit what the organization is about.

Lesson: If you want managers to manage for neither the long run nor the short run but for the run appropriate to the problems they face, manage and evaluate by alignment with purpose rather than by goal achievement.

I have been talking about purpose in rather abstract terms. Let me tie it into something more concrete. The following case study is based on Tracy Kidder's *The Soul of a New Machine* (1981). The case shows that accomplishing a goal—creating a new computer in one year against terrific odds—was practically impossible. It could not have been accomplished unless it was attempted by people who had a purpose that left them no alternative but to complete the task.

Case: A New Machine

Data General has a problem. Its competitor, DEC, has started marketing a new computer called VAX 11/780, a 32-bit machine. Every company wants a 32-bit machine, yet Data General has no machine to compete with the new VAX.

A project called FHP (The Fountainhead Project) is launched to build a new 32-bit machine within the next year.

The project is started at Data General's headquarters in Westborough, Massachusetts, but then is transferred to a new research facility in North Carolina.

Several engineers refuse to go along with the transfer, refusing to pack up their families and move south. Yet they feel cheated. The one opportunity they wanted most—the chance to design a new computer—has been lost. These engineers decide to build a new computer anyway, so they form a working group of five individuals, call their product Eagle, and start competing against the fifty-member Fountainhead Project team in North Carolina.

The Eagle team decides to hire new engineers to work on their product for the following reasons:

1. They can hire inexperienced engineers right out of school. New engineers do not know what is supposed to be impossible.
2. Because the Eagle project has limited funds, unlike the heavily financed FHP project, they need to hire engineers whom they can pay less.
3. They can hire students who have no family commitments and who can commit themselves fully to the project.
4. They can hire engineers who know the state of the art in computers.

Yet the demand for young computer engineers far exceeds the supply. Competition for them is fierce. What can Eagle offer that IBM cannot? Not money but the project itself. Engineering schools prepare students for big projects, yet many graduates end up doing repetitive work with known technology. In the Eagle project, the young engineers can create their own technology. They can create the machine they could only dream of building in other companies. This incentive lures thirty young engineers to Eagle.

There is no pat on the back for these young engineers, no smiles from the boss. It is a mad rush against time to build the machine within a year. No incentives are paid for working overtime.

Fighting against the odds, passing through desperate hours of debugging, they finally announce that the computer is ready for manufacturing.

Although an observer would be accurate in saying that a group of engineers got excited about building a computer, the case represents more than this. The engineers had a chance to escape dull routines and to do something that really mattered to them.

Stonemasons who raise cathedrals work for more than their pay. It is this sort of work that gives meaning to life. It is work informed by a purpose. The young engineers were working with a purpose; they described their true rewards using expressions such as "self-fulfillment," "a feeling of accomplishment," and "self-satisfaction." They would add that they did not need official recognition.

Granted, this is an unusual case. It still shows how easily goals and employee satisfaction can be achieved if there is purpose behind a project or organization.

A clear purpose helps us apply our ethical models because it gives a framework for decisions and a clear path to follow. It is not enough to know rule ethics or end-point ethics. We must know how to apply them in real situations. And the idea of purpose helps us to see a unifying structure underlying our decisions. To tie this to ethics as ground rules, the ground rules of a person or organization should implement the purpose of that individual or organization. If they do not, they are not coherent. Either the ground rules or purpose must be revised, or one of them abandoned.

We can accept the idea that a framework of purpose helps to pull everything together. But this raises an even more puzzling question. Say that we have found a guiding purpose for our organization or division; well, the purpose will stay in our heads unless the organization takes responsibility for implementing it. What does it take to have an organization take responsibility for what it does?

Look again at the Eagle project. The engineers were able to design and put into production a new computer system because all thirty of them shared a purpose—to go where no computer had gone before. If only a third of them had accepted responsibility for the purpose of creating a new computer, the project would have failed. Yet with *all* the engineers taking individual responsibility for completing the product, the purpose developed a life of its own.

For any purpose to be effective, individuals in the organization must accept *responsibility* for it. The problem of individual versus group responsibility has permeated every hard management problem discussed so far. Responsibility is central to gaining the ethics edge, and it is crucial that we understand it.

Responsibility Makes the Organization Work

Japanese management haunts us. Like an elusive ghost, it floats in front of us. We see through it but cannot see it. The Japanese are onto something, and it concerns responsibility. Responsibility solves the Rubics Cube of Japanese management.

Our discussion of long-term versus short-term management leads to responsibility. It matters little whether managers manage for the long term or the short term; he who manages irresponsibly for the short term also manages irresponsibly for the long term. We can adjust reward systems to encourage managers to keep the long run in mind, but like the donkey, they eat the carrot and ignore the thought behind it. They manipulate the reward system designed to encourage long-run thinking to gain short-term advantages.

The same problem troubles our ubiquitous commons problems. We adjust incentives to ward off disasters, and managers respond. But they are still playing "beat the reward system" rather than anticipating commons disasters. We (the knowing critics) rely on our intelligence to say what to reward or punish and on *their* (the managers') Pavlovian character to go along with it. We make the molds and pour plastic managers in. But we are poured as often as we pour.

Solutions to management problems are typically based on the *economic model* of humankind: In this model, individuals—managers, workers, consumers, and others—play against a reward system to achieve the best outcome for themselves.

Since the model stipulates that managers only respond to reward systems, solutions are merely reward-and-punishment
schemes to pull managers' strings at the whim of some knowing
puppet master.

True, managers, like the rest of us, respond to reward systems. But under the economic model, even those who design
reward systems can only be responding to yet other reward systems. Our puppet masters are puppets responding to yet another reward system. *Genuine responsibility begins where mere
response to reward systems ends.*

What it is for an individual or organization to be genuinely responsible for something? Let us look at some ways in
which we think about responsibility.

Causal Responsibility. A car spins out of control on a
slippery highway. An accident results. The slippery condition of
the road, the car's worn tires, the driver's drowsiness, or some
combination of these is *responsible* for the accident. One or
more of these factors *caused* the accident. Responsibility in this
causal sense does not imply ethical blame or praise. It is absurd
to blame the road for acting unethically. But causal responsibility is relevant.

Causal responsibility states: *You cannot be genuinely responsible for something unless you were part of the cause of its
happening. You cannot be responsible for doing something unless you did it.*

The causal sense of responsibility often confuses discussions of corporate responsibility. For instance, it seems obvious
that the Hooker Chemical and Plastics Corporation is responsible for chemically contaminating the Love Canal. Hooker
Chemical, or a historical antecedent of the present company,
did wholly or partly *cause* the Love Canal to contain toxic
chemicals. It hardly follows from this, however, that Hooker or
any current principal of Hooker is now ethically responsible for
contaminating the canal, for it is doubtful that any present
managers or employees worked for Hooker when the wastes
were dumped (1942 to 1953). It is equally doubtful that many
present stockholders of Hooker Chemical (a subsidiary of Occi-
dental Petroleum since 1968) were stockholders in 1942.

The outrage directed at Hooker confuses causal and ethical responsibility. Even officials of Hooker bought into the confusion. An executive vice president said, "We take moral responsibility, not legal liability." It is exactly as if someone proposed subjecting me to child-support payments because the head of my Cub Scout pack impregnated someone in 1956. After all, my accuser says, someone must be accountable, and you did belong to a sexist organization. I plead "guilty."

The confusion of causal and ethical responsibility is sloppy thinking backed by a tendency to believe just about anything of business. Once you get agreement that Hooker, Ford (the Pinto), or just plain "big business" is (causally) responsible for something, the misguided transition to ethical indictment is easy.

Lesson: If your organization is being held accountable for something no individual in the organization could reasonably have done, press the distinction between causal and genuine responsibility.

Intentional Responsibility. If causal responsibility is not genuine ethical responsibility, what more is required to make it so? A clue is found in our system of laws. Under this system, a person can be held responsible (criminally) for something only if the person was in a certain state of mind. The person must have intended to do what he did and must also, perhaps, have intended that it turn out as it did.

It would be a mistake for managers to take their cue in understanding responsibility from the blame-laying legal concept of responsibility. Yet responsible action must include intention. An action without intention is a mere event, no different from natural events such as earthquakes and tidal waves.

Intentional responsibility states: *You cannot be genuinely responsible for something unless, either individually or as part of a group, you intended it to happen.* With intention, an action reflects the human elements of forethought and choice.

The Elements of Genuine Responsibility. We have gathered the elements of genuine responsibility, but how do they fit together? To answer this, we need to recognize that *creativity and responsibility are one and the same thing.* This may sound farfetched. But many of the organizations you think of as highly responsible and highly successful are organizations that still feel the breath of their founders—their creators.

We need to lay out our elements and use creativity to glue them together into the whole of genuine responsibility. There are three elements.

1. Responsibility means the ability to act independently of reward systems. We sometimes get people to act *as if* they were responsible through rewards and punishments. But we cannot buy responsibility. Why not? We can induce behavior that *matches* responsible behavior only if we know well ahead of time what behavior to induce. This made sense when the manager's job was to get workers to repeat actions quickly and precisely. It makes no sense when the manager must guide himself, fellow managers, and employees in exercising good judgment in complex, nonroutine situations.

To decide what to reward and punish requires a manager to see where the firm is going, how it will get there, and what incentives will get it there. An effective reward system reflects the purpose of the firm and consistently implements its ground rules. Using incentives, we can control nondiscretionary behavior, but most behavior in an organization is discretionary. That we cannot control. In good companies, managers and employees understand and accept the firm's purpose. When the appropriate action is not prescribed—which is most of the time—the manager's or employee's actions are guided by the firm's purpose.

2. Responsibility requires effectiveness. You are responsible just to the extent that you are effective. The image of the responsible manager as careful, rule-observing, and uptight is false. Such people think that responsibility means doing nothing for which they can be *held* responsible. Genuine responsibility requires the opposite. It requires that one have power in the literal sense of the ability to do things.

3. Responsibility is based on intention. It is not enough that something happens and you are part of the cause. What happens must grow out of your intending it to happen. Inten-

tions are the way we project ourselves and our purposes into the future.

You cannot be responsible for what will happen regardless of what you do (the sun rising). Responsibility means that you make something happen that would not happen without you. This is *creativity*—making something happen that would not happen without your insight, intentions, and efforts. Although we routinely say that we intend this or that, we have little sense of what intentions are. This is a costly cultural blind spot that obscures the nature of responsibility for us.

Warren Bennis studied sixty chief executive officers and thirty innovative leaders to identify the elements of leadership. He concluded that leaders are distinguished by their "transformative power." The first element of transformative power is not "doing things right" but "doing the right things." The second element of transformative power brings intention into the picture: "The second element of transformative power refers to the 'compelling vision' mentioned earlier, or the 'intention.' The expression of an intention 'takes' an organization to a place it has never been before, the unknown. . . . In the cases of really successful leaders whom I have interviewed, they did create and express an overall set of intentions attractive enough to both involve people and empower them" (1982, pp. 55-56).

Bennis's "compelling vision" or "intention" connects with our account of responsibility. It emphasizes that leadership and excellent management create an intention that empowers people. The intention succeeds because those who must implement it accept responsibility for it *as their own creation*. And it becomes their creation. (See also Bennis and Nanus, 1985, pp. 87-109.)

Lesson: People take responsibility for what they intend and create, individually or as organization members.

Creativity Is the Organization's Life-Force

We have the elements of responsibility: independence, effectiveness, and intention. It is time to see how creativity glues them together. Creativity is the catalyst for responsible action at every level.

How does the responsible manager act independently of the reward system? He does so by creating value for himself in what he does. Howard Roark, the Frank Loyd Wright architect-hero of Ayn Rand's *The Fountainhead* (1943), exemplifies this point. Roark is inexplicable to his group-thinking peers just because he creates value for himself in doing excellent work. He creates value by acting in accordance with his purpose.

We live in material circumstances far exceeding those in which most human beings have lived, yet do we find more value in our lives than our parents did? The value we find in what we do is not a function of the rewards granted or withheld by organizations. The simple truth is: We create value, or we do not. Grasping this point instinctively in our actions, enables us to act independently of reward systems, and responsibly. This is not to commend renouncing material well-being. It is to commend independence from reward systems that deprive you of the value you create for yourself.

It is interesting to observe that reward systems organize themselves around individuals who are already rewarding themselves. The Henry Fords, Frank Loyd Wrights, Tom Watsons, and Soichiro Hondas of the world did not do it for the bonus plan.

Creativity also drives effective action. In terms of business functions, responsibility is closest to strategy. Compare strategy with forecasting. Forecasting concerns what can be expected to happen, irrespective of what you do. A forecast assumes that the intentions of individuals average out. There is no responsibility in bringing about the utterly predictable, the available roles are accomplice or footdragger. On the other hand, strategy assumes that you and your firm figure in what happens. Strategy acknowledges the predictable but prefers to undermine predictions rather than to follow them.

It is commonplace that most strategies live in notebook binders. This happens because there is no intention behind the strategies. Some strategists think that the key to strategy is to have a vision in front of the strategy. But visionary strategies go without implementation as much as blind strategies if no one intends the vision. A vision pictures a *possible* future for the firm, but an intention states what the future of the firm *will be*; whereas a vision promises that something may happen, an intention promises that it will. An intention belongs to someone. A vision starts with a person or group, but it may belong to no one. No ownership, no commitment. No commitment, no action. End of vision.

Notice that the Fountainhead team and the Eagle team had exactly the same vision. But the Eagle team intended the vision, whereas the Fountainhead team merely hoped they would succeed.

Lesson: Strategy becomes effective when its effectiveness is unpredictable but nonetheless intended.

Creativity closes the gap between envisioned strategy and implemented strategy. An intention is a creative force, a vector from the present to the envisioned future. Because the envisioned strategy will not happen in the natural course of events —that is its strength, it must be carried forward by intention. How does an intention make something happen? There is no recipe. Because what one intends opposes what is likely, there is *no good reason* to think it can be done.

The intention is a creative force cutting a path from the present to the envisioned future. The intention must create a path to the envisioned future because no path exists. There is no evidence of an intention's effect until it begins succeeding. Some philosophers have called this force *will*. Practical-minded people call it *purposefulness* or *commitment*.

Few managers are strategists. But what I have said applies as much to first-line supervisors as to chief executives. Each must recreate the intention for himself. Further, each manager must transmit the intention to others. This will only happen if the manager accepts the intention as his own.

Following recent studies of the role of values, superordinate goals, and driving forces in corporate success, many companies attempted to inculcate values. Values are not intentions. It is easy to come up with vague values (typically, quality, service, and excellence) that all employees *should* share, but these values may have little relevance to employees' ground rules (purposes). But intentions grow out of our purposes, as encoded in our ground rules.

How many organizations are purposeful, driven by intention? Apple Computer, Bell Laboratories, and Mrs. Field's Cookies are. But the list does not grow easily. Efforts to inculcate values have not led to much. No one likes to be "modified." An intention cannot be inculcated. The very phrase *inculcating an intention* rings false, which shows the difference between values and intentions. Intentions must be recreated by each individual. Top management must speak to the ground rules (purposes) of its organization's members in order to produce an organizational-individual alignment of purpose that generates common intention.

Lesson: The way to spread intention and responsibility throughout an organization is to base the organization's intentions on its members' purposes, or ground rules.

John F. Kennedy and Jimmy Carter had the same values. But Kennedy was purposeful, and he spoke to our purposes. The difference was not in values, but in intention-driven action.

The One and the Many

With the three hidden factors of responsibility, purpose, and creativity in hand, we turn to the hardest problems of management: Who is responsible? How do you break interest gridlock (the commons)? And how do you balance the long and short runs?

Who is responsible, the individual or the group? This question is at the heart of ethics. Consider Japan. The picture of responsibility developed here emphasizes the *individual* as the source of responsibility. The Japanese are said to view the *group* as the source of responsibility. How can we learn about Japanese management from a discussion of individual responsibility? Appearances aside, I have been discussing responsibility Japanese style. This is paradoxical. Paradoxes arise when our models do not fit reality. Familiar models conflict with new models or models not yet discovered.

Microphysics is the classic case. Most of us think of the basic elements of reality as particles. But experimental results indicate that the basic elements are waves. Nothing can be both a wave and a particle, but in the absence of a consistent model of reality, physicists tolerate the obviously inconsistent idea that reality is both wavelike and particlelike. The same is true of responsibility. The source of responsibility cannot be both the individual and the group, yet the reality of organizations forces us to tolerate this inconsistent view.

If responsibility is individual, then when we say that a group is responsible for something (Ford Motor Co. for the sorry Pinto, or IBM for the happy PC), we must be using an abbreviated way of saying that certain individuals in the group are responsible. So the Nuremberg Trials concluded. Although Nazi Germany was gripped by collective madness, the responsibility for the atrocities committed under the Nazi banner was assigned to the individuals who committed them. Our attitude on this issue is ambivalent. In the wake of the My Lai massacre, we were reluctant to hold Lieutenant Calley responsible; we maintained that responsibility was collective, belonging to all of us (who were conveniently immune to prosecution) and not to Calley. When we assess corporate responsibility, however, we happily assign responsibility collectively but not individually.

Responsibility is ultimately individual; we assign responsibility to groups or organizations only to deflect responsibility from ourselves or our friends. And responsibility is ultimately collective; individuals act almost exclusively as members of groups. A group can do things, for much better and much worse, that no individual or aggregation of disorganized individuals can do. When a group acts as more (or less) than the sum of its parts, it is responsible for what it does. Groups can act independently of reward systems, and they can act effectively and with intention.

So responsibility ultimately resides in the individual, and responsibility ultimately resides in the group. This is impossible, and thus the paradox.

In Japan a group of individuals assembles a defective car door. The defect is in the window flashing. Worker Miko assembles locks. Window flashing is the specialty of worker Hako. Miko would readily say, "I have made a bad door."

Some members of the department in which I work teach poorly. I would not say that I teach poorly. I am an excellent teacher. I am not responsible for teaching that I personally do not do.

Whose sense of responsibility is more individualistic, Miko's or mine? Miko's. Japanese worker Miko, like her American counterpart, is responsible only for what she does or has a hand in doing; however, in Miko's view, she *herself* does what her fellow workers do, and she is thus responsible for what they do. Miko feels responsible for what Hako does in much the way that an American parent feels responsible for what her child does. When we are in a scientific (rational) frame of mind, this may strike us as senseless. In that frame of mind, it is. But the idea that we share responsibility with and literally act through others has outlasted many scientific epochs.

This individual-as-group responsibility requires that creativity be the core of responsibility. Miko is responsible for the defective door *because she created the door.* It is not that she created it alone. That is silly. But Miko views herself as creative enough to affect the quality of what Hako does.

I do not feel responsible for the good or bad teaching of my colleagues. I do not view myself as creating what they do in any sense. Should I change my view? In some cases, I participated in the hiring of my colleagues. Even if I had reason to think that each of them could teach, I was wrong in some cases. Such errors have resulted in poor teaching in my department. Some colleagues teach poorly because of lack of motivation, internal politics (the reward system), or illness.

How can I be responsible for these things? Understood in one way, this is a potent question. I can be responsible by lack of attention to what my colleagues do, by acquiescence in a reward system which undervalues teaching, or, positively, by observing and assisting my colleagues. This broader view of my domain of effect and responsibility is a hard taskmaster.

Lesson: Ask yourself how you can be responsible for the many organizational actions outside your control. Then figure out why these actions are not outside your control or responsibility.

The paradox of individual versus group responsibility is resolved by taking a broad view of individual effect and responsibility. The individual is responsible for what the group does by acting through members of the group. The group is responsible because each of its acts is an act of each of its members. This intense individualism is quite comprehensible to Miko and barely comprehensible to us. Why does this view puzzle us? The reason is that *responsibility conflicts with our conception of the world and of our place in it.*

We assume the potential predictability of everything, possibly excepting totally random events. (Whether there are totally random events depends on the correctness of current quantum physics.) Responsibility presupposes that people can—by intention—do what is, in principle, unpredictable.

We bring human beings within the domain of predictability by viewing their actions as a function of rewards and punishments. Responsibility requires that people act independently of rewards and punishments.

Science tells us that object A cannot act on distant object B unless there is a connection between A and B. Individual and group responsibility is paradoxical unless one person causes what distant group members do.

If there is genuine responsibility, science as we now understand it is not true. If science as we now understand it is true, there is no genuine responsibility. What should we do about this paradox? I suggest living with it. We cannot do without science and we cannot do without responsibility.

This paradox explains why managers and management researchers avoid purpose, creativity, and responsibility. Our paradigm of the rational manager requires him or her to act in accordance with the scientific picture of the world. That is why decisions of consequence in large organizations are backed by substantial, if trivial and de facto, research. For something to count as research in universities, it must look as much like

physics as possible. Management researchers are precluded at
the outset from investigating responsibility, creativity, and purpose. Excellent managers, however, appeal to these concepts,
leaving explanation to others. And they act before explaining
their actions, because the explanation may never show up.

What can we say about commons problems and managing
for the long run? We can say at least this: A member of a commons who acts through the other members of the commons
does not act at their expense. The other members of the commons do not take advantage of a member who acts responsibly.
The model for this is management of common resources in a
family.

*Lesson: Insofar as members of a commons view themselves as
acting through one another, and as responsible one to another,
they will not pursue their interests at each other's expense.*

We want managers to manage for the long run so that
their conduct will at least *mimic* responsible behavior. If one
acts from a purpose in creating something, one manages for neither the short nor the long run. One manages to produce an intended result, with a sense of time appropriate to producing
the result. To demand that managers manage in a specific—
say, one-year or five-year—time frame is counterproductive;
such a specific frame will suit few of the tasks the manager is
responsible for. The manager will perceive the demand as arbitrary and will ignore it or work around it. I repeat one of the
lessons of purpose:

*Lesson: If you want managers to manage for neither the long
run nor the short run but for the run appropriate to the problems they face, manage and evaluate by alignment with purpose rather than by goal achievement.*

Many of the things that we learn by exhaustively studying organizations are things we already know. How many companies had to be studied to remind us of what we know in
our bones but have forgotten in our heads and actions—to know
our customers and keep it simple. Much of what I have said here
is already known but hard to prove. If it seems that what I rec-

ommend is unreasonable and idealistic, it is. Responsibility is. I am reminded of what George Bernard Shaw said: "The reasonable man adapts himself to the conditions which surround him. The unreasonable man persists in trying to adapt surrounding conditions to himself. . . . All progress depends on the unreasonable man" (1930, p. 225). All progress depends on the unreasonable man, and so does all responsible action—all action undertaken with the intention of producing progress.

Exercise: Finding a Group's Purpose

Since the key to both ethics and strategy is purpose, I begin every strategy workshop with a purpose-finding exercise. You cannot attack purpose frontally, because no one will know what you are talking about—or, if they do, they will not engage in a purpose-finding exercise. People are not used to confronting fundamental and partly personal issues in the context of their business lives.

I will tell you how I attack purpose from the flank in my strategy work, in the hope that you can adapt this to your circumstances. I describe a strategy workshop.

The declared topic is strategy.

I open the workshop with some observations.

"One reason that groups come together to discuss strategy is that the goals now in place are not working. Further, new goals may be needed because the internal and external conditions of your organization's environment have changed. We must avoid setting more goals that do not work. And we must avoid choosing goals for the future that do not fit who we are as individuals and as an organization. So we need to discuss what we want out of our goals, and how we should choose them."

I then ask the group to list the present goals of its organization. Once we have a list, I ask the group, "What, if anything, made each goal appear sensible in the first place?"

On reflection, some of the goals may not look so good to the participants. Some participants will say, "We have those goals because we always did that."

"But why did you always do that?" I ask.

The participants may blame it on old fogies tied to tradition, or on changing conditions, or a lack of concern for strategy in the past. I raise the issue of whether it is not likely that we will be someone's old fogies, and I try to get the group to rethink why the old fogies adopted these goals. The point is to get the group to recognize that their goals came from somewhere and that this makes all the difference to what the organization is now doing and not doing. I call the source of the goals *assumptions,* or an *assumption set.*

I ask, "What assumptions shall we make in setting new goals? It is crucial that every one be aligned with the direction the organization is going."

We generate a tentative list of new goals. I then ask each participant to state as clearly and candidly as possible how each goal would benefit that participant. You will get a load of high-minded garbage at first. Call the garbage what it is, and try again, and again, until you begin to see why each member of the group might or might not find each goal in accordance with his or her purposes. Once you begin to see the purposes of the individuals, you can look either for a common purpose or for aligned purposes that can be elected as the purpose(s) of the group.

Once you have gotten this far, the right goals will come easily. You can work from the tentative list of goals, used as a foil in the purpose-finding exercise, or start again to draw up a list of new goals.

This is a powerful and threatening exercise. A version tailored to your organization or unit will work only if you can generate high commitment to the process and a sense of safety. Your job in the exercise is to keep asking "Why?" until you cut through the garbage. Thus, you may appear domineering, arrogant, and intrusive. This will dissipate if the group makes progress. A group with one purpose or with aligned purposes is forgiving. If the group cannot align itself or if there is no area of alignment, you will engender ill will. That is why I get hired to run the process. The person calling the workshop can use me as a sacrificial lamb if necessary, accepting blame only for the choice of consultants. And I have been sacrificed. But I am rehired a lot more often than I am sacrificed. In short, this is a risky process only for those whose purposes encompass having the organization truly work.

In Chapters Nine through Eleven, we use ethics to look ahead by looking around. We use the concept of ethics as ground rules to explore phenomena in the environment of business that are creating internal pressures for change and placing ethical issues at the functional core of business.

Organizations are taking new forms. They are evolving from goal-seeking entities best managed by the carrot and stick to organizations by agreement. They are operating in an ethically charged environment in which accidents are tragedies and errors are instances of evil. These changes are accompanied by the rapid emergence of technologies that shred the ground rules by which we operate and evaluate. Managers can cope only by using ethics to ask hard questions—and by accepting their role in creating the next ethics.

9

Confronting New Threats
to Business

> If we don't change directions, we'll end up where
> we're headed.   —*Chinese proverb*

In this chapter, we use ethics to look ahead by looking
around. We look at what the new technologies of information
and biology are likely to do to organizations. When we look
past hyperbolic promises and hysterical threats made on behalf
of new technologies, we find these technologies posing a challenge to the ethics of business and free enterprise. We find a
predictor of what business will face, and how it may respond, in
corporate tragedies. Corporate tragedies and new technologies
combine to force us to recognize that the ethics we have in-
herited cannot answer the questions posed by a new and more
complex world. We conclude by considering the new ethics that
is emerging and the role that business can play in shaping this
ethics.

Ethics is a good tool for predicting social issues that will
affect organizations in coming years. Because ethics focuses on
the ground rules, or most basic principles, of individuals and organizations, changes in ethics have broad impacts on organizations. And social changes can often be first detected by observing what ethical issues are "in the air." One function of ethics is

to provide a forum for arguing basic changes in ground rules. Ethical discussion does not move quickly; it predates an actual shift in ethics by years.

Many changes that affected corporations in the 1970s were preceded by intense ethical discussion that was largely ignored by business. Intense discussion of obligations to preserve the quality of the environment preceded an effective environmental movement, and regulation, by almost ten years. Active discussion of women's rights preceded the women's movement by at least five years.

When society decides that things should change, there is a cost of lubricating the change. None of us wants to pay for (or be) the lubricant. Since business has said little about the changes, taking a reactive posture at best, it is billed for the lube job. There is no question that the cost of environmental protection has been shifted to business, with business left to whine about it. Similarly, business is bearing a lot of the cost for correcting past discrimination and for our desire to change the role of women in society. This may or may not be good. The point is that executives with a measure of foresight should have seen these shifts coming and capitalized on them. A few did. Contol Data capitalized on the need to upgrade the technical skills of minorities rapidly, and Milos Krofta (inventor of an inexpensive water purification process) capitalized on the need for economical means of cleaning up the environment. Most businesses ran for cover, unsuccessfully.

There are good indicators of the broad social changes that will, in part, determine the rules of doing business in coming years. One of these is the rising popular interest in how to manage. This indicates a sense that the form and legitimacy of management is changing and must change. I argued in Chapter Seven that a new form of organization, the organization by agreement, is emerging to cope with these changes; we will take a further look at the ethics of this new organization here.

A second indicator is the ever more pervasive phenomenon of corporate tragedies, exemplified by the Tylenol case and the accident at Bhopal. The question to ask is why these are judged to be *corporate tragedies,* as opposed to crimes against corporations in the one case and to the inevitable outcome of government meddling (by the Indian government) in the other. The phenomenon of corporate tragedies is partly an outgrowth of the cultures of old organizations. In the organization by agreement, it is at least possible to think about tragedies. But tragedies are also the leading edge of ethical discussion for the near future, for corporate tragedies signal the front end of the radical ethical shifts new technologies are bringing and will bring. I maintain that ethics is the only tool available for grasping these shifts and that our present ethics is not a very good tool.

I have emphasized throughout that the best use of ethics in management is in providing a framework for asking good questions. The less clear the issues facing a manager, the more important it is to ask good questions. The social issues that will critically affect organizations in the future are certainly not clear. Thus, the focus in this chapter is on using ethics to ask good questions about these issues.

Ethics Watch

When we use ethics to look ahead by looking around, we look for perturbations in the environment of business that signal shifts in basic ground rules.

Two obvious perturbations in the business environment are the ever more pervasive corporate tragedies and the rapidly changing technologies. These phenomena are closely connected. The factors that make tragedies hard to foresee and manage are the factors that make new technologies threatening. These factors include entrenched corporate cultures, a management style that precludes asking hard questions, and ethical illiteracy. In both arenas—tragedies and technologies—it is fair to say that if managers do not change directions, they will end up where they are headed.

I will begin with the tragedies, turn to the next technologies of information and bioengineering, and then examine what it takes to manage ahead of the curve of change in each case.

Corporate Tragedies

Ian Mitroff and Ralph Kilmann deserve credit for calling attention to tragedies as an increasingly pervasive fact of corporate life—a kind of fact that managers just cannot handle. Mitroff and Kilmann say: "Most of us are unaware that we have the following unspoken compact with life: 'The world is inherently orderly and predictable. It will behave as it always has; the worst will not happen to me.' Imagine the shock to an individual or to a corporation when something so terrible and unpredictable happens that it shatters our belief in the orderliness of the world" (1984a, pp. 48-53). They go on to say that dealing with this shock is the greatest challenge facing contemporary managers. To help, they offer categories of evil into which tragedies fall. (See also Mitroff and Kilmann, 1984b).

What Mitroff and Kilmann call an "unspoken compact" is a basic agreement, or ground rule. You can see this if you rephrase it: "These unthinkable things shouldn't happen to us," or even "Unthinkable things can't happen to us." And they are right to think of tragedies in terms of the ethical concept of evil. *Evil* is that which falls outside our ground rules; it is that which our ground rules say cannot happen, but which sometimes happens anyway. But it is more. Evil tears our ground rules asunder by demonstrating that they do not run the world and cannot always be counted on.

Thinking About Evil. The association between new technologies and tragedies is through evil. If the thought of bureaucracies tracking your every move from birth to death does not strike you as clearly evil, then the prospect of designing children to make them "better" surely will. New technologies stun our low-tech ethics, violate our ground rules, and invite application of the term *evil*.

Evil is hard to think about. Almost every corporate tragedy from thalidomide to Bhopal was forewarned. It may seem that this is a matter of hindsight. But in many cases, the warnings were so obvious and/or uncannily accurate that we can only conclude that managers *refused* to consider them. Richardson-Merrell may not have been forewarned of the dangers of thalidomide, the drug which caused the birth of countless still-born and deformed children in the late 1950s. But no sooner were the results of this tragedy in than Richardson-Merrell marketed a cholesterol-repressing drug called MER/29, which blinded many of the people who took it. In the face of one tragedy, the company apparently did nothing to prevent the same thing from happening again. To view this as the profit motive unchained requires that we assume incredible stupidity on the part of Richardson-Merrell executives. A more likely explanation is that Richardson-Merrell executives simply could not think through the possibility that their genuinely well-intended products were evil. They could not ask: Will this happen again?

Nor is this an atypical case. In a seminar for executives on thinking about the unthinkable, I reviewed a "minor" tragedy at Warner-Lambert. An explosion at a Freshen-Up manufacturing facility severely burned fifty-four employees and killed six (Sethi, 1982). In discussing this case, the executive group was outraged that Warner-Lambert did not heed countless warnings that just such an explosion might occur. The seminar proceeded with an exercise in which participants were asked to pretend that some such problem could arise in their firm and to substantiate the possibility. At least 90 percent of the participants were shocked to find that they were ignoring warnings in their own corporations that were at least as strong as those in the Warner-Lambert case. Why? After some futile attempts at buck passing, the group generally concluded that they simply could not bring themselves to think about these things.

Other tragedies reveal a similar pattern, from Hooker Chemicals and the Love Canal, to Allied Chemicals and the Kepone discharges, to McNeil Laboratories and Tylenol. And the early reports on Union Carbide and Bhopal suggest that Union Carbide had many warnings of an accident of just the kind that occurred.

The point is not to indict these companies. They do a good job of indicting themselves. The point is that the lack of willingness to think ethics, ask hard questions, and think what the ground rules say is unthinkable, is costly at best, and often disastrous for managers.

There are many foreseeable tragedies implicit in new technologies. Just on the statistical basis of the number of experiments occurring, together with the fact that every industry faces its worst potential accident at least once, it is predictable that the biotechnology industry will produce an environmentally harmful organism. And it is predictable on much the same basis that a factory robot will "go beserk" and injure a number of people. It is not that we should cringe in fear of these events. Rather, we should think them through especially if we work in the industries that will be affected.

How can ethics help business deal with the evil of tragedies? Tragedies are unpredictable in *specific* terms, but they can be foreseen by type. Businesses are ever more vulnerable to tragedies as they rely more and more on new technologies, not only in products but in manufacturing. This much can be foreseen. We can also anticipate, to some extent, the directions from which tragedies will come. To do this, we first have to realize that not everything that goes wrong and not every disaster is a tragedy; an accident or disaster differs from a tragedy in that a tragedy violates ground rules. So ethics tells us to anticipate tragedies by focusing on those accidents that will upset our own ground rules, the ground rules of stakeholder groups, and the ground rules of society at large.

Can ethics help us do more than anticipate? Be a bit hardnosed. Use end-point ethics to assess the tragedy in Bhopal. Many died in Bhopal, but many benefited from Union Carbide's presence in India. It is quite possible that Union Carbide saved more lives in India than were lost in the accident. It might not have done so had it done everything possible to prevent accidents. For there might have been no reason to locate a facility in India if U.S. safety standards had been observed there. This is tough reasoning, but ethics requires as much; we do no favors by preventing accidents at an even higher cost in human life.

Union Carbide would be foolish to press this line publicly; it is too late. But it can press industry organizations to make the point. Companies in high-risk businesses thus need to initiate public discussion of the risk-benefit trade-offs of their industry. And such companies, not individually but through organizations, need to establish agreements with affected constituencies. Who picks up the pieces in case of an accident? (Since it is always the company now, you can hardly lose by raising this issue.) Do you want us here badly enough to insure us? Fair agreements are possible in this domain. Some utilities have made agreements with residents near nuclear facilities to preindemnify them for risk in return for guarantees not to litigate. (Recall our end-point strategy in Chapter Four for defusing issues of justice through fair transactions promoting joint well-being.) Such agreements must be made prior to tragedies.

Business should also seek agreements with consumers. Products have risks, and consumers know it. Our regulatory system does not grant consumers the right to take risks. They are instead protected against risks. When protection inevitably fails, someone gets blamed. Since the consumer could not have assumed the risk and since regulators are trying to protect the consumer, guess who is found guilty? Business must reopen the discussion of whether consumers are to be allowed to take risks. If Rely Tampons had been labeled "New Product," they would still have found a market. If people buy sports cars, they will take other risks for style, convenience, or simply to experiment.

Most importantly, the reciprocity of rights and responsibilities needs to be reargued and reestablished. The Tylenol case was a shock because a part of our ground rules, a part honored even by murderers and rapists, was violated. Who is responsible for this? Can packaging really protect us against psychopaths? If we want products offered in convenient, inexpensive ways, we must accept reciprocal responsibility for the safety of the marketplace.

In short, the strategy is to think ethically, using ethics selectively to make a point with stakeholder groups. What does end-point ethics say about this accident or risk? Are the rules at issue prima facie or categorical? Is there an agreement worth establishing here? These questions will not eliminate corporate tragedies, but they do make it possible to think about them, ask questions that need asking, and assume a posture that is not entirely reactive.

The Threats of New Technologies. This strategy is less

helpful in dealing with tragedies resulting from application of new technologies, such as bioengineering. There is no ethics here to give form to our questions and provide a framework for establishing agreements. Yet these new technologies will be at issue in an ever greater number of tragedies. For this reason, and because of the tremendous impact these technologies will have on business, managers must ask what ethics will govern the advance of these technologies.

You have probably read and heard more about information systems, computers, and biotechnology than you can stand. But no one has looked at these technologies from the perspective that only business can make them work—ethically and economically. These technologies will either make or break many businesses, including businesses not directly involved in these technologies, just as corporate tragedies afflict businesses that in no way court them. The outcome depends on the ability of managers to get ahead of these technologies by thinking ethics.

Let us therefore focus on the new technologies of information systems and bioengineering. We need to look at information technologies because they are changing the ground rules by which we live and work, and we need to look at biotechnologies because they show us what we must do if we are to have a say over the ground rules by which we will live and work. Both technologies can produce tragedies. Information technologies can produce incremental tragedies, tragedies that occur virtually unnoticed. Biotechnologies can produce tragedies that make Bhopal look like a fender bender.

Case: Linda Berman's Fate

At a major computer firm, applicants are being considered for the position of manager for product development, minicomputer division. The division manager favors Linda Berman. She was a bright, articulate, and energetic interviewee. However, the recruiting officer is bothered by what a routine check with Person Search, a computerized screening system, revealed. Ms. Berman was once "genetically profiled" as part of an insurance check. Tests indicate she has a nearly 100 percent chance of developing Huntington's chorea by age forty. She is thirty-seven. A 1973 credit check reports that she is partial to left-wing causes. And Ms. Berman was once fired for "mishandling" secret documents.

This puts Ms. Berman in an unfavorable light. When the results of this check are reported to the division manager, he is disappointed. The manager for product development must hold the position three to five years if the company is to benefit from the person. It takes two years to learn the company's technologies. The person must be absolutely trustworthy. The division manager knows that such checks are often inaccurate. But even if he reviews the information with Ms. Berman and finds it inaccurate, she will likely be resentful and get off on the wrong foot. He hires someone else. Ms. Berman receives the standard rejection letter: "It was a hard choice among strong candidates."

The truth? Since Ms. Berman's father died of Huntington's chorea, she has a 50 percent chance of developing the disease by age forty. This prompted the insurance company to screen her blood. A technician misread the results as positive. Ms. Berman never discovered the mistake. She lost interest in the insurance policy when she received similar benefits through a group plan. Her "mishandling" of documents was reported by a male chauvinist supervisor out to dump a "women's libber." Her left-wing tendencies? She subscribed to *Ms.*

We once would have cried, "Impossible!" We now say, "Unfortunate but unavoidable." We recognize that the overall benefits of information technologies entail mistakes. We are less aware of the benefits of biotechnologies, but we accept on faith that benefits are forthcoming.

Remember that one of the first applications of the computer in the United States was to identify Japanese Americans for internment during World War II (Burnham, 1980). Personnel departments do use screening services, and the services do make grievous undiscovered errors. They assemble data bases by "cleaning" data from tapes supplied by personnel departments, credit companies, insurance companies, and other data bases. Checking data on a case-by-case basis is impossible. Firms deny legal responsibility for the data's accuracy.

Ms. Berman's case shows the potential for abuse of bio-technologies coupled with information systems. Genetic screening to determine your chances of inheriting Huntington's chorea will be commonplace in two years. Genetic tests for a predisposition to diabetes, depression, alcoholism, Alzheimer's disease, various forms of cancer, and hyperactivity may soon surface. The issue of using such tests for insurance and personnel checks is being debated. A recent *Wall Street Journal* (Bishop, 1984) asks whether an employee who knows that his genes predispose him to Alzheimer's disease (which causes premature senility) has the right to withhold this information from his employer. The article questions the *employee's* right to *withhold* the information, implying a presumptive right for the employer to know. Where, or where, did this right come from?

Information Systems: Critical Questions

The manager who wants to manage new technologies, rather than be managed by them, must use ethics to ask some key questions. What questions might the thinking manager ask about information systems? I suggest three:

- Can information networks become communities?
- Where does responsibility reside in an information system?
- Can we manage without individuals?

We cannot answer these questions. But our ethical models give us a start in thinking them through.

Can Information Networks Become Communities? Richard O. Mason argues that we create information networks but not information communities (1983; 1985). Networks link people who share common informational interests and standards. There are networks for lawyers (Lexis), doctors (Medicus), stock brokers (Dow Jones), philosophers (Philosophers' Index), forecasting economists (DRI), owners of Osborne computers (users' group), hackers (bulletin boards), and almost every group of information users. While the information carried by a network should have economic value to justify the cost of the network, it cannot be *intensely proprietary*—critical to the comparative competitive positions of network members. Stock-brokers will not share the names of their best clients, and defense attorneys will not share the details of the defense. Information networks are commons grazed by information-hungry users, each feeding his or her private information herd.

Communities differ ethically from networks. Mason describes communities as being "comprised of many different people with diverse backgrounds who share their whole lives with one another. There are old people and young people, rich people and poor people, smart people and dumb people, butchers, bakers, and people of all different sorts of careers and persuasions in communities. . . . Communities are inefficient, but ultimately they are essential. Communities recognize humanity in its wholeness. Novelties emerge in communities to kill boredom and narrow-mindedness and, in the long run, to lead to survival" (1983, p. 2).

Information networks are not communities because network users have only narrow utilitarian relationships to each other. The fact that information networks are not communities explains why people guiltlessly steal (copy) software, add inaccurate data to data bases (census takers and insurance investigators), and break into systems (hackers and embezzlers). The user has no agreements or contracts with other users—no one to feel guilty about or responsible to.

One solution is to transform information networks into communities. But we might not want to trade the efficiency of a network for the inefficient integrity of a community. There is a middle ground, something more responsible than a network and more efficient than a community. It is an agreement—a social contract among users of a network. An agreement establishes rights and responsibilities without the inefficiencies of a community. What rights and responsibilities should an information agreement establish? Our second and third questions address this.

Where Does Responsibility Reside in an Information System? Recall Linda Berman. Who is responsible for her situation? Is it those who put false data into her files? These data collectors may have done their best to gather the data needed, often at Ms. Berman's request. Is it those who clean data from files and sell it without checking its accuracy? Data clearing houses cannot check the accuracy of all data without making their services inordinately expensive. Is it those who use the aggregated data to make important decisions? People are lying more than ever on résumés, and decision makers need to know who is truthful and who is not. Perhaps Ms. Berman is responsible for not checking the information herself, but even if this were possible, it would be a full-time job for Ms. Berman or the rest of us. In sum, this is the information system as a commons. No one acts irresponsibly, but the outcome is disastrous.

We put the responsibility where it belongs—everywhere. This suggests an agreement emphasizing responsibility for each of our information acts. In practical terms, however, this advice is as good as none. Our third question adds substance to this advice.

Can We Manage Without Individuals? This is the important question. What does it mean? Privacy is one issue. Why does each culture have a domain of personal privacy, even if there is wide divergence about what should be kept private. We keep most of our bodies private; other cultures ignore this in favor of artifacts.

Charles Fried argues in *An Anatomy of Values* (1970) that private information is the capital from which we create close relationships. The closer someone is to you, he says, the more willing you are to share personal information with that person. Fried adds that all cultures value close relationships; all allow individuals a domain of information to use in forming relationships.

We are rapidly encroaching on the domain of information private to a person. The consequences? Without privacy, there is little individuality. Trust is replaced with regulation and enforcement. Organizational processes, such as performance appraisal, take on an adversarial, formal character.

Entrepreneurship, which is business's way of giving expression to individuality, is finally receiving some deserved attention. But at the same time it is being threatened by this loss of privacy. Information systems are giving it no room for failure.

Information systems have already eliminated part of the

ethics of capitalism, the ethics of the second chance. Because entrepreneurs try bold ideas, most fail before they succeed. These failures teach them how to succeed in bold ventures.

W. R. Schulz, formerly the largest apartment developer and operator in the Southwest, tells Harvard Club audiences how failing in the home maintenance business taught him to reject the Harvard Business School approach and succeed. Nothing succeeds like failure (W. R. Schulz). Nothing fails like success (U.S. Steel). How did early entrepreneurs handle failure? They moved west to escape the bad news and try again. It became part of the ethics of business that people deserve a second chance.

No more. Entrepreneurs need capital. Those who supply capital want to know the record. They can now find out in excruciating detail. The same is true within organizations; those who get to try new ideas are those who have *records* of success. The moral: If you want to be an entrepreneur, start out small with sure-win projects. Play it safe. But anyone who accepts this moral is no entrepreneur. We can expect entrepreneurship to *decrease* in direct proportion to the *advance* of information systems.

This is even more troubling because of the great potential of information systems to assist entrepreneurs. Entrepreneurs can now obtain information about markets, financing, and general business conditions at a microcomputer terminal that once would have required a large staff. The ability to perform basic business functions (such as bookkeeping and sales and production monitoring) by computer can dramatically lower overhead for entrepreneurs.

The positive benefits of information systems to entrepreneurs will not be realized, however, if we allow these same systems to cut off the supply of capital.

Kent Greenwalt of Columbia University describes the potential leveling effects of information systems succinctly: "The knowledge that one cannot discard one's past, that advancement in society depends heavily on a good record, will create considerable pressure for conformist actions. Many people will try harder than they do now to keep their records clean, avoid controversial or 'deviant' actions, whatever their private views and inclinations. Diversity and social vitality is almost certain to suffer, and in the long run independent thoughts will be reduced" (Burnham, 1980, p. 47). The tragedy of information systems is a quiet tragedy—the extinguishing of the very individuality that makes our business and governmental institutions work. This is what we choose in using information systems to keep better track of our peers, and they of us.

Information systems also shorten the range of management thinking. Managers can now monitor critical quantifiable factors hourly, and managers respond to what they can measure. When to intervene? If a unit's performance is off for a quarter, is it time to step in? Or for a month? A day? It is hard to resist stepping in, even if your time should be spent on something less measurable—a new product idea, a vague but promising marketing idea, or just your sense that team spirit is down.

Investors like information. If the quarterly figures are down, they move their money. Those who invest on behalf of pensioners, policy holders, or charities have a fiduciary responsibility to move funds based on the most current information; they have no business considering the long-term interests of the companies they invest in. Managers know this and think in quarterly terms. But suppose that investors had the same information on a monthly, weekly, daily, or hourly basis. They would respond, and so would managers.

Quantified information is irresistible for managers and investors. Time perspectives shorten, and the factors considered narrow. The ability of managers to think in strategic and qualitative terms *decreases* in direct proportion to the *advance* of information systems.

Addressing the Questions. Can information networks become communities? We opted for agreements among information users rather than for full-scale communities.

Where does responsibility reside in an information system? Each individual is responsible for each of his information acts.

Can we manage without individuals? We cannot. The information agreement must affirm that information about or created by a person is that person's most valued private property—his or her human capital.

We must halt the march to an information commons. This is not easy, for it is hard to identify items of information as someone's property. It would be easier if we abandoned the idea that everyone has a right to know everything.

The right to privacy is said to compete with the right to know. There is no right to know, only a right to seek knowledge without stealing it. This is analogous to the right to be promoted; there is no such right, only the right to compete fairly for promotion.

Will an ethics of information as personal property impede scientific research? If it does, it is worth it in order to have a society of individuals. But it will not. Science does not advance by accumulating data. It advances by competition among the ideas of individuals or groups. Einstein and Salk were scientific entrepreneurs.

Biotechnology: Critical Questions

There are two key ethical indicators of the future of biotechnologies: the incredible anticipatory wave of regulation of biotechnology and the increasing number of corporate tragedies. How do corporate tragedies, from thalidomide and Three Mile Island to Bhopal, relate to biotechnologies?

What topics could be less connected than biotechnology and the low-tech tragedy in Bhopal? John Naisbitt (1982) is right about one thing—read the papers and learn.

Headline (UPI, Dec. 12, 1984): Wider Governmental Rein Urged over Biotechnology

Story: Rep. Gerry Sikorski said he was impressed by the potential of biotechnologies, but ". . . the Union Carbide disaster in India is all too fresh in our minds to view any technological innovation without due respect for the uncertainties associated with its use." As part of the expanding federal role in overseeing commercial biotechnology . . . .

The inference from Bhopal to biotechnology is a howling non sequitur. But it is understandable in ethical terms: Tragedies violate our ground rules and are perceived as evil; biotechnology exceeds our ground rules and so invites application of the term *evil*. The association is through the perception of evil in each case, and through the ability to rationalize this evil by holding business accountable for it. When we confront unexplainable evil, we seek external factors to explain the evil and revalidate our ground rules; hence, we resort to the Great Satan theory of business: "All evils we can't understand have a common source—the search for profits."

The public debate over biotechnologies has consisted mainly of irrational attacks; for example: Will gene splicing produce Frankenstein monsters? This is analogous to attacking nuclear power as a form of weaponry. Business discussion of biotechnologies is confined to glowing reports of potential benefits and to arguments over whether new life forms are patentable. These issues miss the major impacts that biotechnologies will have on business.

What questions might the thinking manager ask about biotechnologies? While biotechnologies promise to revolutionize agriculture (synthetic animal supergrowth hormones), energy production (synthesized fuel alcohol), and medical diagnostics, we focus on human genetic engineering. These are the questions that shred our ground rules:

- Is genetic self-improvement worth it?
- Will industry's next basic technology be controlled by the public sector?
- Is biotechnology an action item for business?

Is Genetic Self-Improvement Worth It? Biotechnologies will have their most profound impact not on the environment, but on us. For example, a genetic trigger seems to tip the balance between anabolism (growth, development) and catabolism (decline, death) in favor of catabolism. If we learn to jam this trigger (a likely prospect), life may be prolonged indefinitely. Try building two-hundred-year-old people into your pension plan. Once it is common practice to predetermine the gender of children, we may face great imbalances in the work force, predictably with excess males. Affirmative action with a vengeance looms large. Think of the design and manufacturing savings on homes, offices, clothing, and cars if human size variations were reduced. The Dallas Cowboys will have a great "farm system." Why trade when you can grow your own?

Nicholas Wade argues that incremental progress in biotechnology will inevitably lead to full-scale human engineering and to leveling: "The advantages of genetic engineering are going to be demonstrated first in the skillful improvement of crop plants and domestic animals. Next will come . . . the gene-splice treatment of some of the fifteen hundred diseases that are now known to be genetically determined. Means of genetic manipulation may then be discovered that enhance the natural process of development and enable each individual to realize his full genetic potential. . . . By the time the human genome has been improved a little, for the best reasons, there remains no clear barrier against improving it a lot" (1979, pp. 151-152). Incremental progress will produce a radical shift that may go undetected until it is irreversible. We notice that the Japanese are ahead of us, that nuclear physics is close to a bomb, that we are about to make ourselves genetically obsolete after incremental change proceeds to the point where we can only respond or control. We assume that each step is progress; we will meet the problems as we face them.

There is a deeper reason to resist serious thought about biotechnologies. The critical questions stupify our standard positions. For instance, what is a "market approach" to designing our genetic future? Markets produce things efficiently *for people*. Should markets efficiently produce people or their successors? For whom? What is the socialist stance on biotechnology? Allocate "good genes" to those who need them; withhold them from those best endowed by nature? Should we design people for the common good? These questions mock our ground rules and strike us as evil.

Will Industry's Next Basic Technology Be Controlled by the Public Sector? The alternative to letting biotechnology run over us is to control it by regulation. This approach is favored by every governmental, legal, and scientific "expert" who has spoken to date. Business has been silent on this topic, with a few exceptions. These exceptions include: patenting new life forms; attempts by states, particularly California, to ban certain bioengineered products; and a recent attempt to block mixing of the genetic matter of humans with that of animals (using human growth hormone genes to enlarge hogs). This last issue foreshadows larger debates, with critics of biotechnology claiming that "These experiments violate the right of every creature to enjoy its natural biological inheritance." Note the ethical flavor of this comment, and the invention of a rather novel right.

Business accepts massive governmental regulation as a given. Edward Jefferson (1984), chairman of du Pont, noting the rapid proliferation of regulations and agencies enforcing regulations on biotechnology, has called for the appointment of a special counselor to the president on biotechnology just to sort out the already congested regulatory environment. It is not that Jefferson likes regulation. He sees the flood of new regulations and seeks reduction of the inevitable confusion. But centralized regulation in the nuclear power industry has not ended the confusion there.

No nonregulatory approach to biotechnology has been proposed. The broader issues remain untouched, except by those who fan public fears of genetic monstrosities. This silence will cost. The government is already waist deep in briefing documents on and proposed regulation of biotechnology. In addition to current regulatory claims on biotechnology by the Recombinant DNA Advisory Committee of the National Institutes of Health (NIH), the Environmental Protection Agency (which administers the Toxic Substances Act), the Department of Agriculture, and the Occupational Safety and Health Administration, senators Florio, Gore, and Durenberger have proposed new legislation aimed at biotechnologies (Jefferson, 1984). Business is abandoning its next technology for lack of anything to say.

Is Biotechnology an Action Item for Business? Few executives regard biotechnology as an action item. Only those working in biotechnology companies such as Cetus, Genentech,

Genex, and Vega place bioethics regulation anywhere on their agendas. This is a mistake. Biotechnology is critical to business—not just to biotech companies—now. It is critical to those who will give credit, insure, package, market, and produce in the new business environment. What to do?

One strategy is to profit from the ethical confusion about biotechnologies. Find an ethics edge. I consult to a firm that has anticipated the inevitable outrage about unethical informational practices by designing an ethical information system. The system documents the source and estimated accuracy of input data and locates responsibility for data inputs, exits, and changes. As outrage over the abuse of information grows, this system will create a demand among high-image information users (such as insurance companies, brokerages, and health-care institutions). No firm now seeks an ethics edge in biotechnology.

Another strategy is self-regulation. Self-regulation is usually preferable to governmental regulation, and it is in vogue. This strategy might be combined with the first strategy, since there is profit in organizing and managing industry associations. While self-regulation is preferable to governmental regulation, regulation is regulation; it often blocks the market. For instance, established steel companies used self-regulation (price fixing) to squelch more efficient upstart companies.

A meeting of high-level biogenetics researchers at the Asilomar Conference in February 1975 (named after the conference site in Monterey, California) established research safety standards. It looked like self-regulation might work in biotechnology. As the industry has developed, however, interest in self-regulation has waned. It can wait until the industry has its Three Mile Island. Self-regulation of human engineering is not on the biotech industry's agenda. Without an *ethics of design*—a sense of what should and should not be designed—self-regulation would be pointless in any case.

Business must use ethics to think about biotechnology. It is not certain that this technology will be allowed to develop, with regulation causing bumps but not derailment. Why did the Chinese, who once had the world's greatest navy, become a fourth-rate naval power and consequently a technologically backward country? The Chinese navy was regulated out of existence (during the Ming dynasty) because of fear of the unknown and the desire to fund social programs rather than technological exotica (Kirwan, 1984). Closer to home, the nuclear power industry has been largely regulated out of existence. When nuclear power is discussed, the issue of what we have foregone by strangling this industry is not even considered.

The likely scenario is that biotechnology will halt when it has its first tragedy. Because of fear of ethics, no one in the biotech industry acknowledges the obvious—sooner or later there will be a disaster. Why? Probabilities. Although no industry has developed without a single disaster, the chances of a disaster striking any one company are small. But in the aggregate, a tragedy is certain. So everyone in the biotech industry needs to think about what will happen when tragedy comes, even if it does not come to their firm. We have seen critics of biotechnology laying the groundwork for nationalizing and/or outlawing the industry as soon as the industry grants them a good opportunity.

Business is so busy retreating from attacks on its ethics that there is no time for considering such apparently abstract issues as the biogenetic fate of men. The public sector has a strategy for dealing with business on biotechnology—divide business into stakeholder groups and conquer. Business's aversion to thinking about tragedies supports this strategy.

The ethical issues raised by biotechnology illustrate that *many important ethical problems confronting business are not internal to individual firms.* It is easy for critics of business to divide and conquer on these issues. Witness international payments, excess profits, and executive severance pay ("golden parachutes"). Business values must figure in discussions of issues central to our social and economic vitality. The job of business is to solve problems profitably. Business does not think well collective ly, nor should it. Business speaks most eloquently through products, but some issues are settled before there are products to speak of.

This leaves only the ignored marketplace of ideas. Business has lost the ethics edge in this market through reactiveness. The tools presented in this book can help you gain mastery of the ethical issues confronting your business and business in general. But these tools are not adequate to the problems of the new technologies and their associated tragedies. These technologies undo our ground rules.

Our ground rules arose and evolved for two purposes: to define and protect the rights of individuals and groups against each other and to allocate scarce resources. We inherit conflict-resolution ethics and scarcity-management ethics. The problems of new technologies are problems of design. They are problems of designing agreements that will block the continued encroachment of the information commons. They are problems of designing the environment that we will live in and those who will live in it. We have no ethics of design.

The following section speculates on what an ethics of design capable of addressing the problems of new organizations, of corporate tragedies, and of new technologies might say. My purpose is to open the topic, indicate the likely form that this new ethics will take, and invite the thinking manager to do the unpredictable—lead the discussion of what our ethics of design will be.

The Next Ethics—An Ethics of Design

I call the next ethics an ethics of design because the hardest choices we confront are design choices. Since the forms of organization we presently have do not work, as evidenced by intense management interest in almost any new organizational form, we must design new forms of organization. Since the information systems that rest on our existing agreements provoke a plague of abuse and crime, we must design new ground rules—a new ethics—of information. Since our ground rules for new technologies breed tragedies and regulations, but no control, we must design an ethics to give sense to the use of these technologies. Since biotechnologies allow us to design ourselves and our environment, we must either devise an ethics of design or submit to an ethics of willful prejudice.

Revolutions respect the past, if only by reacting against it. The next ethics will respect our present ethics, even though by nature it will arise as a criticism of present ethics. Let me begin by speculating on that criticism and its likely outcome.

Criticism of Present Ethics. End-point ethics is to be criticized for telling us to maximize the common good, without telling us why more is better and what to seek more of. Endpoint ethics tells us to drive in a straight line as fast as possible, but it offers no direction.

Rule ethics is to be criticized for telling us to act on principle, while providing an odd grab bag of conflicting principles. When faced with this criticism, rule ethics becomes inflexible and demands faith. As much as we long for the old principles to work, they do not tell us to whom information belongs, what agreements should govern new organizations, or what we should and should not genetically design. Today, if we are to act on principle, we must first choose the principle. On what principle do we choose principles?

Social contract ethics is to be criticized for telling us to uphold agreements that we would freely and fairly choose, without telling us what to agree about or how to establish fair agreements. Agreements are good for producing orderly arrangements among individuals already bound together by something, but they do not create that something. To look at fair agreements as an end in themselves is to commit the classic fallacy of confusing means and ends. This brings us back to purpose. For purpose is no more than a way of being and acting that is, in itself, worthwhile. If we had that, we would have something worth agreeing on.

If the next ethics grows out of criticism of present ethical models, then purpose will figure centrally in the next ethics. If we are to choose what to design as organizations, information systems, and even people, we must be able to say why we are doing it or what intention guides us. But where is this purpose to come from? Perhaps the question has no plausible answer, or perhaps we should accept the diagnosis that purpose, like responsibility and creativity, is paradoxical and beyond our managerial means? This answer is almost reassuring, since it relieves us of responsibility.

I prefer a radical and difficult answer, namely, that there is already a unifying purpose—that the purpose of managerial and employee actions in organizations is no more or less than to act with purpose.

A New Ethics of Purpose. The guiding purpose of organizational activities is not a specific value or activity, but that the activities of the organization and its members be *purposeful.* The new organization will have many internal and external stakeholder groups; they cannot share one purpose, but they can share a commitment to purposefulness. This means that the organization and its members must take the stance, "What we do matters," while allowing *how* it matters to vary with the diverse purposes of the organization's members.

The new organization will be an organization by agreement. Agreements must be based on an *alignment* of purposes among organization members. The agreements will be judged on their ability to support mutually purposeful actions in the organization. The more broadly and deeply an agreement allows purpose to permeate the organization, the better the agreement provides a foundation for an effective organization.

The new organization will put a premium on principled action. Since the principles by which we should operate in organizations are not settled, principles will be close to the surface of organizational life. We will tolerate different principles but will only have contempt for those who take tolerance as an excuse for ethical opportunism. But to seek one set of principles for all stakeholders is to search for a chimera.

The new organization will not respect an inside-outside definition of its boundaries of responsibility. Because it will recognize that all who have a stake are the legitimate concern of management, it will be able to think through potential tragedies. It will not be blinded by lack of foresight, even when prediction is impossible. It will seek agreements concerning risk that assign both rights and responsibilities to all stakeholders.

In short, the new organization will maximize the sense of purposefulness for each stakeholder. It will emphasize fair agreements and principled actions that provide a fertile ambience in which its members may engage in actions that each views as part of something that matters.

This ethics of stakeholder purposefulness is also likely to guide an ethics of design for new technologies. An ethics of design will view the control and ownership of information not in terms of efficiency, which is unmeasurable, or of justice, which is undefined. It will look at these issues in terms of whether a given use of information promotes a way of being and acting valuable for the stakeholder groups critically affected. It will look at whether or not particular actions can be part of a principled agreement establishing informational rights and responsibilities. This ethics, like the ethics of the market, will realize that stakeholders know their own world better than does any mediator of the common good. Unlike the ethics of the market, it will address purpose as well as needs and desires.

An ethics of design will look at the issues of what kind of environment and people to design in terms of the stakeholder's purposes. It will not favor "improvements" that deprive stakeholder groups of meaning or purpose. It will not automatically authorize purposeless genetic tampering as a necessary cost of improving the estate of man. Nor will it rule out improvement in our genetic character on the grounds that any change is evil. It will acknowledge future generations as critical stakeholders in the design process. Most importantly, an ethics of design will not tolerate our making design decisions in the absence of agreements that correlate rights and responsibilities, stakeholder group by stakeholder group.

An ethics of design will focus not on a common good, but on purposes differentiated by stakeholder group. An element of our present ground rules, and the cornerstone of the market economy, is that there is no set of values which it is everybody's job to follow. This is why efforts to regulate in the name of the common good come to grief. Such regulation conflicts with the ground rule of our society, which says the common good is allowing individuals to pursue their own private goods. An ethics of design will incorporate this ground rule, replacing private good with individual and organizational purposes.

Several recent authors, notably including Robert Bellah (1985) and Alasdair MacIntyre (1981), lament the loss of a communitarian ethos which, in fact, never existed. They urge the forging of some common goal or ideal. But there is nothing in which we are all interested. What they are right about is that there is an epidemic of lack of purpose. The cause of the epidemic is the transition from a world in which we could count on scarcity to motivate our actions to a world in which we bear the responsibility for design. The epidemic is not to be cured by reforging a commitment that never existed. What is needed is the recognition that purpose, not goals, gives direction, and that purpose resides in the stakeholders—not in the government, in dated organizations and institutions, or in the cosmos. And we need an ethics that is not an exaltation of the past but that, instead, addresses questions we have never before faced.

Prospects of Success. So far, I have speculated on what ethics of design might be if this ethics is to meet the criticisms and weaknesses of current ethical models and to address the ethical problems of the present and future. I do not argue that this is the only ethics of design that will work, and I do not argue that the chances of this ethics emerging are great. These arguments require assumptions that carry us from speculation to fantasy.

There is no question that ethics as we know it is as likely to persist as are the steel mills in the hills of western Pennsylvania. We do not know what factors produce and direct ethical change. Thus I have made the only assumption available to someone who accepts responsibility, and choice, in shaping the basic ground rules we live by: We can, through our intentions and actions, determine or influence the outcome in ethical debate. But this assumption is by no means unchallengeable. It is challenged effectively by economic determinists (Marxists), technological determinists (followers of Alvin Toffler), political determinists (Machiavellians), scientific determinists (from physicists to sociobiologists), and realists. The only way to meet these challenges is through intention and action—with no warranty of success.

Despite the fact that these challenges can only be met through intention and action, the thinking manager will ask: "What are the chances that such an ethics of design, or some other ethics of design capable of addressing real problems, will emerge? What role will business, and my business, play in shaping this new ethics? And will the ethics that emerges from the muck of the present allow business, and my business, to survive and prosper?"

The ethics of design outlined here is one that can emerge only if business accepts the role (which it has dodged to date) of affirming its ethical validity and arguing its position in forming a new ethics. The chances that an ethics of design will emerge that allows diversity, enterprise, challenge, and rapid learning through competition are the same as the chances of business practicing what it preaches—by taking some risks to enter the competition over the ground rules.

The evidence suggests that business will not play a significant role in shaping the next ethics. I wrote this book to invite business back into the game. What role, if any, business will play in shaping an emerging ethics will be determined first and foremost by managers and firms willing to lead. I have argued that leading, staying ahead of the curve in ethics, is not only risky but also a source of opportunities. My advice is to take a role in the ongoing debate by finding ethics edges.

Whether particular businesses and business as whole will survive and prosper under the new ground rules depends entirely on the outcome of the debate. The best outcome is an ethics that respects diversity of purpose, stakeholder differences, and the high price of control. The worst outcome is an ethics that emphasizes the perils of stakeholder self-determination, the need to design for the common good, and the need for clear, centralized control. Place your own bets. Whatever ground rules emerge, business and particular businesses will prosper only by becoming adept at reading the rules, asking the hardest questions, in short, finding ethics edges.

The next chapter reviews the tools for finding ethics edges, managing ethical realities, and becoming a thinking manager. It consolidates the lessons we have learned and asks how managers can create an organizational atmosphere conducive to outside-the-box thinking about hard management problems.

10

The Thinking Manager's Toolbox

> It is better to know some of the questions than all
> of the answers.   *—James Thurber*

I began with the assertion that business is adrift without an ethical context to give sense to its activities and without the ability or even the desire to live up to its potential. I stated that business should have a voracious appetite for social problems, seeking those it can solve efficiently and profitably. Cummins Engine Company, Caltex, 3M, Cadbury Schweppes, and Morgan Guaranty Trust indulge their appetites for solving social problems with profit and have generally done quite well with this strategy. But this voracious appetite for solving social problems has largely been missing. Business has been on the ethical defensive so long that it now instinctively retreats from dealing with the ever-growing number of ethically flavored problems that present opportunities for profitable solutions. It is so busy ducking that it does not have time to throw any punches.

Here is where ethics must rejoin American business. Ethics does not offer ready-made solutions for problems. It offers new ways of approaching problems, making decisions, and anticipating future problems. It is not that the manager who thinks ethics has a lot of answers. Rather, this manager asks the questions that enable his or her organization to do its job of finding some answers.

Constructive Explosion

Joseph Schumpeter observed that creative destruction is the essence of capitalism: "Creative destruction is the essential fact about capitalism . . . it is by nature a form or method of economic change, and not only never is, but never can be stationary" (Gilder, 1981, p. 236). I add that not only is economics a driving force in creative destruction, but in a world in which ethics is a fundamental forum for change, ethics must also upend the past to make the future of business possible.

How important is explosion? Look at the Fortune top 100 companies of twenty years ago and compare them with the top 100 of today. Some organizations managed ahead of the enormous social and economic changes of the past decades; others have failed to anticipate or respond to these changes—preferring to think that, if ignored, they would go away. Or consider a study conducted by Louis Grossman (1982) of New York Stock Exchange companies that have never missed a dividend in one hundred years. Not one of them is in the business it started in. And these are high-ethics companies.

Organizations that succeed in the long run have the ability to explode their own realities and create new realities. As a matter of record, the explosion is often triggered by hard questions from aggressive directors, who in turn often ask these questions because of hard conditions in the firm's environment. But the manager sleeps better who can set off the explosions first. Ethics has already been the tool for explosion and creation in some cases. And in most every case it can be the tool—for it promotes the close contact with suppliers, customers, regulators, in short, the environment of the firm that is essential to constructive explosion and creation.

The purpose of this chapter is to consolidate the lessons we have learned as a guide or toolbox for the thinking manager. This chapter reviews the concepts, models, and some of the cases to provide a framework for asking questions that will enable you to probe the ethical reality of your firm and its environment, to find ethics edges, and to convert them into business advantages. In short, I offer a guide to using ethics both to explode unworkable assumptions that constrain thinking in your firm and to replace them with more adaptive assumptions and a more adaptive attitude toward assumptions.

The Ground Rules

We started with ground rules, the foundation of ethics. It is impossible to determine an organization's or a person's ethics unless we know the ground rules they play by. Determining an organization's ethics helps us know what ballpark we are playing in, what the object of the game is, what actions are acceptable, and what actions get us thrown out of the game or benched indefinitely. Determining a person's ground rules tells us what that individual is playing for and what he or she will do to get it.

The fundamental definition for understanding ethics is: The ethics of a person or organization is the set of ground rules by which that person or organization acts.

In truth, even though all of us offer complex explanations of what we do and why, we act from a few simple principles. These principles are called ground rules. Once you have considered your options and reached a decision, that decision reflects the values you attach to different outcomes and what you are willing and not willing to do to obtain the outcomes. The same reasoning applies to organizations.

Thinking managers ask what their ground rules are. They also question the ground rules of their co-workers and of the organization itself. Exploring ground rules is uncomfortable, especially since those ground rules which we publicly endorse and those by which we act may be worlds apart. But exploring ground rules is more comfortable than being stuck in a situation in which your ground rules and the ground rules of your co-workers or organization do not mesh. You will be banging your head against the proverbial stone wall. The only thing good about banging your head against a stone wall is that it feels good when you stop.

That is the point of the Ethics Test in the Introduction. Without a clear sense of your own ethics, you cannot develop a clear understanding of how to view your ethics in relation to the ethics of others and the organization. Once you understand what you view as ethical, you can begin to evaluate the ethics of your colleagues, your organization, and other organizations. To understand the ethics of colleagues and organizations, you need to be as hard-nosed as you are when you read the numbers and assess the competition.

The key to learning the ethics of individuals or organizations is simple: *Do not listen to what they say about ethics. Observe what they do.*

Thus, while a Techtron division advertises its commitment to affirmative action, the all-white all-male management group reveals its true ground rules. And while David Farnsworth tells his employees to develop bold ideas to carry D. F. Venture into new areas, any employee who develops one ends up on the pavement. The flip side to this is that many managers brag about how unethical they are as a way to build their image as rugged jungle fighters. But if you observe them, you will discover that some managers only say this because they think it is expected. Your opportunity may lie in being the only member of the firm who does not demand this tribal ritual.

Knowing your ground rules and the organization's ground rules is important to your career. Do your ethics, as determined by your ground rules, mesh with your organization's ground rules? If they do not, expect frustration and stagnation in a position you would like to move out of. This idea was reinforced in Chapter Two through the example of women executives and how their attempts to move into line management positions are blocked by unwritten organizational ground rules ("It's every man for himself—literally!") enforced by a male-dominated management structure. Chapter Two concluded with an exercise, "Into the Gap." This exercise is critical if you are truly interested in discovering whether an ethics gap exists between you and the organization. It is far better to discover an ethics gap now, before you are stretched across it with nothing to do but fall into the chasm.

The thinking manager is not satisfied only to assess ground rules in the immediate business environment. The thinking manager also probes for disagreements between the ground rules of the business environment and the ground rules of other constituencies in society at large. He or she asks, "Where are there fundamental disagreements between local ground rules and those of outside constituencies?" This enables the thinking manager to foresee the directions from which ethical attacks and tragedies may come.

Nor is the thinking manager satisfied only to uncover the current ground rules of the firm, its environment, and society at large. He or she also probes ground rules to see where fundamental changes in ground rules are being negotiated in the form of ethical discussion. These are areas in which the basic conditions of doing business may shift quickly (such as doing business in Iran) or slowly (such as paying more attention to the quality of the environment). Such areas are sources of grave threats and bold opportunities. One such area discussed in Chapter Nine includes changes in ground rules compelled by changes in technologies. Probing ground rules for instability and change enables the thinking manager to determine the sources and directions of changes, rather than waiting to be run over by them.

Passing the Ethics Buck

If a manager finds an ethics gap between himself and his organization or between the organization and external constituencies, it is easy to ignore it, hoping it will go away. This attitude is pervasive in business and accounts for many of the problems business now faces.

Passing the ethics buck, hoping the problem will fade away, or slapping a Band-Aid on what requires major surgery are ways of ducking responsibility. Ethics Band-Aids are responsible for the Foreign Corrupt Practices Act, the Excess (unethical) Profits Tax, the regulatory stranglehold being applied to biotechnology, and the puzzling array of management techniques inflicted on organizations. Without true responsibility, there is only ethical retreat.

It is a sad truism that we do not act as ethically as we would like because "The company won't let us" or "I would if they would" or "That's business." Chapter Three explored one way this lack of responsibility may have developed. I asked, "Is it caused by something in the way organizations originate and develop?" There is precedent for the unintended development of a situation in which irresponsible conduct is inevitable; it is the historical problem of the commons. To illustrate this problem, I used the example of the herdsman and a common pasture. The common pasture was eventually destroyed because everyone rationally tried to get his own "fair share" without considering the devastating overall effect on the pasture.

The commons problem shows most clearly in business in budget processes. So many people are striving for their fair piece of the pie that they fail to realize that it is impossible to eat an empty pie tin. And if everyone is concerned only with his or her fair share, someone ends up trying to survive on an empty tin. The steel industry's failure to recognize overgrazing of the commons resulted in an industry weakened not so much by outside forces, but by its own herdsmen's demands. You cannot avert a commons problem unless you recognize it *before* it comes to define organizational reality and undercut responsible action by entrenching the ground rule, "You've got to get yours first." Commons are self-perpetuating responsibility solvents.

The issue of the commons is critical today because we are predisposed to regard information as a commons. I observed in Chapter Nine that it is generally believed that there is a right to know. This supposed right says that, other things being equal, everyone is equally entitled to use any piece of information. Just as the right to graze competes with the property rights of responsible herdsmen, so the right to know competes with the privacy rights of responsible individuals. As products increase in informational content and decrease in material content, the supposed right to know competes with the right of information creators to the fruits of their efforts.

The thinking manager asks of supposed rights: "If group *A* claims this right, then which group *B* is responsible for satisfying group *A*'s claims? What is the overall impact of allowing this claimed right to become accepted as an actual right? Does this supposed right create a new commons?'' Thinking managers ask these questions not because they are opposed to rights, but because they are opposed to rights claimed at the expense of others and at the expense of turning ever more resources into depletable commons.

The most important lesson of the commons is to recognize when commons problems undermine responsibility in your organization. Start by asking some key questions. Ask what commons problems affect your organization. Once you have identified the budget, common staff, space, nonbudgeted office supplies, and the other obvious commons, press on. You are likely to identify many of the problems that make your life difficult and the organization's functioning expensive. Unfortunately, like many other business problems, recognizing commons problems does not solve them.

The major obstacle to overcoming commons problems is the issue of justice.

Participants in a commons view their rights to graze their sheep, take 15 percent of the budget, or occupy the tenth floor as God-given. This would not be a problem if *responsibilities* (to maintain the commons, earn the 15 percent, or subsidize the space) were associated with the claimed rights. This is not the case in a commons. When it comes time to reduce rights or to attach correlative responsibilities, each party feels that it is losing a right and gaining a responsibility for having done nothing that it considers wrong.

Any proposal to restrict access to a commons is viewed as *unjust* by at least some of those who expect unimpeded access. In the case of the common pasture, rationing access to the pasture on the basis of herd size will raise cries of injustice on the part of those who have small herds. On the other hand, if the pasture's usage is taxed, those with large herds will contend that they are unjustly penalized for success. Attempts to block access to information commons raise cries of "You are impeding free inquiry for commercial reasons!" and "We need that information to make loans, preserve national security, and calculate the mortality rates!"

What happens when the pasture reaches capacity and disaster is imminent? The herdsmen may call a meeting to determine a formula for limiting access to the pasture. They will not reach agreement. Any restriction of a herdsman's right to the commons will be viewed as unjust. This leaves two solutions.

One way out of a commons trap is for someone (typically a government) to introduce some factor to realign the interests of participants in the commons. This is intended to produce an outcome that someone (usually called "the common good") will be satisfied with. It will also produce an outcome that most participants in the commons will be dissatisfied with, since someone else is telling them what their best interests are. And there is no responsibility in this approach. It is a statement that we cannot manage ourselves, so you manage us. For example, when a river is polluted by factories along its banks, the government finally steps in and says, "OK, it's cleanup time." The factories responsible for the pollution have taken no responsibility for finding a solution and, because they are being "forced to clean up the river," view their cleanup efforts more as a punishment than as a form of responsibility.

The other way out of a commons problem is responsibility. We must let responsibility back in if organizations are to function ethically and efficiently. But how do we bring forth responsibility without the government forcing it upon us?

I recommend a two-step approach to addressing commons problems and other hard problems of ethics and responsibility:

1. First apply ethical tools to determine what you want to accomplish.
2. Then create conditions in which that approach becomes practical.

The summary statement of this approach is: Use ethics to ask key questions, and then be purposeful. Let us review some of the ethical tools for implementing this approach.

Three Ethical Models

Tools are used for a purpose. The purpose of these tools is to allow managers to take ownership of the ethical issues that affect them and to build businesses that are better in the broadest sense, economically and ethically. The way to take ownership of ethical issues is to use ethical tools to ask questions that clarify where you and the organization stand and what you want to accomplish.

Three important ethical tools are end-point ethics, rule ethics, and social contract ethics. These models provide questions to guide managers in making decisions.

End-Point Ethics. In its most plausible form, end-point ethics says that a person or organization should do that which promotes the greatest balance of good over harm for everyone affected. The thinking manager uses end-point ethics to ask of a proposed action:

- What is in this course of action for me?
- What is in it for the others who are affected?

These questions focus attention on the stakeholders in a decision including yourself.

The first step in an end-point decision process is to determine what stakeholder groups are critically affected by the decision and how they are affected.

Identifying stakeholder groups is a difficult process. The end-point approach demands that you press hard to identify stakeholder groups that do not immediately come to mind. Stakeholder groups always come to mind for themselves, and they demand their say. Identifying the stakeholders pays off. In the Big State Bell case, management succeeded by recognizing that responsible consumers and irresponsible consumers are distinct stakeholder groups. Likewise, Mel's shopping mall was approved when he distinguished Bloomington's townies and Bloomington's professionals as distinct stakeholder groups among the present residents of Bloomington.

The second step of an end-point decision process is to identify alternative courses of action. Identify the alternatives you regard as most plausible. Then identify the alternatives that each stakeholder group regards as most plausible.

If practical, you should seek direct input from key stakeholder groups. This has two advantages. First, you may find that alternatives which you regard as optimal meet strong resistance in the stakeholder groups needed to implement them. Second, those with a different stake in the decision may see viable alternatives that you overlooked. It is as wise to listen to the consumers of decisions as it is to listen to the consumers of products.

Do not confuse end-point ethics with its offspring, cost-benefit analysis. There is a fine but critical distinction between the two. Because a cost-benefit analysis should result in a numerical assessment of whether the benefits of an action exceed the costs, the focus of cost-benefit analysis is narrowed to factors measurable in numerical terms. In contrast, the strength of end-point ethics is that it includes all factors that affect success.

End-point ethics is similar to cost-benefit analysis in that it takes quantifiable results into consideration, but end-point ethics goes farther. It takes the intangible but efficacious factors into account. We saw this in the case of Ms. McB. and Central National Bank. From a cost-benefit viewpoint, Central National may have been wise to stick to its knitting. But all things considered, it may be knitting booties for an abandoned child. Tom Peters often says that, in business, soft is hard. He means that factors which are hard to quantify often have the most effect on the bottom line. End-point ethics agrees, adding that soft is sometimes hard with respect to the ethical bottom line as well.

The manager who uses end-point ethics is left with a lot of information and the need to make a decision. The manager knows who he is dealing with, the options available, and what's in the options for all concerned. In our terms, the ground rules of value have been brought to the surface. These determine what outcomes have what value for each stakeholder group. But the ground rules of evaluation, which define the *bounds of action* in pursuit of value, have not been heard from. That is the job of rule ethics.

Rule Ethics. Rule ethics says that a person or organization should do what valid ethical principles require. Further, a person or organization should refrain from doing anything contrary to valid ethical principles. This does not tell you much unless you know what the valid ethical principles are. There are as many opinions about valid principles as there are ideologies, which is to say unmanageably many.

You can unravel this knot by building on the stakeholder process of end-point ethics. Once you have identified key stakeholder groups, correlate with each group its ethical code, or specific rule ethics. The thinking manager uses rule ethics to ask of proposed actions:

- Which of my ground rules are potentially in conflict with this action?
- Which of the ground rules of stakeholders are potentially in conflict with this proposed action?

This enables you to spot points of resistance to decisions not uncovered by specifying the interests of each group. If you are dealing with environmental groups, political bodies, or the media, knowing the ethical codes of these groups will help you anticipate their responses to your actions. These groups often act in ways that cannot be viewed as self-interested. You must unravel their ethical codes to anticipate their actions.

Groups that act from ideology rather than interest are seldom accurately anticipated by business. For example, developers often try to argue for a new project in terms of documentable benefits, only to be surprised by outraged citizens and governmental opposition. These groups can be anticipated in rule-ethical terms by taking a measure of their codes, or rules. Mel and Big State Bell finally succeeded by reading the rule ethics of the opposition and proceeding from there. Some American firms succeed in the Orient; many do not. One significant success factor is the ability to read the ground rules of the stakeholder groups in these markets: Learn the ethical operating systems of those you deal with, and try speaking to them through compatible ethical software.

In discussing rules ethics, I made an important distinction between categorical rules and prima facie rules. Categorical rules

allow absolutely no exceptions. Most ethical rules are not categorical. For example, the rule that one should keep promises
has clear exceptions. A manager who promises an employee a
raise only to find out later that the firm is on the verge of bank-
ruptcy is obligated to break his promise. The manager's obligation to act in the interests of the firm takes precedence. And
other obligations, for example, defending the national interest
take precedence over the obligation to act in the better interests of the firm. The distinction between prima facie and categorical rules would be of only intellectual interest were it not
for the skill that critics of business display in exploiting it and
for the lack of skill that business displays in responding to such
critics.

A strategy for attacking business on ethical grounds is to
indict business for violating a commonly recognized prima facie
rule. The violation is vividly documented—but not the prima
facie character of the rule or the extenuating circumstances.

This seems a simple-minded strategy for attacking business, but the Lockheed bribery case illustrates that it is effective. Although there is little or no ethical basis for damning
these payments, and considerable ethical basis for damning the
law proscribing the payments, American business now lives with
a hypocritical across-the-board prohibition of bribery. Executives typically respond to such attacks in economic, legal, or
other defensive terms, which concedes that they are unethical.
But knowing the underlying strategy, you can take a positive
stand without conceding ethics to the critic.

Rule ethics advises that you reverse engineer your decisions, the decisions of others, and the decisions of organizations
in order to determine your evaluation ground rules and those
of others. But rule ethics leaves you in the same basic position
as end-point ethics, with information and the need to decide
and act. It adds a crucial element to the picture—the bounds defining acceptable actions for different groups—but it does not
tell you how to move the boundaries to remove conflicts and,
perhaps, to get a better deal. Social contract ethics addresses the
nature of basic agreements and how they can be shifted.

Social Contract Ethics. A social contract is an implicit

agreement about the basic principles or ethics of a group. Another way of looking at this is to say that, at the level of groups,
ground rules are a matter of implicit agreement. We find ourselves in a web of implicit agreements whenever we enter an
organization. If these agreements are unbalanced, favoring some
groups at the expense of others, the disfavored groups work to
undermine the agreements. Social contract ethics provides a test
for determining whether a contract is sound: *A contract is
sound if parties to the contract would enter the contract freely
and fairly.*

How can you tell whether the members of an organization would agree to the contracts of the organization freely and
fairly? The thinking manager uses social contract ethics to ask:

- Do I agree to this contract or do I just live with it?
- If I were to occupy the position of a lower-level manager or
  employee, would I accept this contract?
- If I were a higher-level manager, would I accept this contract?

Look at it this way: If you were to have an equal chance of
being assigned to a different rank in the organization, would
you be satisfied with the contract as it applies to the ranks you
might hold? Assume the positions of the various parties that live
by the contract, and assess the contract from their perspectives.

What is the price of not recognizing the implicit agreements? If you do not know the agreements by which your organization operates, it is difficult to institute significant changes.
Significant changes in organizations generally shift the social
contract for those factions in the organization that are critical
to implementing the change. If the shift is not perceived to be
fair, these factions will resist the change. Their resistance is not
always effective, but it is always expensive.

We looked at problems that occurred when Motorola attempted to change its culture without auditing its social contract. Motorola wanted to establish a culture of participation.
Workers liked it and accepted it, for the culture change implied
a shift in agreements that favored them; they got more pay,

more respect, and more say in their working conditions. But the program stalled at middle management. The middle managers perceived that the line workers had gained advantages at their expense. Middle managers had to put in more time, listen to countless suggestions, and work harder for the same pay. Moreover, their outside options diminished. They resisted the change because of the agreement shift implicit in it. Middle managers are effective resistors.

The Motorola case underscores the close connection between the cultures of organizations and their social contracts (agreements). Social contracts are carried by the cultures of organizations and indeed constitute the operating core of the culture. That is why culture change, as now practiced, is difficult; it is attempted over the dead body of the ethical agreements at the core of the culture. On the other hand, organizations that manage ethical agreements can succeed while managing little else. The reason is simple: If the agreements are sound, the organization is willing to do its job without an undue measure of control, force, or atta-boying.

R. L. Carol has almost eliminated management in what is typically an intensely managed business (stockbroking) by working hard to maintain a fair, if offbeat, social contract. Cadbury Schweppes has consistently succeeded against long odds by maintaining fair agreements with everyone in the firm.

If you ignore the agreements, you will find it extremely difficult to effect basic change in your organization. Everyone who does not know whether he or she will be treated fairly will have a stake in resisting the change. On the other hand, if you make a clear commitment to fair agreements, radical change is within your reach. If you know you are not going to lubricate the wheels of change, you can enjoy it. By rigorously pursuing fairness, Jaguar PLC was able in just a few years to change from a lemon-producing subdivision of a huge, state-owned bureaucracy to a quality-oriented private firm.

Think about the basic agreements (social contracts) in your organization. Establish and stand by agreements that are good for you and your firm. Be sure you would work under the agreements voluntarily. The changing nature of organizations is a fact; so is the changing nature of the basic technologies under-lying business. Both facts make establishing fair agreements more difficult, and more important. Since organizations are rapidly becoming organizations by agreement, you might as well start managing the agreements.

Upholding agreements is not a basis for the activities of any business—it is a precondition for conducting these activities. And you can only establish a fair agreement if you are operating in a context in which people will be responsible to the agreement. Responsibility cannot be established by our ethical models. In fact, it cannot be established by any models.

The Key Ingredient

The key ingredient that moves us from models and analysis to decision and action is purpose. To find purpose, we must grasp the distinction between goals and purposes. Esoteric? Perhaps. But this distinction not only provides a place to stand in decision and action; it also unlocks the mystery of strategy.

A goal is a target towards which one aims. A goal no longer exists once it is hit, or missed. Goals answer the questions: Why are you doing that? Where do you expect this company to be in one year? Five years? Goals are typically economic in form and include a target date. You must know whether or not you made the goal at some point; otherwise, you had no goal.

When one set of goals is exhausted, we must think of new goals. Where will they come from? Consultants? Management retreats? Organizations are often unclear where the next set of goals is coming from, and they often formulate unreachable or hopelessly vague goals. The problem is that goals must be set in terms of purpose if they are to fit the organization and gain the support of those charged with implementing the goals.

A *purpose* is a way of being or functioning viewed as valuable in itself. A purpose makes a value (as in a ground rule of value) specific and operational. If my purpose is to have computers support thinking rather than just data collection and manipulation, then this purpose makes concrete for me the value of being a thinker. (This is the purpose of a friend of mine who works at Bell Laboratories.)

Organizations also have purposes. The thinking manager seeking to know company purposes asks:

- Why is the existence of this company worthwhile?
- Why should I and others in the firm perform tasks and seek company goals with maximum commitment?

These questions are philosophical, but the need to address them is concrete. Purposes give a company a sense of who it is, where its goals come from, and why trying hard matters.

Remember that purpose answers one of our most important questions: When you have collected the information and done the analysis, where do you stand to decide and act? The answer is: Stand on your purpose. No one can tell you how to decide. But you can consult your purpose as a foundation—as an assurance that your decisions and actions collectively have meaning.

Once managers and employees accept the purpose of a company as worthwhile, they will assume individual responsibility. They will quit pointing fingers and begin blocking commons problems. They will think short-run or long-run, as appropriate to the problems they face. They will manage and work purposefully.

I asked, "How many organizations are purposeful?" and cited Apple Computer, Bell Laboratories, 3M, Control Data Corporation, and Mrs. Field's Cookies. But the list is not long. Why? Even if the top management sees a purpose for the firm, it is not the firm's purpose until it moves down the line.

But purposes cannot be inculcated. Inculcating purpose makes no more sense than inculcating individuality. Top management must speak to the purposes and ground rules of the organization's members in order to produce an organization-individual alignment. This is the problem of responsibility in organizations. Each individual must be responsible for the purpose.

What is responsibility? How do you spread it? Is it an individual or collective matter?

Taking Responsibility for Getting Responsibility

I have argued that the single most important question the thinking manager can ask about any organization is: Who is responsible here?

Responsibility is the issue in almost every hard management problem, ethical or otherwise. This idea is not novel, just unpopular. Peter Drucker, in a retrospective on his work, puts responsibility front and center when he says: "I stressed all along that organization does not deal with power but with responsibility. This is the one keynote of my work that has remained constant over more than 40 years" (1985, p. 8). Drucker is right. But none of his ideas has received less attention or uptake. It is as if the word *responsibility* jams the mental circuits.

Responsibility is a complex concept that we all have a hard time understanding. One reason is that true responsibility, if understood, is very demanding. It is easy to talk about "taking responsibility" if you can use the phrase to fault others without getting the message yourself. Another reason is that responsibility challenges our entire way of looking at the world by forcing us to deal with paradoxes and to accept the idea that creativity is a part of plain old responsibility.

Responsibility requires *effectiveness, independence,* and *intention* (acting from purpose). You cannot be responsible if you are ineffective; if you cannot do it, you cannot be responsible for doing it. To be responsible, you must act independently of where the payoffs are. Payoffs are unlikely to track the requirements of responsible action in even the best situations. The only way to act independently is to act for a purpose that makes acting independently worth it to you.

Acting for a purpose that makes acting independently worth it to you is a compressed statement of exactly what ethical management is.

It is easy to pull the elements of responsibility together if you make one simple observation: People take responsibility for what they create. People will work hard—for less money, and above their abilities—if they are creating a new company

(Apple), a new computer (Data General), or a new way of working together (Jaguar PLC). Creativity is literally doing something outside of the domain of the laws by which the world predictably works; the ancients said creativity is bringing something into being from nothing. That, of course, is impossible according to our scientific world view but still quite necessary.

The very ideas of responsibility and creativity force paradox on us. Paradox is good for the manager because it forces thinking outside of the parameters that lock in competitors. If you ask good questions—if you are a thinking manager—you find a lot of paradoxes. Learn to love them, or you will have to quit asking. One paradox is that of individual versus group responsibility. This paradox excuses more irresponsible conduct than does alcoholism. We resolve this paradox by embracing it.

The individual is the source of responsibility since the individual is the source of creativity. But the creative individual cannot create by himself, so he or she creates the group as cocreators. Recall the situation described in Chapter Eight: Some members of the department in which I work teach poorly; I am an excellent teacher; I am not responsible for teaching that I do not do. Why do some colleagues teach poorly? Perhaps it is due to motivation, lack of basic skills, a reward system that undervalues teaching, internal politics, marital problems, and so on. *How can I be responsible for these things?* If asked sincerely, this is a powerful question. I can be responsible by participating in the hiring and promotion of teachers lacking basic skills. I can be responsible for lack of attention to what my colleagues do, for acquiescence in a reward system that undervalues teaching, and for a lack of sensitivity to politics and personal problems. I am not so much responsible for the existence of problems as I am for the existence of unsolved problems. If doing good teaching is a purpose for me, and if I am effective in pursuing this purpose, *I am responsible for creating solutions to these problems.*

Any manager who sincerely and aggressively asks, "How can I be responsible for these things?" will find very many good answers.

The Coming Challenge

I have emphasized that ethics can help you manage better, both in the economic sense of getting a better return on the assets you manage and in the ethical sense of getting the right return in the right way. Yet I have also pointed out in Chapter Nine that our ethical tools have limits. They cannot help with many of the ethical issues that already bedevil managers and will continue to bedevil them in coming years.

These tools are limited because they have developed in a world that does not include many of the problems now confronting managers. Our ethical tools evolved to establish rights in the new institutional forms of the industrial revolution, to resolve conflicts among groups forced to coexist despite radically different ethical viewpoints, and to allocate scarce resources. We thus have ethical tools that assign rights to physical property, resolve conflicts, and organize scarcity.

But we live on the front edge of the bio-information revolution. This revolution will produce its own new form of organization and its own new ethical problems. I argued that the new organization will be a flexible organization built on fair agreements, for the new ethical problems are essentially problems of design—how to design agreement-based organizations, responsible information networks, and even people and their environment.

Because our ethical models are mute on issues of design, a new ethics must emerge. I speculated that this ethics will rest on a foundation of stakeholder purposefulness but not on a specific common purpose. The likely alternative to an ethics of stakeholder purposefulness is an ethics of control in the name of the common good. The thinking manager realizes that the emerging ethics will shift the ground rules of business, and of his or her company, and will take a role in the debate to form this ethics. It is only with the participation of thinking managers that an ethics that respects such business values as individuality, diversity, and the right to create has a fair chance of winning the debate.

Armed with these tools and issues, we ask the thinking manager to march forward. But how is he or she to do this and what does the objective look like? Chapter Eleven offers an agenda for the thinking manager and a look at the objective—a high-ethics, high-profit organization.

11

Lessons from High-Profit, High-Ethics Companies: An Agenda for Managerial Action

The great end of life is not knowledge but action.
— *Thomas Huxley,* Technical Education

We have covered a lot of material, addressed some very hard problems, and gathered many lessons. Since the ethical manager is not just a thinker but also a person of action, how do these lessons translate into an agenda for action for the thinking manager? I am committed to avoiding recipes that are substitutes for thinking. So I approach the issue of an agenda for action in a different way.

Instead of offering a recipe, I offer an ideal. It is an ideal for business and business organizations. What should business be like?

Business should be experimental, always seeking nonconformist ideas that will break open or create markets. It should be a hotbed of creativity, harboring no respect for bureaucratic power struggles. It should (to borrow a thought from Steve Jobs) be our internal Ellis Island, embracing those rejected by academies, governments, and accrediting bodies—and anxious

218

to get ahead by producing results. Business should have a voracious appetite for social problems that it can solve profitably. It should be confident in its ability to produce prosperity and unembarrassed in resisting governmental meddling. Free thinking should find its true home and chance of finding application in business.

Things have never been this way, unless by exception. We think of Apple Computer as a free-spirited company even though it strictly enforces its antielitist dress code, antidefense ideology, and mandated gestures towards "team spirit." And Apple does deserve credit, if only for being nonconformist about what it is conformist about. We could list many reasons why business is, and has been, less than it might and should be. These reasons would range from greed to improper education for managers to the demands of intense competition. But the better we explain why things must be as they are, the further we are from having them be otherwise. The value of an ideal is that it shifts attention away from what we know does not work and onto what we want to accomplish.

I noted in Chapter Ten that the thinking manager uses ethics to produce constructive explosion. The purpose of such explosion is to allow the firm to peek over the edge of the world as it is into the domain of how it can and should be. Most of us live with the disappointment that things will not turn out as we once had hoped; that is why the Eastern philosophy of lowering our expectations, and thus our exposure to disappointment, is popular with so many these days. Organizations do the same thing. They lower their sights to reduce the risk of disappointment; they thereby ensure slow catabolism—a diet of day-to-day death. The hard part about consulting to organizations is not addressing the problems, but convincing them that there is a chance for things to be very much better. My purpose in stating an ideal is not to foster a Pollyannaish optimism, but to foster a realistic raising of our sights.

There is a chance to close the gap between business as it is and business as it reasonably might be. And ethics is one way of seeing where that chance is. It does so by allowing managers to penetrate to the ground rules the organization really operates on. This in turn opens the possibility of *choosing* these ground rules or choosing to replace them. It is often necessary to explode the old rules to make way for new rules, but it is irresponsible to explode the old rules unless you have something to offer in place of them. We thus need an ideal—a picture of what could replace the old rules.

I express this ideal as a set of principles for high-ethics, high-profit organizations. I have said that to have ethics is to have ground rules. What then are the ground rules of the *high*-ethics organization? I offer these principles to answer this question.

When I speak of principles for high-ethics organizations, I offer principles for high-ethics, *high-profit* organizations. High-ethics, low-profit organizations do not persist, and high-profit, low-ethics firms should not. These principles are based on the research, consulting, and thought that have guided my argument. The research included a three-year international study of twenty-five firms recognized for both their economic and ethical performance. The firms studied included Cadbury Schweppes, 3M, Arco, Motorola, Hilby Wilson Inc., Northern Chemical Company, Interwestern Management, Apple Computer, and many other fine firms; additionally, we studied several public (governor's office; mayor's office) and semipublic (chamber of commerce; industry association) organizations.

The study was conducted by leading management researchers, practicing managers, and management consultants. The objective was to discover what connections, if any, there are between high ethical performance and high economic performance. The participants carried trial versions of our principles back to our organizations or consulting practices to sort out the wishful thinking from the substantive lessons. We finally settled on a set of principles that work synergistically to promote good ethics and good economics. These principles are good ethics by our standards.

I believe that the ideal embodied in the principles is a practical one. I believe that this ideal is within the reach of able managers because I, and the other participants, have seen these principles work, albeit not all at one time in one organization.

When I say that these principles express an ideal, I do not mean something removed from action, for all responsible action is practically motivated as much by ideals as by interests. Ideals are no more or less than the formal statements of guiding purposes.

The agenda for thinking managers is to take these principles to work and start the process of testing them against hard problems, revising or rejecting them, and trying again. Above all, the thinking manager will carry these principles as questions, not as question killers, and will persistently seek criticism, new principles, and new questions.

The principles are formulated as principles for high-ethics *firms*. Although the study focused more on private than on public organizations, I can suggest with measured confidence that these principles also provide the basis for high-ethics, high-effectiveness public organizations.

Principles for the High-Ethics Firm

Most firms are a closed "reality." Managers are comfortable dealing with peer managers and often not entirely comfortable even with this group. In high-ethics firms managers deal comfortably with the extremely diverse groups who do or should take an interest in the firm's activities.

Principle 1: High-ethics firms are at ease interacting with diverse internal and external stakeholder groups. The ground rules of these firms make the good of these stakeholder groups part of the firm's own good.

The high-ethics firm knows that its success depends on many stakeholder groups not ordinarily encompassed in business thinking. This goes beyond being close to customers, suppliers, employees, and so on. It is an *attitude* of looking inside and outside the firm to see whose interests can be folded into the firm's purpose and activities. It is an attitude of recognizing the perspective most unlike one's own and of seeking to internalize it (Pastin, 1985c; Brenkert, 1985).

Control Data took note of the unemployed minority

youth in neighborhoods where it operated. It knew that these kids were unlikely to acquire the skills necessary to participate in the emerging information economy and started intensive computer training programs for them. Motorola recognized that cost-effective *quality* health care was a priority for its employees and tackled the issue; it shared proprietary cost-reduction and quality-assurance programs with health care providers. Diesel Engines recognized that clean air was a priority for many stake-holder groups; it adopted a strategy to clean the air and enhance its competitive position at one and the same time. Interwestern Management knows that every employee is an individual and wants to be treated as such; its ground rules emphasize auton-omy and uniqueness in all aspects of the business and make a virtue of individualism.

Principle 1 suggests that you look at the true stakeholders in your firm, ask whether your firm has any reasonable idea of how its actions look in the eyes of the stakeholders, and ask whether the firm has overlooked ways of folding stakeholder perspectives into the firm's thought and actions. It also suggests getting some first-hand knowledge of the stakeholders and allowing them some first-hand knowledge of the firm.

Nothing makes most managers more uncomfortable than issues of justice or fairness. In high-ethics firms, however, fair-ness is the bread and butter of management.

Principle 2: High-ethics firms are obsessed with fairness. Their ground rules emphasize that the other person's interests count as much as their own.

These firms waste little energy managing conflicts; thus they appear to be undermanaged. The amount of control and management that you need is proportional to the number of people who feel unfairly treated. A paradigmatic example is Cadbury Schweppes. It has achieved labor peace in a hostile labor environment by assiduously maintaining fairness in deal-ing with employees at all levels. Despite bargaining with over twenty unions, it has better labor-management relations than any nonunionized U.S. firm we know of, and it does this with a lean management cadre. Hilby Wilson, Inc., a land syndication company, succeeds with a similar approach. It offers no deal that it would not invest in as an outsider. Its ground rules emphasize putting its own interests on the line before asking anyone else to do so. Its deals quickly sell themselves. Little management and no marketing function are needed. Jaguar PLC and R. L. Carol succeed by attending mainly to a tough-minded, competitive style of fairness.

Principle 2 suggests that you find the groups within and outside of your firm who may feel unfairly treated by the firm. Look at the firm's actions from their viewpoints, and make adjustments to achieve fairness. Observe situations in which managers spend their time managing conflicts of interest, and ask how conflict and its management could be reduced or eliminated by taking a new view of fairness. This does not mean giving turkeys to the poor at Christmas. It means having the basic confidence that you treat people well and that you can restore fairness when imbalances inevitably occur. Fairness includes fairness to yourself and to the firm. You and the firm have a right to fair treatment and should forthrightly seek it.

Responsibility is impossible to pinpoint in most firms; it stares you in the eye in high-ethics firms.

Principle 3: In high-ethics firms, responsibility is individual rather than collective, with individuals assuming personal responsibility for actions of the firm. These firms' ground rules mandate that individuals are responsible to themselves.

This principle, whose influence has been evident throughout this book, was the most surprising and paradoxical finding of our research project. The emphasis on individual responsibility is a surprising contrast to the nearly unanimous call for collective responsibility in the current management literature. It is paradoxical in that individuals in these firms claim personal responsibility for the actions of the firm itself.

Consider a discussion that we had with line workers at Jaguar PLC. We refer to the new, post-1980 Jaguar, liberated from both British Leyland and the British government and a strong economic and ethical performer. Workers scorned the "we are all one" mentality and personalized actions and responsibility for them. A typical comment: "I am the emblem man; every emblem you see on a Jaguar is mine." An individualistic view. On the other hand, the emblem man said, "That door is crooked; I don't know how that got by me." Joseph Yiu, one of Motorola's best managers, frequently expounds his philosophy, which views every last action of Motorola as one of his actions; he seriously believes that he runs the company from his midmanagement position. In short, we found individualized responsibility, with individuals taking a broad view of what they individually do and an equally broad view of their responsibilities.

Principle 3 suggests that you first look at the degree to which you accept responsibility for what happens in the firm. Then consider what others consider themselves responsible for. Adopt an attitude which says: "If it happens here, I did it. I did it by doing *A, B,* and *C.*" Although this attitude is naturally infectious, it is still worth promoting. Promote it by reviewing the tasks that make up various jobs in order to find their creative component and by drawing attention to that component by every means possible. Let it be known that people create in countless forms in every aspect of their work, and watch the responsibility flow.

The glue that holds the high-ethics firm together is not culture, goals, superordinate goals, participation, employee stock ownership, or leadership. It is purpose.

Principle 4: The high-ethics firm sees its activities in terms of a purpose. This purpose is a way of operating that members of the firm value. And purpose ties the firm to its environment.

We describe the glue of high-ethics firms as purpose, not goals, to underscore an important point. Goals are future-oriented, inviting members of the firm to see present activities in terms of a speculative future good. This does not work. High-ethics, high-profit firms invite members of the firm to see their activities as valuable *in themselves* and *to the world at large.*

3M is, perhaps, the best example of a firm held together by purpose. 3M's purpose is to innovate. *Being* innovative is not a goal, although 3M has goals reflecting its commitment to innovation. *Becoming* innovative is a goal, a goal 3M neither has nor needs. Innovation is a way of life at 3M enjoyed by 3M managers and employees *day to day*. And 3M people see innovation as socially important. At one time, Apple Computer was held together by the purpose of making computers an integral part of the life of common folk; Apple people believed they were leading this process and that it was vitally important that they succeed. The Eagle team at Data General operated from the purpose of being at the creative edge of new computer technology and succeeded against stiff odds.

Principle 4 suggests that you take an honest look at the issue of how many members of your firm view themselves as engaged in work that truly matters. From those to whom the work matters, find out why. From those to whom the work does not matter, find out what does matter, and see if there is a possible alignment with the work of the firm. Purpose is hard to find for two reasons—there is not that much around, and what is around is buried beneath layers of belief, rationalization, and fear of disclosure. The only way to find purpose is to learn to persist in asking why, to try to see the pattern and underlying assumptions, and to become an excellent reverse engineer. But find it you must if you seek the alignment and self-motivation that produces the most ethical and effective action.

An Agenda for Action

The ethical firm operates on ground rules that deal fairly with diverse constituencies, promote individual responsibility, and enact a purpose. This is fairly complicated. A simpler formulation says that the ethical firm thrives on individuality, rather than suppressing it, and uses a grounding purpose to focus and multiply the efforts of individuals. The mark of unethical firms is that individuals lose part of themselves to belong to the firm. The mark of the ethical firm is that individuals gain new dimensions through the firm, without giving anything away. In this firm, ethical conduct is natural and needs no support from codes, slogans, and phony ceremonies.

This agenda calls for the thinking manager to look at his

or her own organization and ask whether its ground rules enact these principles. While I have offered many lessons and tools to aid this process, it boils down to the willingness to ask the hard questions that need to be asked about the hard problems that need to be solved.

We do not offer these four principles as answers. Being a thinking manager and trying to build a high-ethics, high-profit firm or work unit is a bootstrapping operation. You start by questioning the accepted answers: Ask hard questions about the accepted answers, try out some new answers, and then start asking why once again. Since you must stand somewhere to start asking questions, I offer the above principles for you to use in raising some critical questions. Treat these principles, and the ethics they embody, as a ladder to climb up on and then to kick away once you have achieved a better view.

It takes guts to ask questions. Not only do you reveal what you do not know. You reveal what others do not know, and often do not want to know. But if you do not ask, you must manage within the narrow bounds set by what you do not know but need to know. The lesson is to be a thinking manager.

Is it worth the risks?

Remember Elliot, our paradigm short-run manager. Elliot's problem turned out to be not so much his short-term perspective as his obsequious attunement to the reward system. We know that Elliot could easily be made into a long-term manager. But he would exploit the long run just as he exploited the short run.

We did not like Elliot, but we easily recognized him. In an important sense, the issue in life is whether or not to be Elliot, or at least, how much to be Elliot. Unraveling this issue is not simple. Elliot not only gets away with being Elliot; he prospers. By now, Elliot has the wealth, position, and respect that most of us can only dream of. There is truth to the idea that you can be Elliot, or just work for him. Every one of us is Elliot. Many of us turn up our noses at the world's Elliots just because they have out-Ellioted us.

Elliot presents us with a choice. It is a choice that makes

the lessons of this book worthwhile or worthless. If you operate on the ground rule "I must act like Elliot or I will not survive or succeed by my standards," you can still use ethics to find new edges in hard problems. On balance, however, you may have wasted your time. And most of us act on some version of this ground rule most of the time. Yet we also operate on a ground rule "What I do and how I do it is the only thing that matters for me." Given the willingness we display to work irrationally hard for ridiculously little if we just think this may be the project that counts, this ground rule cannot be ignored either. If you operate on this ground rule, the ideal presented here is for you.

The greatest English-speaking philosopher, William Shakespeare, pointed out the risk in playing by Elliot's ground rule. The risk is that you may understand the following speech too well:

> To-morrow, and to-morrow, and to-morrow,
> Creeps in this petty pace from day to day
> To the last syllable of recorded time,
> And all our yesterdays have lighted fools
> The way to dusty death. Out out, brief candle!
> Life's but a walking shadow, a poor player
> That struts and frets his hour upon the stage,
> And then is heard no more; it is a tale
> Told by an idiot, full of sound and fury,
> Signifying nothing.
>
> —*Macbeth* (Act V, Scene V)

A lot of organizational life is a tale full of sound and fury, signifying nothing. What is the difference between the life described by Shakespeare and lived by Elliots and something better? I have found no better word than *purposefulness*.

My purpose is to invite you and your organization to try a little purpose. Stand on a purpose and look around with our ethical models. The world you see will be no less messy than it was the last time you looked, but now you can probe the ground rules by which it works, ask what values are being pursued and how they are pursued, and see where responsibility is and where it should be.

We live in a complex, challenging world that is unfriendly to quick fixes. Our invitation is for those who know that business can make it a better world through sound thinking and sound acting.

Selected Bibliography

Andrews, K. "Letter from the Editor." *Harvard Business Review*, 1985, *63* (5), 1-2.

"Antibribery Act Splits Executives." *Business Week*, Sept. 19, 1983, p. 16.

Aristotle. *Nicomachean Ethics*. (M. Ostwald, trans.) Indianapolis, Ind.: Bobbs-Merrill, 1962. (Originally appeared 335-323 B.C.)

Bellah, R., and others. *Habits of the Heart: Individualism and Commitment in American Life.* Berkeley: University of California Press, 1985.

Bennis, W. "Leadership Transforms Vision into Action." *Industry Week,* May 31, 1982, pp. 54-56.

Bennis, W., and Nanus, B. *Leaders.* New York: Harper & Row, 1985.

Bishop, J. E. "Should Employers Be Told?" *Wall Street Journal,* Sept. 12, 1984, p. 1.

Blodgett, T. "Cadbury Schweppes: More Than Chocolate and Tonic." *Harvard Business Review,* 1983, *83* (1), 134-144.

Bower, M. *The Will to Manage.* New York: McGraw-Hill, 1966.

Brenkert, G. G. "Thoughts on 'Management-Think'." *Journal of Business Ethics,* 1985, *4,* 309-312.

Burnham, D. *The Rise of the Computer State.* New York: Random House, 1980.

Chandler, A. *Strategy and Structure.* Cambridge, Mass.: MIT Press, 1962.

Churchman, C. W. *The Design of Inquiring Systems: Basic Concepts of Systems and Organization.* New York: Basic Books, 1971.

Culbert, S., and McDonough, J. *The Invisible War: Pursuing Self-Interest in the Workplace.* New York: Wiley, 1980.

Davis, K., and Frederick, W. C. *Business and Society.* (5th ed.) New York: McGraw-Hill, 1984.

Davis, S. "Transforming Organizations: The Key to Strategy Is Context." *Organization Dynamics,* Winter 1982, pp. 64-80.

Davis, S. *Managing Corporate Culture.* Cambridge, Mass.: Ballinger, 1984.

Deal, T., and Kennedy, A. *Corporate Cultures.* Reading, Mass.: Addison-Wesley, 1982.

Delgado, J. M. R. *Physical Control of the Mind: Toward a Psychocivilized Society.* New York: Harper & Row, 1969.

Dellheim, C. "Research Report on British Industry." Center for Ethics, Arizona State University, 1984.

Diebold, J. *The Role of Business in Society.* New York: AMACOM, 1982.

Drucker, P. "What Is 'Business Ethics'?" *Across the Board,* Oct. 1981, pp. 22-32.

Drucker, P. "Drucker on Drucker." *New Management,* Winter 1985, pp. 6-9.

Fisher, R., and Ury, W. *Getting to Yes.* Boston: Houghton Mifflin, 1981.

Forrester, J. W. "A New Corporate Design." In J. W. Forrester, *Collected Papers of Jay W. Forrester.* Cambridge, Mass.: Wright-Allen Press, 1975.

Freeman, E. *Strategic Management: A Stakeholder Approach.* Boston: Pitman, 1984.

Fried, C. *An Anatomy of Values.* Cambridge, Mass.: Harvard University Press, 1970.

Gilder, G. *Wealth and Poverty.* New York: Basic Books, 1981.

Goodpastor, K., and Mathews, J., Jr. "Can a Corporation Have a Conscience?" *Harvard Business Review,* 1982, *60* (1), 132–144.

Grossman, L. "Research Report on Long-Term Success." Department of Management, Arizona State University, 1982.

Grube, G. M. A. (ed. and trans.). *Plato's Republic.* Indianapolis, Ind.: Hackett, 1974. (Originally appeared 387–367 B.C.)

Hall, R. H. *Organizations: Structure and Process.* Englewood Cliffs, N.J.: Prentice-Hall, 1977.

Hardin, G. *Exploring New Ethics for Survival.* New York: Penguin Books, 1977.

Hitler, A. *Mein Kampf.* Boston: Houghton Mifflin, 1939. (Originally published 1926.)

Jefferson, E. "Biotechnology Advance Will Require End to Regulatory Limbo." *Financier,* Oct. 1, 1984, pp. 21–24.

Kant, I. *Grounding for the Metaphysics of Morals.* (J. W. Ellington, trans.) Indianapolis, Ind.: Hackett, 1981. (Originally published 1785.)

Kapleau, P. *The Three Pillars of Zen.* Boston: Beacon Press, 1967.

Keeley, M. "Organizational Analogy: A Comparison of Organismic and Social Contract Models." *Administrative Science Quarterly,* 1980, *25,* 337–362.

Keeley, M. "Theories of Organization and Management." In J. B. Wilbur (ed.), *Ethics and the Marketplace: An Exercise in Bridge-Building.* Geneseo, N.Y.: University of New York Press, 1982.

Kidder, T. *The Soul of a New Machine.* Boston: Little, Brown, 1981.

Kilmann, R. H. *Beyond the Quick Fix: Managing Five Tracks to Organizational Success.* San Francisco: Jossey-Bass, 1984.

Kipling, R. *The Collected Works of Rudyard Kipling.* New York: AMS Press, 1970.

Kirwan, J. "Mandarin Mondale and the U.S. Future in Space." *Wall Street Journal,* Oct. 23, 1984, p. 30.

Kluckhohn, C., and Kelly, W. "The Concept of Culture." In R. Linton (ed.), *The Science of Man in the World.* New York: Columbia University Press, 1945.

Kotchian, A. C. "The Payoff: Lockheed's Seventy-Day Mission to Tokyo." *The Saturday Review,* July 9, 1977, pp. 6–12.

Lawrence, P., and Dyer, D. *Renewing American Industry.* New York: Free Press, 1983.

Locke, J. *Second Treatise of Government.* Indianapolis, Ind.: Hackett, 1980. (Originally published 1690.)

Machiavelli, N. *The Prince.* (G. Bull, trans.) New York: Penguin Books, 1981. (Originally published 1513.)

MacIntyre, A. *After Virtue.* Notre Dame, Ind.: University of Notre Dame Press, 1981.

Mason, R. O. "Designing Information Communities: Ethical Issues in the Information Age." Working Paper, Management Information Systems, University of Arizona, 1983.

Mason, R. O. "Designing Information Communities." *The Information Society,* 1985, *3* (5), 229–239. (Update of Mason, 1983.)

Mason, R. O., and Mitroff, I. I. *Challenging Strategic Planning Assumptions: Theory, Cases, and Techniques.* New York: Wiley, 1981.

Mill, J. S. *On Liberty.* D. Spitz (ed.). New York: Norton, 1975. (Originally published 1859.)

Mill, J. S. *Utilitarianism.* Oskar Piest (ed.). New York: Liberal Arts Press, 1948. (Originally published 1861.)

Mitroff, I. I. *Stakeholders of the Organizational Mind: Toward a New View of Organizational Policy Making.* San Francisco: Jossey-Bass, 1983.

Mitroff, I. I., and Kilmann, R. "Corporate Tragedies: Teaching Companies to Cope with Evil." *New Management,* 1984a, *1* (4), 48–53.

Mitroff, I. I., and Kilmann, R. *Corporate Tragedies.* New York: Praeger, 1984b.

Murphy, P. "Business Ethics' Time Has Come in Era of Defense Contract Overcharging." *Arizona Republic,* June 10, 1985, p. 2.

Naisbitt, J. *Megatrends: Ten New Directions Transforming Our Lives.* New York: Warner Books, 1982.

Nietzsche, F. *On the Geneology of Morals.* (W. Kaufmann, trans.) New York: Random House, 1967. (Originally published 1887.)

Ohmae, K. *The Mind of the Strategist.* New York: McGraw-Hill, 1982.

Ouchi, W. *Theory Z: How American Business Can Meet the Japanese Challenge.* Reading, Mass.: Addison-Wesley, 1981.

Ouchi, W. *The M-Form Society: How American Teamwork Can Recapture the Competitive Edge.* Reading, Mass.: Addison-Wesley, 1984.

Pascale, R. T., and Athos, A. G. *The Art of Japanese Management.* New York: Simon & Schuster, 1981.

Pastin, M. "Why?" *Business Horizons,* 1983, *26* (1), 2-6.

Pastin, M. "Business Ethics by the Book." *Business Horizons,* 1985a, *28* (1), 2-6.

Pastin, M. "Ethics as an Integrating Force in Management." *New Jersey Bell Journal,* 1985b, *8* (2), 1-15.

Pastin, M. "Management Think." *Journal of Business Ethics,* 1985c, *4,* 297-307.

Pastin, M., and Hooker, M. "Ethics and the Foreign Corrupt Practices Act." In K. D'Andrade and P. Werhane (eds.), *Profit and Responsibility.* New York: Edwin Mellen Press, 1985.

Peters, T., and Waterman, R., Jr. *In Search of Excellence.* New York: Harper & Row, 1982.

Plato. *Five Dialogues* (G. M. A. Grube, trans.) Indianapolis, Ind.: Hackett, 1981. (Originally appeared 387-367 B.C.)

Rand, A. *The Fountainhead.* New York: New American Library, 1971. (Originally published 1943.)

Rawls, J. *A Theory of Justice.* Cambridge, Mass.: Harvard University Press, 1971.

Reich, R. *The Next American Frontier.* New York: Times Books, 1983.

Russell, B. *A History of Western Philosophy.* New York: Simon & Schuster, 1965.

Ryan, A. *John Stuart Mill.* New York: Pantheon Books, 1970.

Schumpeter, J. *Capitalism, Socialism, and Democracy.* New York: Harper & Row, 1962. (Originally published 1942.)

Sethi, S. P. *Up Against the Corporate Wall.* Englewood Cliffs, N.J.: Prentice-Hall, 1982.

Shaw, G. B. *Man and Superman.* London: Constable, 1930.

Skinner, B. F. *Science and Human Behavior.* New York: Free Press, 1965.

Smith, A. "Theory of Moral Sentiments." In L. A. Selby-Bigge (ed.), *British Moralists.* Indianapolis, Ind.: Bobbs-Merrill, 1964. (Originally published 1759.)

Smith, A. *An Inquiry into the Nature and Causes of the Wealth of Nations.* E. Cannon (ed.). Chicago: University of Chicago Press, 1976. (Originally published 1776.)

Speer, A. *Spandau.* New York: Macmillan, 1976.

Steckmest, F. W. *Corporate Performance.* New York: McGraw-Hill, 1982.

Steiner, G. A., and Steiner, J. F. *Business, Government, and Society: A Managerial Perspective.* (4th ed.) New York: Random House, 1985.

Uttal, B. "The Corporate Culture Vultures." *Fortune,* Oct. 17, 1983, pp. 66-72.

Wade, N. *The Ultimate Experiment.* New York: Walker, 1979.

Waterman, R. H., Peters, T. J., and Phillips, J. "Structure Is Not Organization." *Business Horizons,* 1980, *23* (3), 14-26.

Wright, J. P. *On a Clear Day You Can See General Motors.* Chicago, Ill.: Wright Enterprises, 1979.

Index

235